LEVI'S UNBUTTONED

The Woke Mob Took My Job
But Gave Me My Voice

LEVI'S UNBUTTONED

The Woke Mob Took My Job
But Gave Me My Voice

JENNIFER SEY

All Seasons Press

2881 E. Oakland Park Blvd. Suite 456

Fort Lauderdale, FL 33306

Interior design by Kim Hall

SECOND EDITION: NOVEMBER 2022

Library of Congress Cataloging-in-Publication Data has been applied for.

ISBN-13: 978-1958682241

Printed in the United States of America

10   9   8   7   6   5   4   3   2   1

For my husband Daniel.

The only person who has ever told me to say it all.

To make myself and my voice bigger, not smaller.

I love you all the time.

If evil be said of thee, and if it be true, correct thyself; if it be a lie, laugh at it.

-Epictetus

CONTENTS

PROLOGUE

In February 2022 I walked away from my job as the first female Global Brand President of Levi's after close to twenty-three years at the company. I'd given the better part of my adult life to Levi's because of the product itself – I do love my 501s. (I have always preferred the button-fly on my jeans, rather than the zipper.) But while I may have chosen to work there in the beginning because of the product, I stayed because of the company culture. I believed in their mantras: "profits through principles," "harder right over easier wrong," "use your voice." These oft-repeated refrains were rooted in the company's heritage, one of rugged individualism, corporate philanthropy and populist inclusiveness. I was nothing short of heartbroken to find out that, in practice, these phrases were just empty buzzwords.

The phrases are merely shibboleths of woke capitalism and have nothing to do with the company's current guiding values, which are anything but inclusive or principled.

Of course, woke capitalism wasn't only happening at Levi's. In recent years, in the wake of George Floyd's murder, almost every corner of American business has become frantic to prove its do-gooder, anti-racist status. Immediately following Floyd's death, internal memos and pronouncements on Instagram went out in companies across America. All featured the same buzzwords: social justice, anti-racism, equity and inclusion. All promised to do their part in defeating racism and all forms of discrimination. Only the foolhardy would dare challenge. Any suggestion of any doubt was defined as bigotry. And stories of cancellation were rampant.

My company, Levi's, was among the wokest of the woke. And I was in on it. Until I dared to be one of the few who were foolhardy enough to challenge.

Woke capitalism seeks to build consumer loyalty through social justice stances rather than what the company makes and sells. Woke capitalism tries to convince buyers that companies are in business to do good and make the world a better place, not make money. Woke capitalism seeks to brainwash the world with the message that corporations care about employees, even when they lay them off at the same time as they are delivering unimaginable wealth to shareholders and executives through dividends and stock price increases.

In service of this massive lie, woke capitalism offers free speech to some employees, but not others. And woke capitalism ejects any employees suspected of wrongthink, pretending these "wrongthinkers" are a significant threat to sensitive anti-racist employees, thus creating a "hostile work environment." In reality, the banishments are a maneuver to foster the illusion that the company is highly principled and *really cares*.

It's all a deception that should be in plain view. Woke capitalists say — *hey look over there* — to employees and consumers, while shareholders and executives fill their coffers with obscene wealth. It's like a kid stealing cookies from a cookie jar when nobody is looking, and then lying about it to his mom despite the fact that he has cookie crumbs all over his face, and the jar is left empty. Except the woke corporatists actually convince themselves that they are being honest about what they do, rather than distracting in order to gorge themselves and leave only scraps for everybody else. At least the kid knows he's lying to get out of trouble. The corporate grifters really believe that they are do-gooders. They buy their own thieving charade, and it's why, perhaps, it's convincing to so many.

Of course, woke capitalism is more than just one thing. For some, it is capitalism's road to redemption, elevating business beyond mere greed into the realm of noble altruism. These true believers are mostly young and hyper-active on social media. For them, woke-ism is a quasi-religion, and the workplace is where they seek to proselytize.

Even when these woke employees are laid off, they don't realize that they are being used to further leadership's deceptive message. In reality, these unsuspecting employees are often laid off primarily so that the rich can stay rich and keep getting richer. But the message broadcast to the world is that it was a "tough call" intended to maintain employment for as many as possible. The employees and consumers who believe this "we really care" message are being manipulated and taken advantage of in this woke capitalist game.

For a great many others, us oldsters in the upper echelons of American business leadership, woke capitalism is a ploy. It is a pose, a communications strategy, a way for corporate executives to feel like philanthropic heroes, and be celebrated as such, all while getting rich in the same way that they always have. Only this time, they are selling a side of righteousness and social justice activism to go with their t-shirts, instead of offering a mere assurance that insecure teenagers will look cool and feel confident on the first day of school.

In their cynical way, these leaders are more relentlessly destructive than the most zealous social justice warriors, for they are even more willing to cancel anyone who challenges the narrative of companies as do-gooders. Anyone who pushes back on the causes of the moment is deemed an apostate of the social justice movement, because they risk exposing the C-suiters for the frauds that they are. And so, like all infidels, the challengers must be ousted and shunned.

Which is to say, woke capitalism is, above all, a lie. There is no justice in it. Only protection of intergenerational wealth for the already wealthy, and enforced obedience and conformity of thought for employees to protect the lie. Challenge the charade at your peril.

And while Levi's is not the biggest company to foster this lie, and its executives and shareholders are not the richest from profiting off of it, it is, in fact, the epitome of woke capitalism.

Having come from the progressive side of the aisle, I was caught short and alarmed by the "progressive" savagery in policing their own, by the unforgiving drive to purge the unworthy and heretical. For those on the side that supposedly celebrates diversity, to trample anyone who veers from government-issued talking points – to hold any such dissent as profane – seems such a transparent and obvious trespass against their own stated values.

At Levi's, these "values" of individualism, corporate philanthropy and inclusion were supposedly baked into the company's DNA.

It all started at Levi's inception in San Francisco back in 1853. Levi Strauss himself donated a portion of his first profits to a local orphanage. And in the 1900s, Levi's applied their values internally, seeking to take care of employees by doing the right thing. During World War II, when the company hired black sewing machine operators and laborers in its California factories, it integrated the workforce. And then, in the early 1960s, the company opened a desegregated factory in Blackstone, Virginia, despite local opposition. In 1992, the company offered same-sex partner benefits, before any other large company had even seriously considered such a thing.

The company took to heart the phrase "charity starts at home." And Levi's never sought to take rights away from any of its employees. They just provided equal rights to *all* employees. Giving a gay employee healthcare benefits leveled the playing field. Healthcare was not taken away from those in traditional heterosexual marriages. And, in fact, partner benefits were extended to straight, unmarried couples. It was a win-win.

The other important point is that this approach of ensuring equality and fairness for employees never detracted from the company's purpose: to deliver the best possible product, at a fair price, in order to maximize profits for the company. As we used to say at Levi's, our mission was to clothe the world.

But by 2020, this principled approach of equitable treatment of employees had morphed into a way of being and operating that can only be described as the wokest imaginable version of woke capitalism. The "profits through principles" ideology had oozed into every aspect of our brand image-creation, even though it was now completely untrue.

As the company's egalitarian principles for all employees mutated over time into woke capitalism, it happened slowly, then all at once. I participated. I contributed. I didn't see it. And by the time I did, it was too late for me.

The mob had taken over. And our mission to "clothe the world" had been usurped by employees demanding we fight to change the world instead.

This seemed patently absurd to me. And impossible. We could change the lives of some of our employees by treating them with fairness. We could provide high quality jeans that lasted a lifetime to our fans, who included everyone from blue-state mini-van moms to cowboys and those insecure teenagers who just want to look cool on the first day of school. But the idea that one little jean maker should be responsible for fomenting political change seemed not only ridiculous, but destined to fail. It would limit the size and growth of our business. It would also, eventually, detract from our focus enough to dissipate the thing that people really wanted from us: pants. And the business would suffer, and perhaps even go under.

But not only was I in the minority, I was the only leader who seemed to feel this way. Leadership caved time and time again to the demands of a woke mob of employees.

The company didn't believe that Levi's was for everyone anymore. We only wanted the woke to work at Levi's, and judging by our public stances, we only wanted the woke to buy Levi's.

As someone still committed to traditional liberal values like free speech and due process – those I thought the Left was committed to – I felt as if I'd been swindled and, not so much betrayed, as like an idiot. I worked at Levi's longer than I've ever done anything else, in part because I believed in these things we said. But they were fabrications. And so, my time was over.

What marked the beginning to my end at Levi's? I was outspoken about the policies impacting children during the COVID-19 pandemic: closed schools, closed playgrounds, the masking of toddlers. I'd spoken out since the very beginning – March 2020 – in defense of maintaining as much normalcy as possible for kids and ensuring that they were not carrying an undue burden on behalf of society. I expressed serious concerns, backed with data, about the age stratification of risk from covid (people over seventy were at three thousand times the risk of death as children were) and how that should inform public policy on the matter, but didn't. Restrictions that unfairly burdened low-risk children were driving learning loss, an increasing educational gap between the haves and have-nots, and a mental health crisis among teens due to intense isolation and lack of normalcy.

All of these "unintended consequences" were a direct result of long-term public school closures and other onerous restrictions on kids. I pointed out that this would happen and harms would be done, and then the harms actually happened. I said it again and again, with increasing passion, on social media, in op-eds, on the local news and then on Fox (you guessed it, this is when things really went south).

I was hoping to help bring some sense to these cruel and abusive policies that were hurting disadvantaged kids, those most likely to be in public schools, the most.

My boss at Levi's and my peers all begged me to "just stop," even as their own kids returned to in-person schooling at their elite private institutions while public school kids remained stranded at home.

Only gradually did it dawn on me that our campaign slogan "Use Your Voice" did not apply to me.

I was challenging all-knowing public health authorities – the same public health authorities who kept playgrounds closed in San Francisco – where Levi's is headquartered and where I lived – for the better part of a year. The ones who closed beaches and disallowed surfing, filled skate ramps with sand to make them unusable, boarded up basketball rims to prevent kids from shooting hoops. Those all-knowing public health authorities.

For saying we should focus resources on the most vulnerable – the elderly being at the top of that list – while letting low-risk children have their lives, I was deemed a granny-killer. In saying that closing hiking trails and gyms was a bad idea, and that perhaps public health authorities should consider a "get healthy" outreach effort given that obesity is a primary risk factor for poor covid outcomes, I was attacking the overweight. I was also denying science. The "science" behind the mandatory masking of diapered toddlers, and the bleaching of groceries, and plexiglass barriers and shuttered schools.

Though Levi's prides itself on being a company unafraid of taking controversial stands, standing up for kids was apparently a bridge too far. Employees in the company called me every name they could think of: racist, ableist, eugenicist, fat-phobe, anti-trans. These sentiments were reiterated and given force by anonymous social media trolls outside the company, as well.

And eventually, in January 2022, I was told that there would be no place for me in the company going forward. Despite my years of service, my stellar work performance, the rapid recovery of the business post-lockdowns (led by me, in large part, as the Brand President) and my unofficial role as an embodiment of the ethos of the company – an inspiring leader and "culture carrier" – I no longer represented the company's "values." My views were out of sync with Levi's political ideology. And I was deemed a risk to the company's reputation.

I chose to quit rather than accept Levi's framing of my exit. I wanted to leave on my own terms, without one million dollars in hush money and a non-disclosure agreement to ensure my silence on the context of my departure. I felt the aggressive silencing of debate on matters of public concern, the viewpoint discrimination within supposed bastions of liberalism like San Francisco, and the general obliteration of a culture of free speech were too important, and needed to be discussed. In fact, alarms needed to be sounded. And so, the most important thing to me was to leave not only with my integrity intact, but my voice as well. So that's what I did.

I've said much of this publicly – maybe you've read it or heard it or maybe you haven't. But there is more to it, and I'll lay it out here. It's about me – yes – and that's an egotist's endeavor no doubt. But it's also about so much more than me. I know it's not such a big deal that one well-paid executive got pushed out of a company for spouting off on Twitter. It is a big deal, however, WHY I got pushed out. And this should, in fact, concern us all.

I was pushed out because I stood up for kids during covid, in direct violation of the progressive mainstream's manufactured narrative. I said kids should be in school when Democratic leaders, the media, the Centers for Disease Control, local public health officials and teachers' unions all said schools must stay closed or else we'll kill all the kids and teachers, and anyone who wants them open is a very bad person.

They were wrong. I was right.

The wrong ones contrived consensus by silencing doctors who offered another perspective and "normies" like me who just knew how to read and interpret data. But I dared to continue to shout about it all, even after I was warned to stop. I failed to heed their warnings, again and again. And so, I was a person unworthy of employment.

I am loyal to principles, not party. I am against hypocrisy. I think that there are a lot of people who feel the same way. And that, in fact, we are the majority.

I hope that reading this book will make it less scary and more urgent for other reasonable people to say what needs to be said. To call out things that are false, even – *especially* – when a most vocal and punitive minority says otherwise. I hope it will inspire them to say what they know to be true but haven't dared to say. Yet.

CHAPTER 1:

A DAY IN THE LIFE OF ME LIVING IN, AND AT, LEVI'S.

I loved my job. I was really *really* good at it. Before my final promotion to Levi's Global Brand President, I'd served as the Chief Marketing Officer (CMO) from September 2013 until October 2020. The median tenure for a CMO is about twenty-five months. It's a high-profile role with even higher expectations, and most don't meet them. They either get fired, or leave when they see the writing on the wall. Of course, corporate life being what it is, many fail up, moving on to CMO roles at bigger companies. Especially for CMOs, one is often rewarded less on merit than on talking a good game.

Some consider the CMO role that of chief brand storyteller. Many CMOs weave entertaining tales, position themselves as wacky creative visionaries in a land of analytical number-crunchers and salespeople. These CMOs spend their time giving talks with flashy

Power Point slides at trade conferences and going to ad agency parties that culminate with a musical performance by an artist at least ten years past his prime.

But I took my responsibilities seriously. I wasn't there to party and build my personal profile. I was being well compensated to sell product, not with cheap gimmicks like "buy one get one for free," but through brand-elevating storytelling deeply informed by data and consumer research. I also wasn't there to build my own reel with moody short films that might win me a prize at one of far too many advertising awards shows.

In my younger years, as I was moving up the ladder, I attended all of our photography and film shoots. In order to cut costs, we made ads all over the world, in places where labor was cheaper than in the U.S. because it was not unionized. We went to Buenos Aires (not once, but three times), Budapest, Vancouver and more. Although this may sound fun and exciting, we were there to work, and these shoots often took several weeks. I was heralded by the then-Brand President – who was himself not a parent – for being so deeply committed to my job, and to Levi's, that I spent significant time away from my young children. This was positioned as a necessary sacrifice for the company, one that all employees should have been willing to make without complaint. Indeed, I never complained, but I hated it.

Sometimes, we did actually film in Hollywood, which I preferred as it allowed me to make quick trips home to see my family on break days. At one of these L.A. shoots, I got into an argument with the creative director from our ad agency. As the client, it was my job to come home with ads that worked to grow our business. I was responsible for making sure we got the film "in the can" (a left-over phrase from the days when movies were actually shot on real film) and captured everything in the storyboarded concept we had finalized, before "rolling tape."

This was a night shoot. It was 3 a.m., I was six months pregnant, very tired, with many hours to go. We had live buffalo on set, and more than a few PETA representatives to make sure that we didn't harm the animals. We'd spent the last two hours shooting the moon. Literally. I'd had enough. There were at least a hundred people employed on the production, and we were wasting precious time and money filming the moon, not the jeans. I was the one who had to call it.

"We need to move on. We've got the shot," I said. I had the authority to make this happen. It didn't mean the agency would listen to me.

"This is the most important shot. We've got to get it right," the creative director/frustrated wanna-be film auteur barked.

"It can't be the most important shot. There are no jeans in it," I retorted. "The butt shot is the most important shot. That's the money shot. Every time."

In every Levi's ad there is a shot – at least one – of the back of the jeans on a human. The red tag, the leather patch at the waist and the "arcuate" stitching that together signify that they are indeed a pair of Levi's – that's what made it a Levi's ad. Indeed, that's what makes Levi's jeans a pair of Levi's. My job, in part, was to make sure that that shot was always present, had the utmost impact, and made people only want to wear Levi's. A butt in a pair of jeans that didn't have those signature branding elements had to be seen as hopelessly uncool. We needed youth and hipsters to covet the red tag and think of the Wrangler "W" on the butt as lame, even if cowboys preferred it.

"But the moon, the sky, it's the whole mood. . ." he pressed.

"I don't care about the moon. If you want to make movies, do it on your own time. We're making a Levi's ad." And that was that. They were all mad at me. But I had a job to do. And it wasn't to make this guy into the next Martin Scorsese.

As CMO, I no longer regularly attended shoots. I sent my Vice President of Marketing to bring home the goods, and I always guided her with these instructions:

Bring home the film as we've envisioned it. Do not be intimidated. Your obligation is to the company. The money budgeted for these ads comes from the company, and the company expects a return. This is not a million dollars (yes, that's the budget for a high-quality TV ad, often more) to help some ad guy fulfill his dreams as an art house director. Our job is to deliver a return on that investment. If we don't do that, we don't get to work here anymore.

I didn't suffer fools. I made myself clear. Get it done, or you might not get another chance.

I was tough but encouraging. I prioritized my role as coach and mentor. As CMO, I managed a team of about 750 people in more than a hundred countries. I had anywhere between seven and twelve people reporting directly to me, depending on the year. I had an open-door policy. Come in any time. Ask me anything. Bring me your ideas. I also dedicated at least an hour a week to coaching sessions for each of my employees who reported to me. This time wasn't used to go through their checklists. It was used to focus on career development: what are the skills they need to build, what are their goals and how can I help to make those aspirations a reality?

It is not easy to get that many people all moving in one direction. Strong leaders have clarity of vision and an ability to inspire belief that that vision will work to achieve a goal. In our case, that goal was to sell more product, and to get people to fall in love with the brand, to be loyal buyers for life.

Every employee also needs to feel that they can make a meaningful contribution, that their ideas will be heard, that they own a little piece of the whole pie, for the team to be effective. If employees know that they can make actual decisions on the stuff that they are responsible for, and not have to run back to their supervisor for approvals on everything, they feel engaged, empowered and committed. They like their work more. Everyone on my team knew that I wouldn't micro-manage them within an inch of their life. Everyone felt useful. Don't we all want that?

But for this to work, there needs to be a framework within which to make those decisions, so that everyone isn't running in a different direction. Think of it this way, everyone on a basketball team has to play their position, but they are all working towards a common goal: score baskets and prevent the other team from scoring them. The same is true in business. Everyone has a position to play. And the common goal is growing the company's sales and profits.

When I started in the CMO role at Levi's, it was clear to me that there was no unifying vision – everyone just did whatever they wanted. A junior person could just decide that she thought Levi's ads should be all about the history and heritage because that's what she liked about Levi's. Someone else, in some faraway country like Russia or Indonesia, could decide that Levi's was all about baseball caps. And make that the focus of the seasonal ad campaign. This is a recipe for inconsistency, inefficiency and poor financial performance.

So the first task at hand was to create what we called a "north star" – what is the thing we want to say that is more than the product itself? For instance, Disney is all about "the magic of childhood." Every movie, every theme park experience, is supposed to call that to mind for everyone who experiences them. At Levi's, I put a stake in the ground. We were all about "authentic self-expression" (oh the irony). We didn't tell people how to wear their jeans. We made styles for everyone. We didn't dictate the "look" – you, the guy or gal wearing them, decided exactly how you wanted to rock your jeans. Maybe it was with a white t-shirt and a pair of sneakers, or maybe it was with heels and a ruffled blouse.

I didn't come up with this idea of standing for "authentic self-expression" on my own. This came from consumer research in ten countries around the world. When talking with fans of the brand – "Levi's loyalists" – they all said: "I feel like my best and most authentic self in Levi's." This is what we in marketing call a "unique selling proposition." We had one without even trying or having to make one up. We just needed to amplify it, and get more people to want the brand because of it.

For the framework to gain traction, for everyone to understand it and work towards it, my job was not just to come up with it, but to say it again and again, until everyone embraced it. I scheduled regular meetings to reiterate what we were going for. We had town halls to share the framework and the work that it generated. I had staff meetings every Monday to ensure that we were all connected. And then, of course, I had my weekly one-on-one meetings with each of my direct reports. I repeated myself over and over again. Repetition and focus are the lifeblood for successful business leaders. The key is to do with it with verve, to keep people excited about it. To not get bored yourself.

That wasn't hard for me. One of the best things about my job as CMO at Levi's was that there was no such thing as a "typical day." It was never boring. The job wasn't just one thing. And it expanded as I became more adept, becoming more wide-ranging, more fun and more interesting. I might spend my day flying to New Jersey to convince Alicia Keys to work with us. Or I might spend it at our ad agency around the corner, reviewing and providing feedback on our new ad concepts. Or, what might seem less interesting to some but was my favorite part of the job, I might spend it poring over consumer research to identify where our next growth opportunity might come from. Were we faltering and failing to resonate with consumers in the UK? Why? Was it product, marketing or where we were (or weren't) sold? Was there an opportunity in the southeastern states in the U.S.? Were our sales faltering there because a major wholesaler had shut down, or was it because we weren't "tweaking" our marketing message for consumers in that district? I found this part endlessly fascinating. It was a giant puzzle. And I liked solving it.

Once we'd gotten the hang of what "authentic self-expression" looked like in our advertising, we expanded our marketing efforts to include associating the brand with music. I often said to my team: "We didn't choose music, music chose us." What did I mean by this? Levi's had always been worn by artists with original voices. Everyone from Elvis Presley to Elvis Costello, from Bruce Springsteen to Beyonce, wore Levi's on stage and off. Another phrase I often uttered (again, repetition was key) was: "We are at our best when we are at the center of culture." When we were present at key cultural moments – like Woodstock (everyone there wore Levi's or nothing at all) – we were at the height of our relevance. We'd lost this by 2013, but we could re-engineer it back into existence with focus and effort.

What did it mean to associate the brand with music? It meant partnering with musicians on product collaborations ("collabs" are the key to cool in fashion these days) – people like Tyler the Creator and A$AP Nast (you may not know who these rappers are, but, believe me, the kids do). It meant showing up at music festivals like Coachella, not just with a big Levi's sign, but with a whole set-up letting attendees customize their jeans in fun ways – adorned with rhinestones, or tie dyed, or air-brushed with paint. The point of these sorts of events was to generate PR and social media "buzz," so that all the kids who wished they could come to Coachella to see Travis Scott or Lady Gaga but couldn't afford the $500 entry price could watch their favorite celebrities on Instagram Live getting their jeans customized. Then they'd copy at home what they had seen on the livestream.

Every year that we did this customization project at Coachella, we generated well over one billion impressions in the press and on social media from folks who didn't attend the festival. This was a winning formula. We replicated it at music festivals around the world – events like Glastonbury in London and Strawberry Music Festival in Beijing.

This focus, combined with analytics, data and discipline, in addition to a well-planned product calendar to ensure we marketed the same products at the same time all around the world, was serving us well. We had secured leading "share" with men all around the world. "Share" measures what percentage of overall jeans purchased are Levi's. We'd lost our lead spot in many countries in the 2010s, but gained it back with a "north star" and music to guide us. We were also scratching at the door of the #1 spot for women in many of our top markets, something we'd never gotten close to in the past.

By 2018, we'd had a successful initial public offering (IPO) – we took the company public – earning our CEO, Chip Bergh – tens of millions of dollars and intergenerational wealth. Of some note, despite leading the brand's marketing efforts that led directly to the successful IPO, I received no stock payout, just my regular salary.

While I received no special financial reward for my efforts, I was recognized by *Forbes* in 2018 on its inaugural "CMO Next List," which highlighted marketing leaders redefining the role and shaping the futures and business trajectories of companies. *Forbes* wrote about me:

. . . she's clear on her mandate: to define the vision for the company's brands. Under her watch, a key success: a significant comeback reflected in five years of consecutive topline revenue growth and a third consecutive quarter of double-digit revenue growth. She's led award-winning campaigns, overseen the launch of Levi's Stadium and made music a brand focus. She relaunched the women's business in 2015 and by 2017 had achieved $1 billion in sales.

Then, in both 2019 and 2020, I was named to *Forbes*'s "real" list: The "Top 50 Most Influential CMOs." As a result, even amidst my open schools advocacy and despite the pushback for it by my boss and peers, in late 2020 I was rewarded with the title of Levi's Brand President. Now I would oversee not just marketing, but product, as well. What we designed, how we priced it, how we "assorted it" (that means what items show up where, and in what stores). Further, I oversaw the design and buildout of our owned and operated stores, our research, our brand "go to market" (which we were always trying to make shorter and shorter to be better able to respond to trends) and our overall brand strategy for growth. My team now ballooned to about a thousand people.

I also served as a key member of the company's executive team. I spent more time in business reviews analyzing our profit and loss statements, in executive team meetings debating our path forward and in board meetings convincing the board that we were actually headed in the right direction.

I was able to do these other things only because my team was a well-oiled machine. They knew what to do without me being there to guide them every minute of every day. They'd embraced the framework that we'd created and built together, delivered against it expertly, and felt a strong sense of loyalty and connection to the brand and company.

I'd taught my team to fish, as the old adage goes, and now they could feed themselves, hopefully for a lifetime. And nothing makes me prouder of my time at Levi's than having built a team that could operate without me. Pretty soon they were going to really need to, not because I was toiling away in some boardroom, but because I would be banished from the hallowed halls entirely.

CHAPTER 2:

THE LAST CALL.

I was expecting this call, had been for some time. I'd received warm-up versions repeatedly from various peers, executives, members of the leadership team of which I was proudly a part: *please consider, maybe don't say that, you really can't say **that**, why are you doing this, you know you could be CEO if you'd just stop.*

But this was THE call, the final one. I'd delayed it, feared it, pushed it out, provoked it, welcomed it, cried about it, had nightmares about it, all in equal parts. And now it was here.

"We finished the background check. I've been dreading having to tell you this. But there just isn't a way forward for you here," said my boss, the CEO, Chip Bergh. "You can't be CEO given your history on social media for the past few years, and you can't stay in your current job as President if you can't be CEO. You're a blocker."

Being a "blocker" meant I was sitting in a seat that someone else needed to occupy, someone worthy and capable of being the CEO when Chip retired in a few years. It's called "managing the talent pipeline." For me, it meant lights out on my career at Levi's.

Chip and I had worked together for over a decade, since he started at the company in 2011. He'd been the first man in leadership to truly recognize, appreciate and reward my skills, intellect and ability to lead. He saw me as someone, and told me as much, who had it all. He told me I was creative, but could also translate my ideas into action, unlike so many with vision but no discipline. I understood culture and could figure out how our brand could intersect with it to stay relevant. But (and here's the unusual part), I was also analytical. I understood data and could translate it into insight that could, in turn, be translated into product and marketing. And I could do math. The basic retail math necessary to understand and grow our business. Lastly, and most importantly, I could lead. It's not easy to take all these skills, weave them together, and use that to inspire an organization. He believed I was capable of that, and he was the first, and last, of my supervisors who saw this in me.

When Chip started at the company in 2011, he read my first memoir, *Chalked Up*, that had come out three years earlier. Then, in 2018, when I told him that I wanted to make a documentary about the abuse of children in the sport of gymnastics, a film, called *Athlete A*, that would go on to win an Emmy in 2020, he said: "Yes. You should definitely do it!" He felt proud to support a woman who spoke her mind.

Chip was a veteran of the military, which is where his tremendous discipline was instilled. He didn't have an MBA from some fancy school. He learned on the job, in his two decades at Proctor & Gamble prior to joining Levi's. He grew up in the Midwest with traditional Midwestern values. He'd voted Republican his whole life, or so he told me, until he moved to San Francisco. His views had changed, he said, when he moved to a more Democratic city. He'd had a third child in his fifties, the result of his second marriage, to a woman who was born in China. This made him think differently about diversity and inclusion than he had in the past. As had working at a company with a large LGBTQ employee base in a city that led on gay civil rights issues.

He read books. He was a life-long learner, always trying to better himself. He was open to changing his mind, unusual for people in their sixties, often set in their ways, convinced that they are right about everything. Chip wasn't like that.

He was also an obsessive exerciser and an off-and-on-again vegan. He tracked his sleep compulsively, always striving for a sharper mind and better health. He often practiced "dry January," giving up drinking for a month, to prove to himself that he could. Having grown up with an alcoholic parent, it was important to Chip to know that he could maintain control.

However, during the past two years he had apparently become intolerant and closedminded. He found my views to be dangerous and unacceptable. And ultimately, he decided that as an employee, I was dangerous and unacceptable, as well. I was disappointed that

Chip seemed to no longer be the person that I had always thought he was.

My most childish inner voice reared its head:

I don't want to work here anyway. This is a speech- and thought-suppressing shithole and a total travesty and a farce and I can't believe I've spent over twenty-two years of my life in this place that is a total LIE.

"It's ok. I expected this," is what I actually said. My years of practicing a diplomatic I'm-not-an-angry-woman voice were coming in handy.

Chip was relieved. I was going to be reasonable and accept the details of my fate delivered through Microsoft Teams. His shoulders dropped, his face softened, he even smiled a little.

"We'll give you a soft landing (code for severance). A year and a half's salary. If you stay until we find your replacement, of course. And keep it down on social media until then."

You might think I had been using the N-word or ranting about how Democrats eat babies in underground pizza restaurants or something.

You're all hypocrites and liars pretending to care about equality and diversity and inclusion, but you don't. It's a just a communications strategy. You don't mean any of it. And why would I stay quiet now? Have you learned nothing about me?

"What will you do next?" he asked, hoping I'd let him off the hook with some promising notion of my self-charted future.

You say you care about civic engagement and are inspired by those who dare to challenge. But you don't. This is what you really think: "Our view is the right view and if you don't uphold it, well you're a racist alt-right lunatic and we will take you down and you'll deserve it." This is closer to reality than the progressive doublespeak you're all so fond of, eager to prove your "woke" bona fides to cover up the fact that business is as it always has been – about profits. Plain and simple.

You can put on a "we care about profits through principles" face, and you can post about BLM and LGBTQ and all the other letters, but when the rubber hits the road, it's all about the Benjamins, as they say. And, desperate to maintain this "harder right over easier wrong / we really care" ethos, you strike down any view that veers from the orthodoxy. The San Francisco bubble, Democratic Party orthodoxy. Because yes, you're about Party, NOT principles. You're about appealing to the "woke" to sell jeans, because they seem cool to you, like they might buy more and spend more than some Midwestern unstylish self-avowed patriot.

And you do it to satisfy your Gen Z employees who get very noisy when you fail to take whatever Instagram stand of the day is popular – whether it's Ukraine or reproductive rights or posting black squares for some unknown reason or calling Latinos LatinX even if they don't want it. You don't do it because you actually care about equality. You just want to seem like you do.

I naively misunderstood but now I understand. It's all a pose. A pose to make money. You abandoned the principle of equality when you sent your own children to private schools in fall 2021, while remaining silent on the matter of 50,000 mostly disadvantaged San Francisco public school children being trapped at home. And then you told me that I had to remain silent too, because my speech might make you look bad.

From your gated communities, you post IN THIS HOUSE WE BELIEVE signs while quite literally never having had a black person in your home. You genuflect to the obedient useful idiot thought police, letting Twitter and employees strike down anyone who veers from the covid cultism and woke corporatism. They hurl epithets like racist and anti-trans and anti-science at anyone who dares have a point of view anything short of total working-class-destroying lockdowns until no covid. Which, if it isn't clear by now, is and always was an impossibility.

You're all cowards parading around as morally courageous leaders, as "good trouble," but you're no trouble at all. You check to your right and left before taking pretend bold stances that are really just conformist, obedient, state-sponsored talking points, and craven marketing strategies.

Good riddance.

"I'll make movies, write a book," I said.

Chip knew I could do it because I'd done it before while working full time at Levi's. But he had no idea what that meant in the current context. Or could mean.

"Oh, that's great. A second career. You'll be happy. And successful. You've always wanted to do that."

"Yes. Since my twenties."

"That's great. I know you'll be great. Even better than you are at this. Because it matters more to you."

We hung up.

Chip was off the hook, in his mind. Not in mine.

CHAPTER 3:

MY ASKS.

At this juncture, you might be wondering where I stand on the political/ideological spectrum. Of course you are. We live in a binary world and, all too often, we determine what we think of others based on their political affiliation. Unfortunately, both "sides" are often unwilling to concede that those on the other have any integrity, or even basic human decency. And so, each side refuses to listen to the other, an utterly dysfunctional state of affairs which should raise alarm bells for us all, whichever "side" we are on.

For this reason, I'm asking you to set political ideology aside as you read this. Because this story really isn't about politics or political identity or my defection from Left to Right. I voted for Elizabeth Warren in the 2020 Democratic primary election because of her advocacy to protect consumers from corporate malfeasance. My life experiences have left me with an especially strong emotional connection to the issues of women's rights and racial equality. Yet more and more I find myself deeply at odds with much of the Left's "progressive" platform. Which also puts me at odds with most of my longtime friends and traditional allies who, these days, are often not only harshly censorious, but are passionate defenders of ideas that strike me as ranging from destructive to deranged. I find myself "all over the place," politically speaking, even as I have remained true to my long-held principles.

"What's happened to you?" I'm sometimes asked by an erstwhile ally. And I think: *What's happened to me? What's happened to YOU?!*

There's a writer named Liel Liebowitz who captures the feeling in an essay in the online magazine *Tablet*, discussing what he calls "The Turn." He writes:

> You might be living through The Turn if you ever found yourself feeling like free speech should stay free even if it offended some group or individual but now can't admit it at dinner with friends because you are afraid of being thought a bigot. You are living through The Turn if you have questions about public health policies—including the effects of lockdowns and school closures on the poor and most vulnerable in our society—but can't ask them out loud because you know you'll be labeled an anti-vaxxer . . .

This last scenario is of course what led me to where I am. I DID ask those questions, repeatedly and unapologetically. I asked them not in betrayal of my longtime beliefs, but in passionate support of them. For doing so, I was cast as a "*Covid denier*" – a monstrously dangerous ignoramus regurgitating the misinformation spewed nightly by Tucker Carlson. This person – one who believes that covid doesn't even exist – was like no one I've actually ever met, and it certainly didn't describe me.

Lines have been drawn. If you believe lockdowns and school closures were harmful, you're cast as a right-wing lunatic who only cares about freedom (free-dumb!) and doesn't give a damn if people die. If you believe in locking down as long as possible and wearing masks forever to eliminate covid, it means you are a deeply caring and humane person because even if kids don't learn to read or graduate from high school, hey at least they're alive! But these assignments of political ideology based on covid views are not only incorrect, but irrelevant. Please, set them aside, at least for the duration of this book.

Furthermore, I'm not asking you to necessarily agree with me on covid and kids and schools. Or covid policy overall. Chances are, you have well-formed thoughts on these covid matters already. Or maybe you did in the beginning of the pandemic, and shifted your thinking mid-way through. Either way, you know what you think now, and this book probably won't change your mind. Although you never know, maybe it will.

I know there are still plenty of people out there who remain terrified, who stand firm in staying home to stay safe, and double mask when they risk venturing outside, and believe, even now, that the real issue is that no one followed the rules and that we never locked down hard enough, and what we really needed to do was more like what China did – sealing people in their homes, removing infants from their families if parents tested positive, even killing pets – to stop the spread. They'll never shake hands again and think worrying about kids getting an education when people are dying is selfish and short-sighted and monstrous (in which case you probably aren't reading this book and surely think people like me are the problem).

But what I *am* asking – and I realize that for some, in the current environment, this is a big ask – is that those on whatever side of covid issues be given a full hearing.

For nothing is more central to our democracy than a culture of free speech. Nothing is more key to finding truth than open debate and the open expression of ideas. Are some ideas just so dangerous that they need to be shunted, quashed, eliminated from the public sphere? To the contrary, long experience shows that good ideas invariably drive out bad.

In regard to my case, should a Republican (even had I been one – which I'm not; I'm currently registered as "unaffiliated") be able to hold a job in a "progressive" company like Levi's? Shouldn't I have the right to air views at odds with others at my company on my own time without losing my job? Things like this:

Jennifer Sey ✔
@JenniferSey

This makes me so sad. And mad. The private schools will all open. The kids in SF public schools, which includes my own, remain virtual. Which is to say with 'virtually' no schooling.

This is the death knell for public schools in San Francisco.

> **𝕏ₓ SF Examiner** ✔ @sfexaminer · Oct 20, 2020
> San Francisco public schools won't reopen to students for the rest of this year due to issues including limited COVID-19 testing capacity, officials told the Board of Education on Tuesday. sfex.news/31rauPw?utm_ca...

10:10 PM · Oct 20, 2020 · Twitter for iPhone

ılı View Tweet analytics

1 Retweet   **2** Likes

Or this, a direct quote from an op-ed in the *Chicago Sun Times:*

Jennifer Sey ✔
@JenniferSey

"We cannot understate the serious psychological harm that prolonged virtual school has had on many children. We are seeing an epidemic of serious psychological illness that has reached a crisis point." How many more opeds from drs do we need? #openschools chicago.suntimes.com/2020/12/29/222...

6:57 AM · Dec 30, 2020 · Twitter for iPhone

8 Retweets   **29** Likes

Or this:

Jennifer Sey ✔
@JenniferSey

...

I can't believe that bars in SF are open but my son can't go to high school.

6:51 AM · May 7, 2021 · Twitter for iPhone

1,896 Retweets **172** Quote Tweets **13.7K** Likes

This is the broader issue at the heart of my story. In a culture where free speech is recognized as crucial to a democracy, my speech protects yours and yours protects mine. When we only allow the speech of those we agree with, that culture ceases to exist, and so does democracy.

We live in a time when even reasonable and widely accepted ideas get called "hate speech," and when people who veer from various orthodoxies get cancelled. We all have work to do if we want this to change.

Given all that is at stake, and all we've learned, I'm hoping that even some of those who most angrily opposed me on covid have by now come to see things in a new light. For some that will never happen. But I'm hoping that for others, one of the following will resonate:

- Maybe you had an "aha" moment when you were required to wear a cloth mask while walking from the front door of a restaurant to your table, but then you took it off for the next two hours, to drink and eat and laugh.

- Maybe you were fine at first keeping your kids home, but then your daughter told you she was depressed, and you found her report card and, though she'd been a straight A student before, now she was getting all Ds and Fs. And when you questioned her, she told you: "None of it is real. School on the computer isn't real and neither are these Fs." But the depression was real, and so you recognized that because of school shutdowns your kid was suffering, without anything to look forward to or anyone to see or anything to structure her day around.

- Maybe you didn't understand why, although you were "fully vaccinated," you weren't allowed to say goodbye to your friend who was dying of cancer in the hospital.

- Maybe you started to question all the restrictions and requirements (and perhaps even asked yourself if there might be something else at play) when Novak Djokovic was barred from entering the U.S. to play tennis in the U.S. Open because he is unvaccinated. Even though he had recently had covid and recovered, and unvaccinated fans were free to attend matches and cheer on the players.

- Maybe you asked yourself in the spring of 2022: Why are toddlers in preschools and daycare centers still being forced to wear masks all day? And you couldn't come up with any good answer to that question.

But, alas, even among those who have had such revelations, far too many are afraid to say so out loud. That's the *real* danger to America. Staying quiet for fear of the consequences of speaking up. That's not just a betrayal of what the "side" I spent my life on always professed to believe, it's just plain wrong.

Call it a fool's errand, but I do hope and believe that even as we continue to argue about everything else, those on both "sides" will arrive at a point where they can at least agree to hear what the other is saying.

By August 26, 2022, New York Governor Kathy Hochul had stated that closing public schools was a mistake:

> "When the decisions were made to have all the kids go home and learn remotely. Wow. Wow. What a mistake that was."

If we'd listened to each other and had a societal conversation, rather than demonizing the open-schoolers as murderous fascists, might we have reached a different decision and opened the schools sooner? Further, did I deserve to lose my job because I said what I said two years earlier than Governor Hochul? These are the central questions I'd ask you to ponder as you continue. Not, is she Left or Right? Not, do I agree with her about covid? Rather, *Do I support a culture of free speech and open debate*? Or not?

CHAPTER 4:

LEAVING GYMNASTICS.
THE FIRST THING I QUIT.

I am fifty-three years old, and I've quit three things in my life: gymnastics, my first marriage and my job at Levi's. The truth is, I tend to stay in bad situations way too long. I tend to stick with endeavors until I am bleeding on the ground, and I have no choice but to stop. Because I simply can't get up. I should probably do a lot more quitting for my own sanity and self-protection. Better yet, I shouldn't look at it so much as "quitting" as transitioning to a new phase. It's not a failure. It's moving on to new opportunities. I still have work to do on this reframing.

I am also not a contrarian. I don't come by whistleblowing or speaking up against the crowd easily. I spent many years trying to oust the obedience instilled in me by unrelenting coaches who had no regard for the grave responsibility endowed to them when parents hand over their children.

I don't think I spoke in class more than a handful of times during my four years in college. I attended Stanford and was haunted by feelings of inadequacy, or imposter syndrome, as I'd later learn it was called. Having spent most of my adolescence in the gym, training as much as ten hours a day, I wasn't a confident student. I turned in my work, I mastered the complexities of college paper-writing and I got good grades, but I didn't dare debate the other students who seemed WAY smarter than I could ever hope to be. My view was: do my job as a student – get good grades, but don't argue, challenge or rock the boat. Be seen, but not heard. I learned this as a young athlete. It worked for me. Until it didn't.

I was an elite gymnast as a child. I loved turning cartwheels and flipping through the air. As I wrote in *Chalked Up*: "I felt unfettered and invincible."

But then I moved away from home when I was fourteen to train at one of the best clubs in the country so that I could not just qualify for the National Team (I'd already been on it for three years at this point) but rank in the top six. I trained forty to fifty hours a week as a teenager. I endured a forced starvation diet of less than four hundred calories a day, public humiliation and fat shaming (our weight was announced on the loudspeaker at the gym if we gained a quarter pound), training on a broken ankle among other maladies, and coaching cruelty that eventually drove me to the brink of collapse. But I didn't quit; I stayed. For a full two years after my body, mind and spirit rejected the sport, I toiled on, under the belief that I was an abject failure if I couldn't stick it out.

I graduated high school in 1987, and deferred my college start for a year to continue my training and, hopefully, earn a spot on the Olympic team. It was an undertaking that seemed doomed to end in failure as soon as I decided to take it on. Though I'd won the title of U.S. National Gymnastics Champion in 1986 – a feat hugely impressive to outsiders, and one I am proud of to this day, close to forty years later – I had little confidence that I was up to the task.

There were two years until the Olympic squad would be selected. In the life of a young gymnast, two years can feel like ten. If I could maintain my composure and prowess, I seemed a shoo-in; I didn't need to maintain the number one slot, I had six spots I could land in to make the team.

By then, the intensity of the training and the abusiveness of the coaching made every day an impossible slog. Add to that, I was working on a deformed and shattered ankle, I had stress fractures in my shins and wrists, and I suffered from an eating disorder and a mind that was unraveling from the pain of these physical and emotional injuries. So, two years, a full twelve percent of my life thus far, felt inconceivable. My choice became, as I saw it, to walk away from the sport or to walk away from life.

And so, in the spring of 1988, just a few months before the Olympic Trials, I made the sensible decision to "retire" from gymnastics. My retirement was not a celebration of a career well spent, it was a humiliating and undignified escape out the back door. I felt like I'd never deserved the accolades, and this ignominious ending was proof that I was never any good anyway. I mostly felt shame.

I limped away, physically and emotionally broken from the years of abusive training. My left ankle was the size of a baseball, permanently purple and distorted. I was anorexic but transitioning to bulimia, and every time I got in my car to go teach at the gym I no longer trained in, I thought of closing my eyes and pulling my car across the median of the highway and just being done with it all. I could no longer do gymnastics, but I had no value without it. What was I to do?

At nineteen, I was exhausted and hopeless and saw no future for myself without the sport that I no longer wanted any part of. I'd experienced a whole career, before I was twenty, and I was entering the downward spiral of retirement with little to look forward to. I didn't want to coach or get my judge's certificate. My spirit was drained. I'd trained my entire life, had reached the highest of highs, and was now left with nothing but a broken body and distorted mind and a crummy trophy claiming I'd been the national champion.

It didn't help my emotional state that my own parents had rejected me when I quit gymnastics. Upon my leaving the sport, the response from my mother was to sob and go on about how hard it was. For her. She'd dedicated her life to my gymnastics, an obvious mistake in my opinion, but it's only obvious to me with hindsight and twenty-one years of being a parent under my belt.

My dad quickly "forgave" me which caused no end of consternation from my mom. It was easier for him to just move on. He hadn't spent over a decade in the gym with me, as she had, although he showed up at every meet to support me. It was easier for him to keep it all in perspective, because he had a life of his own.

My dad had a job he loved as a pediatrician. He owned his own practice in Northeast Philadelphia, and he treated tens of thousands of children over his nearly sixty-year career. Beyond medical care, he paid to send kids to camp and sporting lessons if their families couldn't afford it. He treated the babies of moms, and even grandmoms, he'd also treated when they were children.

I'd always admired my dad's commitment to his patients, to kids and to the community he practiced in. I knew I didn't have the chops to be a doctor, but I wanted to have an impact as he had.

At the time of my quitting, his forgiveness of me felt like an unearned gift, as compared to my mom's ongoing rejection, which I felt that I deserved. My mom treated my dad's forgiveness of me like a betrayal. I can only imagine that it must have seemed like a repudiation of her choice to subsume her own identity in my gymnastics career.

My mom volunteered at the front desk at the many gyms I trained in, a coveted spot, holding court and engaging in gossip – who was hitting routines, who didn't make weight and might not go to the next meet, who might quit or get kicked out of the gym for "bad" behavior (that generally meant anything short of total submissiveness). She built her social life around gym meets and gym moms, and she derived her sense of identity from having a champion as a daughter. Me being an Olympian would have been the ultimate capper, an accolade to last a lifetime, and that didn't happen. It had all been for naught. I was now the subject of the gossip, not the shining example. I went from golden girl to bad girl and cautionary tale. I was what happened when puberty and personality reared their heads, a double whammy in my chosen sport.

She couldn't see past her own grief, the loss of forever bragging rights about an imagined but now unrealized Olympic berth, to see my devastation. I vowed never to let this happen to me. I would not live my life through my kids. I would have my own identity, outside of being a mother.

When I said I wasn't going to participate in the 1987 USA Championships, my mom threatened not to attend my high school graduation. I told her I wasn't going to the gym anymore. I was done. "I'll make you go!" she shrieked. She'd always been the nice gymnastics parent, the normal one, not a stage parent screaming from the sidelines. She got so nervous at my meets that she usually didn't even watch, let alone shout from the bleachers. This new forcefulness was out of character.

I said I'd eat and eat and gain weight and my coaches would just throw me out and she screeched: "I won't let you! I'll lock the refrigerator!" She seemed not to care that I walked with a limp, dragging my left leg behind me. Or about the permanent stress fractures in my shins, or that I took ten Advil before every practice just to be able to walk. That I got steroid shots every six weeks like some sort of drug addict so that I could train. She didn't care, or simply didn't notice, that I lived on Diet Coke and chewing gum and apples divvied up into four portions to make up four separate "meals" throughout the day. She definitely didn't know I ate Ex-Lax like it was candy, tricking my mind into believing that the chocolate variety was actually a treat, gagging all the while.

My mom didn't notice that my late career surge, when I mastered all manner of new skills, happened because I'd simply given up trying to keep myself safe. I'd always been a cautious gymnast. I understood the dangers. From a very young age, I knew that, if told by a coach to perform a new "trick" that I wasn't ready for, I could land on my head, suffering a broken neck, a broken back, paralysis, even death.

Julissa Gomez, an American gymnast from my era, rose through the National Team ranks in the 1980s. She traveled to the World Sports Fair competition in Tokyo in 1988, with a member of my club team, one of my closest friends. As Julissa practiced her vault, the Yurchenko – requiring a backwards entry to the horse on the vault – she kept missing her feet on the springboard, and her hands on the horse. She managed to escape unscathed, with commonplace head-landings. Until she didn't. One time, her feet missed, and her head slammed full-speed into the vaulting horse. She was instantly paralyzed from the neck down. An accident at the hospital in Japan, in which she became disconnected from the ventilator supporting her breathing, resulted in severe brain damage. She died three years later at home in Texas.

These stories were everywhere, we all knew them, and some of us feared these outcomes, rightly so. Others seemed not to think about the danger, hurling their bodies through space, regaled for their fearlessness. To me, fear seemed sensible.

What many people don't realize about gymnastics is how dangerous it is. And how living in fear can wear on your mental health. After more than a decade of being terrified, my body rejected the sport. And I simply lost all ability to do it. I could no longer do skills I'd been doing since I was eight years old: a backflip on the beam, a double twist on the floor. The "twisties," as they're called, entered public consciousness in 2021 when Simone Biles, the 2016 Olympic Champion and winningest gymnast ever, ejected herself from the covid-delayed Olympics. She didn't know where her body was in the air. She couldn't decipher up from down, floor from ceiling. Severe injury, not a slow time due to an off day at a track meet, was a distinct possibility. She refused to put herself in danger. And so did I, back in 1988.

My mom and I barely spoke between my quitting in the spring before the Olympics and my boarding a plane to California to go to college in August that same year. I arrived at Stanford on crutches, having just had surgery on that mangled ankle. The orthopedist who'd plied me with cortisone for years, bringing his black doctor's bag to the gym every few weeks, finally acknowledged that maybe there was something amiss. He scraped the ankle joint clean in the summer of 1988. He held up bone chips with a tweezer-like utensil during the surgery, for which I was awake but numbed with local anesthetic, saying: "Oh, I guess this is why it hurt!" Gee, you think?

Twenty years later, after my ankle had deteriorated even further, hampering everyday activities – like walking – I went to a new orthopedist. He ordered an MRI. Upon reviewing the films, he queried: "When was the car accident?"

"What car accident?" I asked.

"Your ankle was shattered at some point. I can only imagine the force of a bad car accident did this."

"No. I was a gymnast. I trained on it for two full years after I first injured it."

I was forty years old when I learned the facts of my teenaged injury. At this point in my life, after years of therapy, I thought I'd wrestled my childhood demons to the ground. I was dismayed and alarmed that the physical repercussions would be life-long. Some days simply walking was a painful ordeal. Running and jogging were out of the question. Skiing – no way; the boot couldn't make its way over my lumpy appendage. The doctor "cleaned" my ankle up as best he could with surgery, removing more bone chips and smoothing out the rough edges within the joint. But I had to simply accept that the training on a broken ankle close to twenty-five years earlier had led to grade four arthritis and the need for an ankle replacement, which I was avoiding. I had thought when I trained in pain it was temporary, and it would end when I walked out the door of the gym and stopped tumbling. I realized in that moment, when the doctor looked at me and said the word "shattered," that some injuries, both physical and emotional, leave scars.

My experiences as a child have informed my understanding of the dynamics of abuse. When you are a child and you are hungry from not having eaten for several days, and your coach screams at you that you are fat, you internalize the blame. It's your own fault. The coach wouldn't yell if you hadn't eaten so much. When you are exhausted and training with severe injuries and feeling you are toiling beyond what could ever be expected, and you are told that you are "a lazy piece of garbage," you come to see the castigation as brought on by your own doing. If you weren't so damn weak and pathetic, none of this would be happening. You learn not only to accept poor treatment but to think that you deserve it. And you don't quit. Quitting would be acknowledgment of your own weakness. You keep going and going, battered and broken, to prove your worthiness, and to try to ward off the shame.

My therapist explained to me that when a parent hits a child, she will often say to that child: "I wouldn't have to hit you if you weren't bad." Understanding this was a lightbulb moment for me. But it would take years to put that understanding into practice and learn to "quit." Or, framed differently, to have the good sense, confidence and fortitude to walk away from an unacceptable situation.

While I'd proudly adopted the title "feminist" in my twenties, a partial response to the abuse I'd endured as a child athlete, my instinctive reflex was to continue to blame myself for most things that went wrong well into my thirties and forties. I'd been doing it for so long, it was an ingrained habit. I was already a Vice President at Levi's. Anything that ever went wrong at work, whether it was in my sphere of accountability or not, I felt responsible for. When in-store signage was cut to the wrong specifications, a multi-million-dollar mistake, I took the blame, even though it was the producer's blunder, not mine. No one ever had to worry about who to point a finger at when an error was made. I was all too happy to point it at myself.

This had been a long-standing pattern with men as well. When a consistent hookup in college, a guy I'd fallen for, demanded we keep our "relationship" a secret, I obliged. He offered no good reason, just vague rumblings about a girlfriend back home in New York, three thousand miles away. I could only surmise that I was embarrassing. And I accepted it as true, acquiescing to his terms of engagement, as I was eager for his scraps of affection. Showing up at two in the morning for a "booty call" while ignoring me in class and social settings was far from anything resembling kindness or affection, but it felt acceptable, and all I deserved. When he went public with a girlfriend on campus, I was wrecked. Not angry with him, though. I was angry with myself for not being worthy enough.

These self-doubting, self-sabotaging behaviors were remnants from the abuse in my childhood. But I was getting better. I was learning that not everything was my fault. I walked away from "toxic friendships." I repaired things with my mother. I learned that parents make mistakes, that they are human. If they apologize, we accept, and then work together towards building a better relationship. I dated a few nice guys, who weren't "the one," but treated me with kindness.

But it would take another decade for me to fully understand this dynamic of abuse, to truly unwind it. I was in my early fifties before I could not just identify the inclination towards crushing self-reproach, but stop doing it entirely. Finally, I learned to halt the progression of destabilizing self-incrimination before it ever got to my brain from where it had started – my gut. I just rejected it entirely, once and for all.

So, when the shrieks of "racist, granny killer and science denier" came as I called for open schools during the pandemic, I simply said to myself: No, I'm not. I'm standing up for children, as I wish someone had done for me when I was a child.

When I left gymnastics thirty-four years earlier, I'd felt intense shame. But as an adult, I would stand my ground. I would stand in the breach for kids. I would leave the company with my head held high knowing I'd held on to my values. Not because I was a bigot or whatever else they wanted to call me. I no longer had to accept other people's definitions of me. I defined who I was.

CHAPTER 5:

I'M JEWISH, BUT BARELY.

Both my parents are Jewish, but I grew up celebrating Christmas. Not in a religious sense. We didn't celebrate Jesus being born in a manger, we didn't go to midnight mass or sing carols or open the little flaps on an advent calendar. We decorated a tree and hung stockings and put cookies and milk out for Santa. That was the extent of it. We didn't even sit on Santa's lap at the mall.

My dad was orphaned by the time he went to college. His childhood was rife with death and loss. His parents had gotten divorced before they died, a fact that I was not even aware of until I was an adult and his sister told me. We didn't talk about my dad's family. We were his family: me, my brother, my mom.

Unlike us, what was left of my dad's side of the family celebrated Jewish holidays. And we joined, on occasion. But not often. We only sat through a handful of Passovers at my Aunt Ruth's. I never asked the four questions though. I didn't know what they were. We never celebrated Hannukah, my brother and I didn't have a Bar or Bat Mitzvah, and we didn't go to synagogue. Ever. We didn't own a menorah or affix a mezuzah to our front door to signal that ours was a Jewish home and that God was inside.

I knew I was Jewish, but I can't say I knew what that meant. The strongest sense of Jewish identify I ever felt as a child was watching a mini-series called *The Holocaust*, in 1978. I was not yet ten, and I watched alone as the gaunt bodies lined up for food in the ghettos and then, later, were ushered to the gas chambers. It scared me. My mom found me sobbing in the den, but I couldn't explain what had caused my breakdown. I understood vaguely that those people were my people. I knew we hailed from Russia and Ukraine but had been in America for several generations. I didn't know anything else. I'm left wondering: Why didn't I? Why didn't we talk about it?

In college I often described myself as "culturally Jewish but not religious," which to me meant: I liked corned beef sandwiches and Woody Allen movies, didn't eat mayonnaise and favored bagels and lox if brunch was in order. And I laughed at things that I considered "goyisha," which according to my dad was not having books in one's house, and according to my mom was having bookless bookshelves filled with glass figurines of bunnies and garden gnomes, and giving daughters names like Tiffany and Courtney.

My mom's father, Poppy, was an alcoholic, an enthusiastic gambler and a bookie. He ran the books out of the back of his dry-cleaning store in Atlantic City. My grandmother, Nanny, aspired to higher status, and she worked hard to keep up with the Joneses, which in Jewish neighborhoods in Atlantic City were Rosens and Maurers and Kleins. They were not dry cleaners, but jewelers and small-time real estate moguls and doctors. She was always perfectly coiffed, collected Ferragamo shoes stored pristinely in her closet, and saved money in a shoe box under the bed for rainy days when my grandfather's luck ran dry at the craps tables. Which was often.

Nanny and Poppy had three children: my mom, my Aunt Jill, and my Uncle Bobby, who had severe Down syndrome. When pregnant with Bobby, my grandmother had been seriously ill, and sensed that something was wrong. She begged her doctor for what would then have been an illegal abortion. She was denied.

For several months after Bobby was born in 1952, no one knew precisely what was wrong. But he didn't progress – he didn't smile, hold his head up or meet other key milestones. Once doctors determined he had Down syndrome, he was both the all-consuming focus and the embarrassment of the household. This was close to forty years before the Americans with Disabilities Act. There were no support services for families with special needs children. Culturally, people with disabilities were often treated with either contempt or shame or both. Many families hid the children at home or hid them in facilities. My grandmother chose home. And she and my grandfather loved Bobby like crazy. But no one could come over. He was a secret to be concealed from the world.

Bobby required non-stop care and attention, and there was little left for the girls. My Aunt Jill was a star athlete, as much as was possible for girls in the 1950s. My mom was popular and pretty. She met my dad as a freshman in high school, and while she went to college and majored in biology, her professional life consisted of working in a lab to help put my dad through medical school. Then she had me, and she never worked again.

Nanny and Poppy came to our house on Christmas, pretended Santa had been to visit us, and brought gifts of their own. My dad's family did not come for Christmas. I'm not sure they even knew we celebrated it – if so, they would not have been pleased. When my dad's aunt announced that she was coming over to visit, we scurried to hide the tree in the backyard. I was confused. What's wrong with a Christmas tree? Everyone has one! But we're Jewish, my parents explained.

This begs the question: *Then why do we have a Christmas Tree?* I didn't think to ask it.

Like so many other things, this just wasn't discussed in my family. Why did we seem to pretend we weren't Jewish? Why didn't I know anything about my dad's parents? Why didn't we talk about Bobby? He was there when we visited my grandparents, he was obviously different, why didn't anyone explain it to me? I didn't know how to ask any of these questions, I just knew that there were certain things we weren't supposed to talk about.

My junior year, I started at a new high school, my third school in as many years. I attended Allentown Central Catholic when I moved to Allentown to train in gymnastics, because there was a nationally recognized club there called Parkettes. I was a national team member when I headed to this club in 1983, ranked in the top ten in the country for my age. I hoped that they'd get me to the top six by the time I turned fifteen, so that I would qualify for competitions like the World Championships. They did.

First, I moved there on my own and lived with a coach. Eventually my mother moved with my brother, also a gymnast, and we lived in an apartment together. Later still, my father joined us, and commuted back and forth to his pediatric practice in Philadelphia.

Most of the Parkettes attended Allentown Central Catholic because they let us out early to train. We trained six, seven, sometimes eight or even ten hours a day in the summer. The public school didn't allow anyone to skip gym or study hall. Which meant staying in school until 3:00 p.m. every day, missing two hours of practice, and being on the wrong side of our coaches before even setting foot in the gym.

It was 1985, and there was a gang of us that chose "Central." Two of us were Jewish. My teammate Alyssa and I were the lone Jewish students roaming the halls of Central in the mid-eighties, in our pleated skirts and penny loafers. We all looked like sixth graders, stunted from enforced anorexia, and socially immature from doing nothing other than gymnastics for the last ten years of our young lives. Alyssa looked more typically Jewish than I did. She had darker hair and skin and a stereotypically "Jewish" nose; I was dirty blonde, pale with a button nose. I also weighed less than a hundred pounds, having dropped ten pounds (thus delaying my menstruation), upon starting to train at Parkettes a year earlier.

Allentown was not an enlightened place back then. It was a former steel town that had come on hard times as many rust belt communities had in the eighties, famously referenced in Billy Joel's 1982 song "Allentown."

When Alyssa got a note in her locker disparaging her Jewishness, threatening some vague violence if she didn't get out, signed KKK, we weren't alarmed, or even surprised. Whatever. We weren't welcome there. We already felt unwelcome as tiny freaks, referred to as "Porkettes" by the cool/mean kids, a reference to how *not* porky we actually were.

Neither Alyssa nor I thought much of it, not even enough to tell our parents. We weren't afraid (did these morons know the KKK hated Catholics also?). Still, I was relieved that they hadn't come for me. I passed. They didn't even know that I was Jewish. And I certainly wasn't going to mention it. If my own parents didn't embrace it, why should I? If we didn't go to synagogue on High Holy days, or celebrate Passover, why did I need to open myself up to even more mockery and make myself feel like even more of an outsider? I mean I basically *wasn't* Jewish. And if we didn't regularly visit the practicing side of the family, there must be something shameful about being Jewish, right? So why not just keep the secret?

Though my husband Daniel is also Jewish, and not religious, his Jewishness is a major part of his identity. The dignity of difference, often strong in Jewish families, is something he and his family are proud of. I envy this pride in his heritage, this deep sense of history and strong connection to the past. For me, there was just my immediate family, in the right now, nothing more.

Since we met in 2012, I've adopted some Jewish practices, if not the faith. One of the few rules Daniel has in our house is no Christmas tree. Ever. We celebrate Hannukah every year, and each time, we light the candles on all eight days, and Daniel tells the story of how the Jews fought for freedom over two thousand years ago when they revolted against their oppressors.

Daniel often says I have less of a religious impulse than anyone he's ever met. And he's right. There is no part of my being that believes or wishes to believe in any higher power. I am neither religious, nor spiritual in a secular sense. I don't like yoga or chanting or praying or seeking. I don't like being told that there are fixed rules to being a good person. I prefer to make that calculation on my own. I've never wanted a framework from religion or any other organized group to tell me how to think, or how to be virtuous, or how to achieve the moral high ground. Perhaps that's why it's been easier for me to have rejected the dictates of the Left and the Democratic Party.

Yet it does seem to me that we all feel the need for guidance, and sometimes I do wish that I could embrace Judaism and find direction from an external source, as religious people do. Indeed, it is precisely because the need for a moral compass is so universal, that in an increasingly secular world so many seek desperately for other ways to find it – whether through political affiliation, blind adherence to "the science," or self-help gurus.

As I've tried to teach myself a bit more about Judaism, I've learned about *Tikkun olam*, a central concept in modern Jewish thought. *Tikkun olam*, in Hebrew, literally means "repairing the world." It teaches that we must behave constructively, through good deeds and everyday kindnesses, to make the world a better place. I didn't know what it was until I was forty-two years old, but it felt like something I could get on board with when I happened upon it, more so than any other religious principle I'd ever encountered. Try to do good in the world in your daily existence. That's it. And that's all I want to try to do. A little good. Every day. In the world.

Which is sometimes very hard. But I keep trying.

CHAPTER 6:

MY EARLY WORK YEARS. HUMILIATING, BUT NOT TERRIBLE. AND NOT WOKE.

Though I spent close to twenty-three years at Levi's, I didn't begin my working life there. In the year or so following my graduation from college in 1992, there was a full-fledged recession, and jobs were hard to come by for liberal arts graduates with no obviously marketable skills. I had dreams of being a writer and a filmmaker, though I'd never actually written anything or learned to use a camera, although I did take film theory classes in college. So, I first worked as a production coordinator on commercials, getting odd jobs here and there on car ads filmed in Napa Valley. Then I worked for close to a year on an independent film called *Nina Takes a Lover*, first for free, then after explaining I couldn't make rent on "free," for peanuts. Since it wasn't enough to make ends meet, I taught gymnastics in the evenings.

I didn't like myself as a gymnastics coach. I'd had terrible mentors. I was impatient with the kids. I didn't understand those who lacked total obedience and commitment. Mostly I was tired by the time I got to the gym in Redwood City, a half hour south of San Francisco, where I lived, having worked a full day running errands for grumpy assistant directors, and driving crew around in the wee hours of the morning.

Production crews tend to be very male. Boys enamored of high-tech toys often grow up to be gaffers and sound guys. On one shoot, I was the driver. I steered a large van around on the windy roads of Sonoma looking for scenic backdrops for the latest minivan iteration, with a location scout and various other members of the production team. On one early morning jaunt, it must have been right around 4 a.m., the lights on my unwieldy vehicle went dead. As I attempted to navigate the slippery roads, I could see no more than a few feet in front of my face. I fiddled with the lights, less panicked about driving blind than about failing in my responsibility to get the men I was carting around where they needed to be. From the back, they all started yelling at me, assuming I just didn't know how to drive. I didn't want to seem incompetent. And I *really* didn't want to cry.

I didn't. I got us where we were going. A small incident, really, but there's a reason it has stayed with me. Even then, uncertain as I was, I was disciplined and determined, and overcame obstacles. And I'm sure this resolve, too, was in part a legacy of my gymnastics past.

The production gigs were irregular, and I realized that I wasn't good at financial insecurity. I needed a real job and a regular paycheck, otherwise my anxiety would get the better of me. I wasn't aspiring to massive wealth, just an ability to reliably cover my expenses, such as an unexpected car repair.

I got an entry level job at an advertising agency called Foote, Cone & Belding (FCB). Upon being offered the job I remember saying to my roommates, of which I had many, as was the common practice then and now for a twenty-three-year-old living in San Francisco: "I better not be doing this in five years." That was 1994. I would keep doing some version of "this" for close to thirty years.

I worked on many accounts during my time at FCB: Taco Bell, Clorox and, eventually, Levi's. My salary, which I was very proud of, was $16,000 a year. I relied on free hot dogs at gay bar happy hours and pizza at late night work sessions to feed myself. I didn't care. The agency was filled with young people, and it was fun. And I was good at it. I kept my head down and my mouth shut, and managed budgets and production details. In the days before sending links to view, I flew back and forth to the Taco Bell corporate offices in Southern California delivering VHS tapes of thirty-second ads.

And I had an amazing mentor. Dominic regularly called me into his office to view new work before sharing it with clients. I didn't understand it. Why did he want to know what I thought? I didn't know anything. He showed me storyboards for new ideas and said: "What do you think?"

I was dumbfounded. *I don't know what I think*, I thought, but usually didn't say. He was literally the first person at work who'd ever asked me such a thing. I'd make up some nonsense of strung together marketing-speak I'd picked up in the halls.

But one day I summoned up the courage to ask him: "Why do you ask me what I think? I'm nobody. I balance budgets."

"Jen, if you lined up ten six-year-olds and told them to do cartwheels, would you be able to tell which one had talent?"

"Sure," I said. "Of course, it's obvious."

"That's why I ask you what you think. I can tell too."

Ultimately, I found myself on the Levi's account at the agency, a prized placement at FCB in the nineties, the height of Levi's relevance. I was thrilled that I would no longer need to immerse myself in the Taco Bell "competitive set" (all the other fast food restaurants Taco Bell vied with for consumer attention) – which meant eating way too much fast food and which was not good for my waistline or overall health. I'd never been a big fast-food eater, but I was a Levi's wearer, and had been since my childhood.

My first pair of Levi's were baby blue corduroys that I wore with pride until they were floods, several inches above the ankle (this was before cropped was cool, they were just too small). Throughout college I wore vintage button-fly 501s found at used clothing stores with names like Wasteland and Afterlife. What makes 501s unique is that they button up to the waist, rather than zip. Finding the perfect pair, worn-in just so, with the right depth of holes at the knee and whiskering at the button-fly was a triumph. You had to try on every pair because the sizing was all wrong, because the jeans had been worn and stretched out by another wearer. But if you had the patience for it, you could find a pair of Levi's to comfortably spend your every waking moment in, and look pretty cool while doing it.

I made friends at FCB on the Levi's account who remain friends to this day. Anna was brazen and smart and just about the sassiest person I'd ever met. Everything that came out of her mouth was funny, and almost everything would today be considered wildly inappropriate. Shannon always had solid advice for those twenty-something romantic entanglements going nowhere. Her advice usually amounted to "dump him," and she was almost always right. (It's no wonder she ultimately became a therapist.) The three of us still meet up whenever we can to talk about where our kids are going to college and what our husbands are up to. For the past decade, Anna has emailed me regularly to ask what fit of Levi's she should get her kids for back to school and for her husband so he could avoid looking hopelessly dated. I've always been ready with advice. The perfect fit for every family member.

I worked for close to three years at FCB with Anna and Shannon, and then left for a job down the street on the "client side" at Banana Republic, the more sophisticated apparel upstart recently purchased by The Gap. I negotiated a $10,000 raise which was too much to pass up. The free hot dogs were getting old as I rounded the corner to thirty. And I didn't want to ask my dad to loan me money when my car broke down, as had recently happened.

Banana Republic had a female CEO, Jeanne Jackson, who took an interest in talented junior employees but was known for making the product team cry if they didn't have answers to her very detailed, sometimes unanswerable, questions about things like color palette. About a year into my tenure, she called me into her office. I couldn't imagine why. I was terrified. She was terrifying. She'd just recently, notoriously, made the accessories merchant sob and flee the room at a seasonal line review. (This didn't halt his career, he went on to run several faltering companies, including Mervyn's, Charlotte Russe and Sears, cashing in with every bankruptcy, failing up the ladder, as they say.) I went up to the top floor, to the executive offices, and took my seat.

"One of my jobs as CEO is as chief cheerleader for promising young employees."

Who me? I strained to smile and seem relaxed.

"What do you want for your career?" I had no idea. Did I even *want* a career

"I'd like to be a Chief Marketing Officer." I pulled that out of my ass. Seemed like the right thing to say.

"Okay! You've got to learn the business." I had no idea what that euphemism meant. I hadn't gone to business school or worked at McKinsey. It had something to do with gross margins and return on invested capital. At that time, I had limited understanding of what those concepts were.

"Yes, I know."

She wrapped things up with: "And never forget, our most important customer is the shareholder." Though I didn't really understand the implications of this statement at the time, this summary is both truthful and important. It was also prophetic in how it would ultimately end my career because, by the 2010s, this admission would come to be seen as ugly, and corporate leaders would try to conceal it.

And that was that. I got out unscathed from Jeanne Jackson's office, wondering what I'd done to deserve such a gentle interaction. I should have been more grateful than I was. It was 1995, and she was the last corporate leader who would express unconstrained support for what *I* wanted from my career. She was also the only leader I've worked under who was so forthright about who we really served and why we were actually in business at all.

The Gap was a culture led by women, except at the very top. The CEO was Mickey Drexler, a guru in the apparel industry who had turned The Gap into an icon in the 1990s with khakis, white t-shirts and casual Fridays. No one knew what The Gap "stood for." There was no such thing as "values-led" marketing. No one cared. They just wanted the khakis and logo tees.

Everywhere but the tippy top – women ran the place. I worked for a female CMO and a female V.P. of marketing and, of course, there was Jeanne, the head of Banana Republic, who reported to Mickey. I could have thrived professionally, embraced the role models afforded to me. But I hated it. *Mean girls gone mad* best described the culture.

When my gay bar escort and best friend, Lance, came to visit me for lunch one day he started laughing hysterically.

"What's so funny?" I said, awkwardly swathed in my silk twinset, not in keeping with my personal style in the off hours, which could have best been described as "goth."

"It's just funny that you were so anti-sorority in college and now you work in one. It's like one big Pi Phi party here. And no one is eating. It's lunch! Where's their food?"

He was right. Functional anorexia presented as lettuce with lemon juice and a Diet Coke for lunch. I was emerging from my own gymnastics-induced eating disorder and feasted on a plate of pasta drenched in butter as an act of rebellion.

Though I was generally silent in the hallways and avoided socializing, I sometimes attempted an interaction by complimenting someone's outfit. I tried it one day in the elevator. "I like your suit, is it Banana?" (This articulation, which we all used, still makes me laugh. I picture someone in a big banana suit, like might be worn at a theme park for Fruit of the Loom.)

She scoffed. "Ha. No. It's Jil Sander."

I had no idea who Jil Sander was. But this colleague, many levels my senior, made it clear that wearing the clothes we made at the company was beneath most executives. They flaunted multi-carat rings and Prada handbags themselves, while hocking knock-offs for those who would never be able to afford such luxuries. I thought it was gross.

Conspicuous consumption ruled the hallways. No one talked about their politics or their charitable giving, only their vacation homes, their new handbags and their "push presents" which were generally diamond tennis bracelets. I had to get out. This was definitely not me.

Yet even as I resisted integrating myself into the culture of business and fashion and fake luxury goods, my fear of not having a job and a steady paycheck always won out. In mid to late nineties San Francisco, the brazen young pioneers, including my boyfriend at the time, who later became my first husband, pursued start-ups and independence from the corporate grind. Out of anxiety, low self-esteem and the need to pay my rent, I kept working at the corporate grind. Still, I hoped that I'd one day find the confidence to write something.

It all finally got to me. One day I stormed out of The Gap not long after a senior leadership meeting that I hadn't known would be happening that day, because I didn't care enough to keep track of meetings that I wasn't invited to. I lost my temper when I was quizzed by my boss on the outcomes of this meeting that I had no idea existed. The most eager and ambitious young employees always knew what was happening in every corridor of the building. Who decided what, who yelled at whom, what seasonal concept was rejected, what window idea was approved. That was not me. I couldn't wait to get out of there every day.

"I have no idea what happened. I wasn't there! I'm busy working, unlike you!"

I literally said that, which was completely out of character. But the rage had bubbled over, and a little while later I was waiting for the bus on Market Street wondering what I'd do next.

I soon found myself a job as an account executive at an upstart marketing agency servicing all the tech start-ups. We did have some non-tech clients, and one of those was Nike. On a trip to Portland one day to meet with the client, I opened our presentation, as is common practice for account executives. The "account" person starts with the messaging strategy, then the "creative" takes over. Before I could even start, the client interrupted me, though he looked at my creative partner, a man.

"I don't want to hear from her."

He pointed at me, barely able to contain his impatience and, frankly, disgust.

At the time, I figured that he didn't want to hear from a know-nothing kid. He wanted to be wowed by the creative genius of my older and more experienced colleague. I stayed quiet, looked at the table, ashamed at what must have been my unconvincing setup. I'd let my agency down.

"Let her finish," my partner Jon said.

"No," the client said.

And that was that. Jon presented the creative. The client didn't look at me the entire time. Jon and I packed up our stuff and flew home to San Francisco.

I assumed that the client rightfully dismissed my youth and inexperience, though I wasn't really that young or that inexperienced.

I refused to acknowledge that it was sexism that drove this guy to tell me not to speak, to assume that whatever I had to say was not worth hearing. I didn't let the possibility that there was even a tinge of misogyny creep into my mind, because noticing it would have been a sign of weakness on my part. And saying something would have been bratty and difficult, and nothing would have been done. It took me twenty years to recognize that it was sexism, and to admit to myself that it was unacceptable bigotry.

With the tech boom flailing and Nike declining our work, the little agency faltered. Worried I'd be without a job when it went under, I took a call from my old FCB friend, Shannon, who was now at Levi's.

It was the summer of 1999. The job was an entry level marketing position, with a reduction in title for a job beneath my experience. But I thought nothing of taking a step backwards. It was Levi's, and they were near the top of their game.

Well, actually, more precisely, they were already a few years into a decline from their peak that would last another twelve years. But I didn't care. I could ditch the twinsets, leave my nose ring in each day, dust off my favorite 501s and at last be myself.

At Levi's we used to jokingly call fashion the "F" word. We sat outside and above the superficial ephemera of fashion. We were a *real* business. Therefore, it was imperative that serious-minded men run the place.

Though still the exception, it's not all that unusual for women to lead fashion companies. Rose Marie Bravo led Burberry back to relevance from 1997-2005, making plaid bikinis all the rage. Coco Chanel famously started her eponymous luxury brand in 1910 in Paris selling hats on Rue Cambon. She touted individual style with the words: *Beauty begins the moment you decide to be yourself.* She exhorted women towards individuality rather than conformity: *You were born an original, don't become a copy!* (Ironic given fashion's appeals today.) In the mid 1990s, at the height of its fame and popularity, The Gap touted "Everyone in Color" in an ad campaign. It was a call to conform, urging everyone to wear the same colorfully striped sweater, with slight variations to allow for some personal choice. This was arguably the death knell for its relevance.

The trick in fashion: get people to all *want* to look the same and buy the same stuff with only slight variations, while telling them they are being themselves. It's a remarkable sleight of hand if you think about it, one only the very best corporate storytellers can pull off (no wonder they're so good at woke capitalism, lots of practice). Fashion weaves a tale of authentic self-expression, no brand more so than Levi's, while moving everyone towards a single trend, the conformity cloaked with individualism. Fashion brands need people to believe that they are all originals, even when they all look the same, because companies can't make one unique item for every person. There's no scalability in that. It's an unviable business model. The Gap said the quiet part out loud, and it set them on a path of decline for over a decade, one they have yet to recover from.

Despite the fact that the fashion industry is geared towards women, Levi's was, and is, male dominated. Throughout the eighties and nineties, it was salesman-led, garmento-modeled and pretty inhospitable to female employees. And despite the current social justice warrior presentation, as of this writing, only 25 percent of the board is made up of women, they've never had a female CEO and the leadership team, while made up of close to 60 percent women, seats men in all key decision-making roles – CEO, Chief Financial Officer (CFO) and Chief Commercial Officer. Women occupy support function seats like the Head of HR, the Head of Corporate Communications and Chief Transformation Officer (you're not alone if you don't know what that is). And there are no black people or Latinos on the leadership team.

CEO Chip Bergh hails from Proctor & Gamble. He is credited as a great innovator for bringing the Swiffer to harried housewives everywhere, which was his crowning career achievement before taking the helm at Levi's. A former Levi's CEO, Phil Marineau, spent his career at Quaker Oats and Pepsi before taking over at Levi's in 1999, when I started there. Men, who know how to run businesses, "innovate," and sell things – mops or oatmeal or colas – lead Levi's. Not women who love clothes and getting dressed and expressing themselves, their individuality and power, through personal style.

But Levi's is not such an outlier. Still today, 86 percent of fashion companies are led by men, even though two thirds of clothing sales around the world are made to women. It's even more lopsided in cosmetics. 100 percent of the top CEOs of cosmetics companies are men, while nearly 100 percent of lipstick buyers are women.

I started in this male-dominated environment in 1999. I didn't know any different. I'd been trained on my production jobs and so the slights and soft misogyny that came went relatively unnoticed by me. It was the world. I simply had to be better than the others if I wanted to succeed.

I'd embraced this challenge from a young age as a gymnast. We were judged (literally) in competitions. A judge may like you, she may not. You just have to be better than everyone else to succeed. You got the benefit of the doubt if you came from a well-known club. Maybe you didn't get the full three-tenths of a point deducted that the code of points required for a stumble if you hailed from Bela Karolyi's team, which I did not. But no matter what, don't ever complain about unfairness.

We were trained to fix our hair into perfect pin curls. We used spongey pink rollers, piled high on our heads frozen with Aqua Net hairspray the night before a competition, impeding sleep, to achieve the just-so pixie look. I was told to lose two pounds overnight, "by any means possible," or I could forget about going to Nationals, because "we don't coach fat gymnasts." I was sixteen, weighed exactly ninety-nine pounds, and already limited myself to four hundred calories a day, while working out for a solid seven hours. I was told by a prominent judge that I should grow out my bangs because they made my face look fat.

That was the world. I was told I'd have to be more perfect, thinner, prettier to win. I'd have to just be better by a longshot, so that I simply couldn't be denied a winning score.

I brought this ethos into my professional life. Put up with the bullshit. Endure any unfair, superficial criticisms. That was the unspoken remit. Just keep going. I truly had no qualms about it.

CHAPTER 7:

LEAVING MY FIRST MARRIAGE.
THE SECOND THING I QUIT.

I 'd met the man who would become my first husband when I was twenty-five and working at FCB. Shannon told me not to put up with his inexpressiveness. But I didn't listen to her. I'd barely dated up until that point and desperately needed validation in the aftermath of gymnastics.

Though I'd graduated from college with a 4.0 grade point average, I had little confidence in my own intellect. But I respected intelligence more than any other quality. I didn't want to be a dumb jock. Or perceived as one. But some part of me thought I was one.

I don't want to get into the tos and fros and who did what to whom. I mention this part of my life only because quitting is a theme in my narrative. Although quitting is often framed as a failure, it can also be framed as successfully exiting a situation that no longer serves its primary purpose – whether gymnastics at age nineteen, or Levi's at age fifty-two. Indeed, it is sometimes necessary to prevent the obliteration of the self. If you can't say what you think and be accepted by those in your life for who you are, the choice should be clear-cut: walk away.

From the minute I met my soon-to-be boyfriend and eventual husband, I was agog and in love. For the first time in my life, I loved someone "like a field on fire," an unimprovable description that I read decades ago in a novel called *The Story of a Marriage*.

My ex was the smartest person I'd ever met, and I had so much admiration for him. I needed him to want to be with me. He quoted Dante and Greek philosophers, and taught himself computer programming languages despite being a chemistry major in college. He held court on everything from politics to philosophy to child-rearing, and I just took it all in.

I loved him like a field on fire.

"How did I get one of these?" he would say, pointing at me, if we glimpsed sight of our reflection in a passing mirror or window. I felt like a whole person for the first time in my life.

He didn't play games. He asked me out. He showed up when he said he would. He cooked for me and introduced me to his family. We talked for hours as young people with fiery brains and hearts do. We were together for five years before we got married. And then we were married for eleven. Much of the time we were unhappy. But not all of it. There were perfect moments of perfect young love.

We had two amazing children together who are now adults and make me proud every day. My ex deserves so much credit for making them into the admirable young men that they are: sensitive, curious, independent. Both are able to sit and draw for hours and have avoided the lure of screen addiction. From the time they could hold pencils, my ex would sit them down and tell them to draw. Here's a comic book, copy it. Here's a still life, you can do it. Both boys have an ability to sit still for long periods of time and just be, with their own thoughts, with a pen in hand. This is such a rarity today. He gave them that, I believe.

But I felt lonely all the time. I needed someone who wanted to talk to me about his day, however mundane, who would hold my hand at the movies, and would grow old with me not in bored or stubborn silence, but engaging in conversations as lively as we'd had when we first met. Ultimately, my first marriage did not stand the tests of maturity, waning passion and the divergence of our individual goals for our life together. I tried to be the person that my ex wanted me to be, but I needed someone who would go on family vacations with me, rather than insisting that they were unnecessary indulgences. I tried to transform myself for him, setting vacations – and all other "indulgences" – aside for a decade. I craved intimacy, and fun, and a willingness to try to make the other person happy, but it felt like there was only *his* way. It wore me down. We were both terribly unhappy, and I felt like a miserable failure all the time.

Our kids were seven and nine when I walked out the door. The guilt of being the bad parent unwilling or incapable of enduring my own dissatisfaction and unhappiness to sustain my kids' sense of stability eats at me still.

The day after I moved out, to an apartment around the corner, I planned to go to work. But I couldn't stop crying. By then, I was the head of marketing for Dockers, the second largest brand in the Levi Strauss and Company portfolio. I texted my boss at the time and said: "I can't come in today."

"Are you ok?"

"No."

I couldn't bring myself to tell him. I was so ashamed.

He called me immediately. Damnit. I had to pick up.

I answered the phone but said nothing. I couldn't find my voice.

"What is it?" he asked.

I was silent.

"Jen?" he prodded.

I opened my mouth. Nothing but a choked sob came out. I waited until I could calm myself.

"I'm getting divorced. I feel like such a failure."

I'd blurted it out. I had to tell someone. I hadn't told anyone yet.

"You're not a failure, Jen. I know you. Do not think this about yourself," he said.

I didn't believe him, but I still needed him to say it.

In the coming months, as my ex and I were sorting the ins and outs of joint custody, I often had to call into early morning staff meetings after dropping the kids at school, on my drive into work, whereas in the past I'd always been the first one in in the morning.

Sometimes I had to leave early, to pick the kids up from school, again taking meetings from the car. When I was married, my husband had handled school drop-off and pick up, since he was a stay-at-home parent. Now we split that responsibility.

I was always running behind, and my heart raced constantly. I could never calm myself and I felt like I was failing everyone.

In fact, "I'm sorry" were the words I uttered most often during these hectic months of transition. I was sorry if I was two minutes late to pick the kids up after school. I was sorry if I got dinner on the table late because I was finishing up a Power Point presentation for the next day. And I was sorry if I had to hurry my team along in a meeting to get to the punch line. I was sorry about everything.

I did less coaching, and more insisting that deadlines be met without a lot of guidance from me. I begged off after-work celebrations. "Team building" happened in the office, during work hours, never after. I actually got very efficient at getting all the work done.

No matter what, I refused to fall behind in my duties. After that one missed day, right after I moved out, I never missed another. And I never missed a deadline. I worked late at home after the kids were asleep, often until well after midnight. I got up at 5 a.m. to answer emails from the night before. On the days I didn't have the boys, I stayed in the office until nine at night. I never failed to deliver on my responsibilities, but I felt like I could never catch my breath. My work product never suffered, but I was not myself. Until I was again.

The work actually kept me going and gave me focus. I liked having something to distract my mind from my divorce woes. And ultimately, I liked keeping work focused on work. Less chit chat, more *get it done*. And the *get it done* became fun once I got my bearings. We were a tight-knit group on Dockers, and I considered many on my team to be my friends. Because even with less chit chat, you squeeze in some during coffee breaks and work trips

For all my ups and downs at Levi's, I made friends across the years and decades. That place was my community, my support system. I don't attend any house of worship, I don't join clubs, or play on a recreational sports team. Levi's was my place.

We were in each other's lives and we knew each other's business. How can you not when you work together sometimes ten or twelve hours a day? During the frenetic and frantic months following my separation, this "work friend," my boss, gave me the thing I wanted and needed more than anything. He told me that I wasn't a failure. And I played it back for myself over and over, just to get myself out of bed.

Before leaving my marriage, I used to think: I have two amazing kids, I have a good job, I have loads of friends. I just don't get to have this. I don't get to have a good marriage. And that's okay. I was trying to convince myself that it was just fine if the person you love most in the world, the one you are supposed to confide in and draw support from, didn't provide that. It really was no big deal, I'd tell myself. I should be strong enough to endure. In fact, I thought of it as weakness that I needed so much from him.

When I left, I knew that I needed something that he couldn't or wouldn't give me, but I felt it was my fault for needing it in the first place. And I desperately missed the idea of what I thought we'd be when we grew old.

As we grew up together in our thirties, and became parents, it became clear that what I wanted and what he wanted for our life together was not the same. I was the breadwinner, in a corporate job I felt ambivalent about, so that we could pay the rent on our rapidly dilapidating apartment. I never cared about being rich, but I did need financial stability to stay sane and comfortable. As a VP of Marketing, I drove a Toyota Corolla with a hole in the trunk from when someone had tried, and succeeded, in breaking into it. I didn't want an upgrade to a Porsche, but I wouldn't have minded an upgrade to an intact Toyota Camry. My ex viewed that as wasteful. He wanted to make art and fulfill his creative passions, having left his tech start-up days behind. I wanted to own a home, and make it pretty, while he disavowed all material goods. When two people can't agree on the basic facts of how they want to live, it's not really a viable relationship any longer.

But it really broke me for a time. At forty-one, I felt lost, having no idea what life held for me anymore. The only time I've ever prayed in my entire life is in the months following my divorce. I prayed to no one in particular, to just please let me recover. Let it not hurt so much. Please, let me breathe again without hating myself.

Even in my darkest hour, quite literally on my knees, I had faith I wouldn't spend the rest of my life alone. Somewhere deep down, I knew I wasn't damaged goods. I wasn't broken. I wasn't too needy. I just hadn't found the right person.

CHAPTER 8:

THE RIGHT PERSON.

I met Daniel at a reading in a bookstore. The author we'd both come to see was a mutual friend. I almost turned my car around to head home and didn't go but, luckily, my therapist's voice was in my head. I'd recently bemoaned my online dating experiences – I dated like it was my job for about a year after getting divorced – as unfruitful. My therapist's advice: "You will meet someone. Just do the things you love." I love books. So, I did a U-turn on the Embarcadero and entered the bookstore alone to find my place in the audience.

Daniel and I went to dinner that night after the reading, along with the author we'd come to see. Prophetically, the first conversation we ever had was about public schools. I told him a story about something that had happened that day at work. A fellow mom in the office was looking into schools for her kids and asked me which school my kids went to. Expecting me to regale her with stories about the city's elite private schools – Live Oak or San Francisco Day or Children's Day, or one of the others featuring gardens and flexible learning schedules and "diversity and inclusion programs" – her jaw dropped when I told her: the public elementary and middle schools in our neighborhood.

"You send your kids to New Traditions? I wouldn't send my dog there," she said.

Really. What's so special about your dog?

What I actually said was: "We like it. The kids are doing well. The teachers are great. We've had a good experience overall. And it's an inclusive community."

I resisted the impulse to point out that my kids' schools didn't *need* "diversity and inclusion" programs. Their school *was* diverse and inclusive.

I was of no use to her. If I thought New Traditions Elementary was fit for my kids, I clearly didn't understand how delicate and special hers were. And her dog, for that matter. She turned and walked away.

Daniel almost didn't believe me when I told him this story. He had not only attended public schools, but like many of his family members, had worked in them. His family members include not just public school teachers, but principals and social workers, as well.

He thought I had to be exaggerating. But he didn't know these people who found public schools to be beneath their children. Though they think of themselves as "of the people," they are snobs, and their snobbishness bleeds into racism, whether they know it or not.

At the time I met Daniel, I had two children, both students in the San Francisco public school system. I believe in contributing time, energy and money (if you can) to improve public schools, not fleeing for the pristine halls of a $60,000 per year private school, where kids are coddled and protected, and shielded from – the horror – less well-off kids. I'd rejected private schooling for my own kids since my oldest entered kindergarten in 2006, though even then I could have cobbled together the money. Later, when I had more in the bank and I could unquestionably have afforded ritzy academies with headmasters and lacrosse teams, I still chose public. I don't mean to make this sound heroic. I just wanted them to go to the neighborhood school where they'd be part of the fabric of their community.

Public schooling is the backbone of our society. It provides the foundation for equality of opportunity, a truly American concept. I believe in this project, and I've always wanted my family to be a part of it. We are not too good for public schools.

We are part of the city in which we live, and we don't wish to be cordoned off from it. All too many say that they believe in public schools as a concept, but then, when it comes to *their* kids, they want nothing to do with them.

"The truth is, she'd never send her kids to a place with that many brown children," I told Daniel on that first night.

"No way. That's not it. That's crazy. No one thinks that way," he declared.

He was sure I was being incendiary just for conversation's sake.

"I'm telling you. All she had to do was look at the schoolyard and she said: *No way, not my kid.*"

We both ended up going on about how much we believed in public schools – so enthusiastic in the absoluteness of our agreement we were practically shouting.

It was a match from the get-go. And I was thrilled to meet someone who felt as strongly about the issue as I did.

The problem with online dating is you need to check a bunch of boxes about the "facts" of a person you're hoping to find. Checking boxes doesn't get at the heart of the person you *need* to find. I'd check boxes about age (close to mine), parent status (divorced, has had kids, doesn't want more), and employment (stable). Daniel would have checked only one of those three. We're the same age, though since I'm three months his senior he likes to say I'm an older woman. He had never been married and had no children when we met. He's an attorney but was an under-employed one, working irregular temp jobs doing document review. But what could never have been captured by the "facts" included in any online form was his kindness and fierce loyalty.

From the very beginning, he lavished me with compliments. Every time he offered one – "You're smart! You're amazing! How did I get so lucky!?" Or even just "what a great question!" – I'd balk. I'd say: "Why are you messing with me? You're mocking me. You can't possibly think that's a great question." He'd look at me with dismay, explaining that he was being serious. Even more than twenty years after leaving gymnastics, I felt so undeserving of compliments that I was distrustful of anyone who offered me one.

But Daniel changed that.

A few fun facts about him that wouldn't have found a box on any form, though they might have wended their way into his profile description: he taught himself a handstand at the age of forty; he was a medic in the Israel Defense Forces in his twenties when he wasn't sure what to do with his life; he's read more books (and can quote them) than anyone I've ever met; he has the heart of a rebel. Also: he will cut off his nose to spite his face, just to not have to follow any arbitrary rules; and he cares less about what people think of him than seems humanly possible. Except me. He cares deeply about what I think.

But here's my favorite descriptive life event from Daniel's past: in high school other students paid him to take the SAT for them. He knew all the answers and could get any score requested. Not too high, or it would prompt suspicion. Not too low, or the intended result (getting into a good college) would not be achieved. He did a low-tech version of Rick Singer's 2019 college admissions scandal that ended with celebrities and hedge fund managers being sent to jail for paying Singer to fraudulently inflate their kids' SAT scores to get into the University of Southern California. Daniel's low-tech version involved just walking in the test room, saying he was the other guy, and taking the test. He used the money to further his gambling habit. He was a smart bad boy. What else could I ask for? I longed for a bad boy to match my own good girl status. And so, we had a match.

Daniel asked me out after that first meeting at the bookstore. I didn't know if it was a date or a friendly get-together. Part of me thought he might be gay as he showed no signs of aggressive lasciviousness. He didn't hit on me in a crude fashion. After a year of creepy sexts from one-time Match.com meet-ups I didn't have much faith in the male species. I assumed that they were all a little untoward and inappropriate in their sexual proclivities. But Daniel was ever respectful.

We went out. Daniel isn't gay. We now have two children of our own, in addition to my two from my first marriage, and we have been married for five years. The marriage came after the kids, as I was hesitant to embark on that journey again. But in the end, he convinced me. He's very convincing.

When I first started my dating excursions post-divorce, I prioritized "nice" above all else, setting "smart" aside as my number one criterion for a mate. I also looked for "divorced with kids," because I didn't want, or think I could have, more. But "nice" proved insufficient. And modern science proved helpful in the having kids over forty part. Ultimately, smart *and* nice was the winning ticket. Nice, specifically, as it pertained to me. His kindness is what knocked my socks off, and ultimately transformed how I thought about myself. Not until I met Daniel did I truly believe I was worthy of kindness. In my heart of hearts, I believed any meanness directed my way was deserved and that I'd done something wrong to provoke it. I don't think that anymore. At least not as a guiding principle, though it creeps back in every now and then, and he sets me straight.

Daniel stated vociferously his relationship goals from the outset: "I want us to have the best relationship. I want us to be closer, share more, be more supportive of each other and have more fun and more sex than any other couple." A few months in, he literally said that. Who says that?

Our relationship is the only area in his life where he is competitive. I'd never imagined such a goal. But I embraced it once presented with it as an option.

Daniel has less traditional ambition than anyone I know. He pursues learning for the sake of it, not to advance his position in the world. When I was younger, I thought ambition to match my own mattered. Now I view it as one of the least interesting qualities a person can possess.

In the beginning he took issue with my tattoos. I have my oldest kids' names displayed prominently on my forearms. "Why words?" he would say. "Why not a rose or something less readable? Why your arms? Why not somewhere that would draw less attention?"

At first, I thought that had to do with Judaism, as traditionally you can't be buried in a Jewish cemetery if your body is marked with ink. That wasn't it, though. I think it was just a reminder of my prior relationship. If ours was going to be the best, how could I have married someone else when I hadn't yet met, let alone agreed to marry, him? When I explained that my tattoos – there are a few others beyond the names of my kids – were my little way of signaling that I was not a conformist (though now arguably having tattoos is the norm) while climbing the corporate ladder (an utterly conformist thing to do), he understood. They were evidence of my subversiveness.

Daniel also values family above all else. Throughout the pandemic, we stayed connected to his family, even though we disagreed with them on some of the restrictions. His two siblings' marriages are of a similar bent to ours – they support each other no matter what. And enjoy being together. Always. In this regard his parents' marriage set the example, as they also did in their approach to child rearing.

When my mother was visiting us in San Francisco and inadvertently sent me a nasty text about the two of us – one that was intended for a friend of hers, and believe me, it wasn't kind – I was furious. We had just spent the day together, visiting museums and parks with the kids, and she'd returned to her hotel room where she sent this text criticizing our parenting. I thought we'd had a lovely day. Apparently, she did not. I immediately responded with a text of my own: "You can go home to Philadelphia now. Don't come over tomorrow."

But Daniel said simply: "It doesn't matter. She's your mom. It was a mistake."

He called her, told her to come over in the morning straight from her hotel, and all would be smoothed over. And she did. And it was.

He's a mensch. And comes by it honestly.

When I met his parents for the first time, they were overflowing with welcoming joy. No interrogating, no suspicion. No worry that I was not a good match for their oldest child. They trusted him. If he loved me, I must be something special. He'd waited a long time to find the one. He was discriminating and precise and refused to settle, and they knew this about him.

It is hard to describe how grateful I am to have become part of this family. When Daniel's father Michael died, my mother-in-law instructed the rabbi delivering the service to say that Michael had eight grandchildren. No asterisks or clarifying clauses for the two step grandchildren, my kids from my first marriage. Michael had eight grandchildren. Period.

In modern relationships when the woman makes more money and has more public status than the man, couples often present a front that this is all great. But many times, behind the scenes, the man bristles. Traditional gender roles, which are difficult to relinquish, make this an affront to his manhood, though in his oh-so-modern and progressive consciousness he wishes this were not the case. In 2003, my ex and I were actually featured in a Newsweek article on this subject. The gist of the piece was that more and more "alpha females" are the primary breadwinners. Men are getting laid off, and women are picking up the slack. But, the article posited, it is not without a cost to the relationship. I definitely believe that in most instances this is true. It is possible to overcome but it's a thing, for sure, even amongst the most open-minded couples.

Daniel truly doesn't mind at all. He's proud of my achievements, all of them. My athletic prizes, the Emmy that I won for producing the documentary film *Athlete A*, my President title at Levi's. When it comes to what I am capable of, he encourages me to think bigger, not smaller. And it has no impact on his belief in himself, which of course it shouldn't. He appreciates that he learns from me, and I appreciate learning from him.

Of all his remarkable qualities, the thing that has saved me in the last few years of my pandemic rebellion is Daniel's firm belief in doing the right thing, repercussions be damned.

"Why do you care what they think of you? Who cares if they don't like you?" he says often.

I don't know. I just do.

"Well don't. They're wrong. They're morons. Obedient sheep. They're the 65 percent in the Milgram Experiment who would have continued to inflict electric shocks even when they thought the person might be dead."

The reference is to a seminal 1960s study that measured the willingness of people to obey an authority figure even when they were instructed to administer painful shocks (fake, but the participant didn't know that) on a "learner." Amidst screams of pain and, later, silence, which indicates that the "learner" was either dead or unconscious, most of the participants in the study continued to obey instructions.

Daniel's refusal to obey instructions has interfered in his life's trajectory at certain points. But his determination to continue on his own path, firm in his own beliefs, has modeled that behavior for me. It is a gift. And it has saved me from my own worst inclinations.

I'm so glad that I heeded my therapist's advice, turned my car around and went to that reading. I found a true "partner in crime" – Daniel's least favorite phrase, one used quite frequently on dating sites as something being searched for. I didn't expect someone with a history of criminal activities would have a heart of gold (another dating site cliché) but good things can come in unexpected packages. I'll be forever grateful for real world meetups, and forever skeptical of an online, virtual lifestyle. A love of books and a fortuitous real-life encounter led me to my one true love. And there is simply not a box to tick on Match.com that would have steered me in his direction.

CHAPTER 9:

MY LEVI'S TREK. A MARATHON, NOT A SPRINT.

I started at Levi's in 1999, when I was engaged to be married to my first husband. I had no idea my time at Levi's would outlast our marriage, which at eleven years was not short by any means.

In fact, I worked at Levi's longer than I've ever done anything in my entire life. I did gymnastics for fifteen years, and it defined my childhood. I've been a mom, thus far, for twenty-two years. By halfway through my tenure at the company, I was sure I'd retire from the place, sent off with a big party complete with balloons and a cake. That didn't happen. Instead, I walked out the virtual door, with an uncertain future but with a clear sense of purpose.

When I started at Levi's, not only was woke not a thing, it wasn't so much as a blip on the horizon. And like so many other companies, the place was riddled with soft, and less soft, sexism; men who were jerks just because they could be.

Most of both the everyday mortifications and the obstacles to career advancement that I endured during my time at Levi's directly related to my being a woman. These incidents – some minor, some not – are by no means the unique purview of Levi's. And I'm not whining, only pointing out that the wind was very much in my face, not at my back, in my career trek at Levi's.

Do I wish I knew, as young women do now, that "no" should always be an option? By "no" I mean: no, you can't treat me that way; no, you can't ask me to take on a larger scope, call it a promotion but not give me a pay increase; no, I don't accept that bit of feedback that contradicts what you said last week; no, I'm not too quiet, too loud, too fast for people to follow what I'm saying, too this too that too everything too nothing at all.

Yes. I wish I knew that this was possible, as many young women do now. Though I don't think things would have gone that well for me. It wasn't acceptable then, and I don't think that I would have progressed in my career. Did I sometimes go along in cases where I didn't want to, because I felt I had no choice? Yes. But frankly, after a childhood of near-obliterating obedience, noncompliance felt too wayward and wicked. So, for many years I simply held my tongue and kept going. It took me until exactly fifty-one years of age to stand firm in saying: This is who I am. This is what I believe. Deal with it.

Here's a taste of what life was like in corporate America, not so long ago. Which, looking back, might also be taken as a testament to how some things have actually changed for the better:

In 2000, just one year after starting at Levi's, I returned from a brief eight-week maternity leave after having my first baby and was moved into a job that would be "easier." Less travel, fewer long hours.

"We're going to move you into a job just handling packaging and in-store signage," said my boss.

The most charitable way to interpret this move is that he assumed that I was not the primary breadwinner, and that I'd probably leave the workforce soon to be a full-time mom. Though I'd never indicated as much.

But like many women, I *was* the primary breadwinner. In fact, in my case, also like many women, I was the *only* breadwinner. Not only did I not want to stay home with kids full-time, I couldn't afford to.

I was mistakenly grateful when this happened. But not for long. Because it set me back at least three years in my career trajectory. Men with fewer qualifications and shoddier work product got promoted ahead of me, while I languished in a less prestigious job.

When I returned from that maternity leave, I was still nursing. There weren't "mother's rooms" at the time. I had to pump milk in an unlocked closet with my back against the door to prevent intruders looking for product samples and promotional materials from barging in. I often cried from the sheer stress of it, and I usually came away with little milk to show for my trouble. The body just doesn't produce under those circumstances, or at least mine didn't. But by 2016, when I had my fourth and last child, I was able to retreat to a quiet "mother's room," replete with a locked door, curtained stalls, and a refrigerator for storage. We'd come a long way.

Back in 2001, there was one top executive whose sole way of relating to women, especially young ones, was flirtation. I refused, keeping my head down, avoiding eye contact and otherwise sending strong signals that I did not want to be bothered. But it was those women who engaged with this executive who got promoted. I stagnated in my role, unnoticed, for some time.

Hardly incidentally, this same guy later came under internal investigation for an episode at a sales meeting. He was one of three senior male executives seen late at night, frolicking in the pool with topless entry-level female employees on their shoulders. The incident became known internally as the "naked chicken fights." For women at Levi's twenty years ago, the batting away of drunken advances was a routine part of sales meetings and sometimes even of office life.

Beyond the everyday mortifications, I was repeatedly prevented from advancing in my career by a whole host of men who felt confident that they knew what I was, or – more accurately – wasn't, capable of.

When I was the U.S. Marketing Director, the Brand President, who was leaving the company, took it upon himself to give me some advice before he departed, though he had barely spoken to me during his tenure. But now he had pearls of wisdom to offer.

"Do you want to know what people really think of you?" he said after inviting me into his office.

I hadn't asked this question, so no. He leaned back and continued:

They don't think you're a leader. They don't think you're creative. They don't think you have any vision. You're an operator [a not so nice way of saying my potential was limited]. You get stuff done but you'll never lead anything. You'll never be a Chief Marketing Officer.

I think I was supposed to thank him for setting me straight, lest I have any aspirations which were not to be realized. I didn't. Instead, I decided to speak:

"That seems not totally fair. I pursue creative endeavors outside of work. I've made two short films. At work, I've led successful ad campaigns."

I was warming up to the idea of pushing back on his stupid feedback.

He was unconvinced.

"I'm just trying to be helpful. It's good to know where you stand."

I asked him if that was all, and then I left. He wasn't the first man to tell me that I needed to lower my expectations, and he certainly wasn't the last.

Yet another Brand President decided a few years later that he needed to have a similar heart to heart talk with me, just in case I still had any delusions of grandeur.

"You'll never be a CMO here or anywhere else."

Okay. I'd heard this before. I was unfazed. But why did all these men think they needed to break it to me that I was at the end of my career road? The implication being that I should just be grateful I had the job I had. Why did they think they got to decide? In fact, they did get to decide, but they were both wrong about my potential, and I knew it even then.

When I was finally "promoted" to Chief Marketing Officer at Levi's in 2013 and dared to ask what the increased compensation would be, I was told "zero." The head of Human Resources said: "You're getting the best job in the company. Just be grateful." Most people don't want to take on more work and more responsibility without more pay. But I did it. I had no choice in the end, really. I pushed and pushed and was repeatedly met with the same response:

"Why are you asking these questions? It's a great job. Very high profile!"

I responded with: "Would you accept a job without understanding the benefits and compensation?"

"No. But that's different. I came from outside the company," he said.

Yeah, it was different. He was a man. And I wasn't. I took the job. I had no choice, really.

After having performed for several years in the CMO role that I was told I'd never be capable of, I was told by Chip, who always claimed to have faith in my abilities, that I was in line for a Brand President role if one were to open. In fact, he literally promised me the President of Dockers role if it were to become available. It would be leading one of the smaller businesses but a step up to a general manager role that came with a seat on the executive team. When that day came because the President of Dockers left the company, I was giddy. H.R. reached out to say I was indeed first in line.

But when I was on vacation visiting family in New York, pregnant with my fourth child, Chip made the decision that the job would not go to me. I learned this in a companywide email announcement, which I read in the back seat of a taxi. I was not even given the courtesy of a one-on-one conversation to break the news. The announcement said that the new Brand President of Dockers was in fact the current Brand President of Levi's. His scope would double, and I would be staying put. Chip was persuaded by that Levi's Brand President throwing a tantrum in his office, arguing that he deserved it more than me and that he'd leave if he didn't get it. And so, in spite of Chip's stated commitment to me, he decided that it mattered more to give the guy a promotion than to give me one, though I'd earned it.

People get passed over all the time. But the fact that I was told it was mine, and then no one even bothered to tell me it wasn't before making the internal announcement, is what really hit me hard. I sobbed for a week not because I didn't get the job, but because I felt like such a sucker for believing that I would. Then I dusted myself off and got back to CMO-ing. Two years later I was named by *Forbes* as one of the fifty most influential CMO's in the world. And then again the year after that.

In 2019, I attended a business/social event hosted by the San Francisco 49ers. The president of the team invited sponsors of Levi's Stadium to a weekend in Napa as a thank you. At the main event, a dinner, I was seated next to the president of the team. With Levi's being the lead sponsor of the stadium, I garnered a premier placement. My husband sat with me.

There were about thirty couples at the event. There was no easy way to decipher who was the invitee – the corporate executive – and who was the plus one. At some point during dinner, my husband, a little tipsy, decided to ask our host. He asked loudly.

"So, who here is the executive and who's the spouse? How many women are the actual executives?" he queried.

As it turned out, I was the only one. All the rest of the women there were the spouses. Daniel was stunned, but I wasn't surprised in the least. Daniel simply couldn't believe, in 2019, that men represented 96.67 percent of the executives present. He started to rant a bit, as he is wont to do. I shushed him. It wasn't the 49ers' fault. These people all worked at other companies. Places like Safeway, United Airlines, and Intel. Daniel was making people uncomfortable as he persisted in wondering aloud about the gender imbalance. You weren't supposed to question their Bay Area, dyed-in-the-wool, feminist bona fides. They said they were progressive. *Trust them*!

I shushed my husband some more. Even at this late date in my life and career, as the highest-status executive at the table, I still didn't want to make anyone uncomfortable.

It's no wonder that all those men felt justified in telling me that I would never be a CMO. I was the only female executive at the table at this event, as was often the case at others like it. One must ask though: what came first, the chicken or the egg? Was I the only one because we were all persistently told we weren't capable? Or did the men assume we weren't capable because they saw no other women in these roles? It's an unsolvable puzzle, but whatever the answer, sexism is at the root of it.

If only I had a dollar for every time that I was told that I didn't speak up enough, or I spoke up too much, or I wasn't analytical enough, or I wasn't creative enough, or I was too "values led" (which supposedly made me naïve to the ways of running a profitable business), or my expectations were too high, well I wouldn't need to worry about how I was going to make a living going forward. I think all this often-conflicting feedback was never the starting point. The starting point was – you're a woman. What *you* are, isn't what we need. Then they back into the why.

How much did my being a woman have to do with how subsequent events played out? Might my outspokenness on the matter of schools have been more palatable if I were a man? There's no way of knowing. But it's certainly more than possible.

Men are allowed to speak their minds. Women are expected to be nice and do as they are told. It's also possible I was just too disruptive, whatever my gender.

In spite of the many obstacles that I faced at work over the years, I kept going. And ultimately, after starting as an entry level marketing assistant twenty years earlier, I became the President of the Levi's brand. No matter how unfortunate the ending, I will always be proud of the work that I did.

What I miss most is my colleagues. I took great care to actually tend to people's aspirations in the workplace. I tried to treat everyone fairly, provide opportunities, listen, help them build meaningful careers. I took mentorship and coaching very seriously. And sometimes we became friends.

I attended weddings, hosted baby showers, even went to a few funerals, sadly. My friends at work helped me get through my divorce, the low point in my life. I miss having colleagues and work friends. I miss the camaraderie of setting and achieving a goal together. I miss them. The actual people.

But no one stood up for me when the going got tough. Out of the more than one thousand employees at the Levi's headquarters in San Francisco, not a single person said to me "I don't agree with what you are saying [outside of work], but I defend your right to say it." Out of the hundreds in the group that I led, not a single soul said anything in my defense. Two employees I'd known for a long time urged me to reconsider.

"Is it really worth it? Why are you doing this?"

I believed, and still believe, that it was not only worth it, but it was also necessary. But I was toxic, and everyone distanced themselves from me in my last year. I felt totally alone.

The humans who I thought were my actual friends were really just "work friends" in the end. And conditional or contextual friendship is not really friendship. I was, in fact, a sucker after all.

CHAPTER 10:

EVERYONE HAS A LEVI'S STORY.
EVEN ALICIA KEYS.
AND SNOOP DOGG.
AND JUSTIN TIMBERLAKE.

It was two years after Chip started as CEO that he put me in the role of CMO. At this point, Levi's had been in decline for over a decade. The company's revenue had decreased 29 percent, from $6.8 billion in 1997 to $4.7 billion in 2011.

We were floundering and were at real risk of fading into oblivion. The company that had invented the blue jean had lost its way.

According to a *Harvard Business Review* case study entitled "Levi Strauss: A Pioneer Lost in the Wilderness," published in 2020, after we'd turned things around:

[Chip] Bergh faced some urgent decisions. Should LS&Co. focus more on the wholesale channel or direct-to-consumer channel? What parts of its product mix should the firm emphasize? In which geographies should it invest? With only a short window of time in which to build momentum, Bergh knew that he needed to prioritize, given the firm's limited resources.

We'd been slow to respond to the changing marketplace in the early 2000s. We held tight to a failing model. We were afraid to open our own stores because it might anger our wholesale partners. We lagged in investing in e-commerce because we dismissed it as a blip, a small part of the business that wouldn't ever really amount to much, so why bother. Consumers would never buy jeans off the internet because they needed to try them on. Right?

Wrong.

At the core of our missteps was our failure to translate the heart of the brand into modern day relevance. Boomers and Gen Xers had embraced Levi's in the 1980s as a mode of self-expression. They weren't their uptight dads, in suits at work and khakis on the weekend. They were rebels, charting their own course in life, emulating rock stars and cool kids. Some had even gone to Woodstock, damnit!

I was one of them. We knew we were still cool, or wanted to be, into our thirties and even forties. The 501 Blues campaign, launched in 1984, was the embodiment of this ethos, and paired a custom blues track with young people in urban settings enjoying life. They traipsed through city streets, in sunglasses and 501s, looking impossibly cool.

But our rugged individualism faded as theirs did. We aged with the Boomers and Xers, and never brought new youngsters into the fold.

At times during the early 2000s-2010s, we were so scared of seeming old, we too obviously and desperately chased young. We put an image into the market that was aggressively hip but ultimately inauthentic, and failed to convince consumers we'd updated our products for their generation.

In 2012, when I was leading our e-commerce business and just before I was appointed as CMO to take over marketing, we'd launched the "Go Forth" campaign. "Go Forth" was the epitome of Levi's marketing at its nadir – a dark and depressing short film that didn't actually sell any products. It was pretentious and moody and featured twenty-somethings looking grungy and dissatisfied. The stated consumer target: young pioneers, hip dreamers and doers.

Even now this campaign is often cited as a favorite by advertising creative directors who hail from hipster havens like Brooklyn and Portland, and who are completely out of touch with everyday Americans and teenagers nervous about the first day of school, also known as jeans buyers. The frustrated creative directors wish they made art films but are stuck making thirty second ads. So, they pour their unfulfilled artist souls into irrelevant and overwrought short films for brands, hoping to win a Cannes Lion one day. (Cannes

Lions is a second-rate festival – not the famous one – that awards advertising creative directors with prizes for making these overwrought short films that don't actually sell products.)

The TV ad was set to a scratchy recording of a Walt Whitman poem, "O Pioneers!," originally published in *Leaves of Grass* in 1855. It began:

Pioneers! O Pioneers!
Come my tan-faced children
Follow well in order.
Get your weapons ready.
For we cannot tarry here.
We must march my darlings, we must bear the brunt of danger,
We the youthful sinewy races, all the rest on us depend.
Pioneers! O Pioneers!

It almost mocks itself. Young people don't read poetry, though I suppose many might like to pretend they do. In reality, I don't know that very many old people read poetry anymore. The ad is dripping in haughty self-importance. Nonetheless, it managed to traffic in juvenile images of semi-naked women. One of the ads within the campaign features a woman, topless from the back, running through a field of grass. Most women don't do that. But male creative directors sure like to think they do.

The ads in the "Go Forth" campaign were not pieces of art. They were ads. And they failed to sell jeans. The ads were all but inciting revolution, and in such a pompous fashion. Don't people have fun in jeans? Not according to the Levi's "Go Forth" campaign, created by Nike's ad agency, Wieden+Kennedy.

Beyond the bad ad campaigns, we never got women's jeans right. As women embraced wearing denim for play, going out at night and brunch on the weekends, we missed the mark repeatedly. Our history was rooted in a weathered, tough masculinity, and when we tried our hand at women's jeans, we just made them smaller and pinker with cursive-y writing on the label, and we never addressed what women really wanted: jeans that make their butts look great. Premium brands like Seven for All Mankind got this right and grabbed market share in the 2000s.

We'd swung to and fro for a decade – either persisting with a dusty cowboy western image or teetering on the edge of embarrassing with a "trying too hard" approach, like that kid in middle school who tries to fit in but just gets it all wrong.

Chip was brought aboard as a change agent. He was a brand guy from his days at Proctor & Gamble. He knew that for us to do all the stuff cited by *Harvard Business Review* – make clear choices around new selling channels, geographic expansion and which products to sell – we had to frame a compelling story about our brand. One that was not only compelling but true, or close to true, if people were going to believe it.

This is where I came in. Though I'd been at the company since 1999, only now did my career at Levi's seriously begin to take off.

Chip hated the "Go Forth" campaign as much as I did. He hated that there was no product in it to speak of. He hated that it was dark and depressing and took itself way too seriously.

And so, in September 2013, Chip tapped me with this all-important assignment. He told me he wanted me to take over as CMO. In this new role, if I were to accept it, I would be responsible for all that storytelling meant to revive our illustrious brand.

Unbelievably to some, at first I said no. I was running our e-commerce business and liked the job I had. I was the first-ever leader of this newly formed division. And I was getting the experience that I thought I needed to generate the required respect as a sensible, practical leader who could run a business. I felt my e-commerce position was my path to CEO. Because CMOs, however high profile, rarely become heads of companies.

After the kerfuffle with the head of Human Resources, with me asking questions like "well what's the compensation?" and him saying "same as you have now, it's a cool job, just take it and stop asking so many questions," I realized it wasn't really a choice. I was being "volun-told." I had to accept it. And so I did.

This is when I made my mark. As the CMO, I had influence over our overall trajectory, and I hit the ground running. After poring through all the research that had been done but ignored over the years by failed CMOs who thought they knew better than to listen to what consumers were telling them, I came across a magical insight from a consumer, and jotted it down:

I wear other things, but I live my life in Levi's. They are with me through thick and thin. They play with me, dance with me, party with me, fall in love with me. *I live in Levi's.*

This was it! "I live in Levi's!" This was the concept, the notion that could cut across generations, genders, attitudes about style (fashionable vs. functional), geographies. It had the most vital of virtues: it was true.

I was convinced that if only we could just get more people to see and understand this, we'd be back!

With Chip's support, it became our signature campaign – Live in Levi's. From the moment it launched in 2014, it worked. Our return on investment with this campaign tripled in just a year. What does that mean? It means having lost money on the advertising we ran in 2013, we made a whole bunch of it off the ads we ran in 2014. People saw the ads and went out to buy Levi's. The campaign is still running almost a decade later.

Around the same time, we were planning a revised approach to finally gain favor with women. This time we were going to get it right once and for all. We'd show women their butts *did* look best in Levi's! How to signal that change? Bring that understanding to all those women who had tried and dismissed us in the past? We had never used celebrities before – a choice meant to convey our everyman (or every woman) brand status. But it seemed to me that the world had changed, and celebrity marketing might be the ticket to breaking through in a cluttered market.

But who? *Which* celebrity?

To my mind, there was only one choice: Alicia Keys. She embodied exactly what we needed, and we never seriously considered anyone else. She was, and is, soulful, real, an icon, above trend. Timeless. She was in her thirties, but *everyone* loved her, both the younger fashion-involved twenty-somethings we coveted and the somewhat more practical forty-plus crowd we needed. She alienated no one, but didn't do it by being milquetoast and boring. Her appeal was in her strength, not her inoffensiveness.

I had to have her. I found her agent, had one conversation with him and he called me to say "Alicia wants to meet you. Tomorrow."

Tomorrow? In New Jersey? I had a newborn at home in San Francisco. My son was only four months old, and I hadn't traveled at all yet.

"I'll be there. Just tell me when and where 'there' is."

I hopped on a red eye, bringing just my breast pump and a carry-on bag, and landed in Newark at 6 a.m., then ran to my hotel to pump and shower. A car soon arrived to whisk me to Alicia's.

The black car pulled up to the gate, the driver gave my name, and we made our way up the long, winding driveway. I was brought inside by one of the many black-clad security staff. It was some sort of guest cottage, a receiving room for the main house. It was unadorned; there was a bar that looked unused, and a seating area. My photo was taken. The security and house staff chatted while I waited.

I had to use the bathroom at one point. There was a Basquiat featuring a polaroid of early-eighties Madonna. A Basquiat was throw-away art, hung in the visitor bathroom. What had I gotten myself into? I'd never met and talked to a celebrity. I wasn't nervous though. She was just a person, right?

I was called into the official meeting room, which was near the kitchen in the house. And waited there some more.

Alicia entered not long after I sat down, a huge grin lighting up her unmade-up face. She apologized profusely for making me wait.

"I'm so sorry, Jen. The baby was hungry!"

She'd just had a baby, too! Hers was even younger than mine, just two months old. We bonded instantly over sleepless nights, sore nipples and shapeless mid-sections. She asked what we wanted with her. I told her. I sold her the story. How everyone lives in Levi's. How we were re-launching our women's business and we wanted her to represent us because she was the embodiment of beauty, authenticity and strength. Then I asked her what her Levi's story was.

She told me.

"When I was growing up in New York City, everyone wore Levi's. All the cool kids. The b-boys, the punkers, the skaters, the rappers. Everyone. Levi's brought people together. Made us realize what we had in common. I wanted to be a part of that. I wanted my own pair. But they were so expensive." Alicia's story of Levi's was one of want.

Snoop Dogg told me a similar story a few years later. He said he stole his first pair of Levi's from a mall store in Southern California. He starched those 501s within an inch of their life, with a perfect crease right down the center of the leg. That's how it was done, he said.

I always asked the same question going forward: what's your Levi's story? If they didn't have one, it wasn't a good fit, and we'd move on to find someone who did. I believed the authenticity mattered if we were going to forge a partnership.

When I met Justin Timberlake in 2018, he had a story too. He told me, when growing up in Memphis, he wore nothing but Levi's and Air Jordans.

"What were your favorites?" I asked.

"Well 501s, obviously. And Jordan 3s. Or 1s. Or 4s. I love 'em all."

Alicia was the only one to ever ask me what my Levi's story was. And of course, I had one. In 1986, when I was seventeen, I'd traveled to Moscow for the Goodwill Games. This rogue competition was a response to the Olympic boycotts of the early 1980s, created by Ted Turner to take politics out of sports, so that the athletes could just compete. I told Alicia:

I brought a bunch of 501s in very small sizes to the meet,
to trade them with the Russian gymnasts – for pins and

sweats and leotards. On the face of it, it wasn't exactly an equal exchange. But to me, it was the deal of the century. The Russians were the best in the world at the time. And I emerged with mementoes of having once been good enough to share the competition floor with them.

Alicia and I hit it off. I left her Basquiat-adorned home and went straight to the airport, arriving home that evening. I was gone less than twenty-four hours, but I closed the deal. I got the confirmation call the next day from her agent.

"Alicia loved you. She thought you were a badass. She's in."

The feeling was mutual. And it pleased me that she only wanted to work with people she liked and respected. It all felt less mercenary that way.

"She wants some time to get back into shape before filming."

Knowing we didn't have a lot of time because we aimed to launch in about nine months, I encouraged the agent to tell her not to worry about it. Wherever she was, was just fine. If she was curvier than pre-baby, that was real. And women relate to and are inspired by real women. We filmed just a couple of months later.

We launched the ad less than a year later. It opened with Alicia saying:

"All women are naturally badass."

Some thought it was too risky to lead with this, but it felt honest and relatable, which I had to explain repeatedly to all the men, including Chip, who were concerned about it. We'd always gotten it wrong for women. We failed because we spoke to women how men thought they wanted to be spoken to, and not how women talk to each other.

The "Go Forth" ad of the topless woman running through a field was the perfect example. I imagine (I didn't work on the campaign, although I know some of the people who did) the male creative director saying: "She feels free! This is what women want!" If I'd been the marketing leader at the time, I would have responded with: "No. She feels naked. And that field looks scratchy. That is NOT what women want."

I reassured Chip: "Trust me on this. This is how we cheer each other on."

We went with it. And we also debuted The Levi's Music Project to complement the advertising. This program, still running to this day, sought to bring music education back to schools and community centers through partnerships with celebrities like Alicia, then Snoop Dogg and, eventually, Justin Timberlake. The inaugural program with Alicia built and instituted a music and technology (so the students could record and mix their own tracks) curriculum at Edward R. Murrow High School in Brooklyn. The school and the details of the program were chosen by Alicia. And she showed up at the unveiling to sing with the kids at the school. They went wild.

In an article about the launch of the Levi's Music Project, Alicia said:

The excitement for learning, and for the potential and possibility, is the best thing ever. I don't think there's anything more important than loving to learn and the passion that you can have for learning, which happens forever—whether in school or outside of school.

In 2016, a year after the campaign launched, I was named by *Billboard Magazine* as one of the "25 Most Powerful People in Music and Fashion."

This article also quoted Alicia talking about me:

She's there to continue to grow the brand, but it's not just about the brand. It's about people relating to each other—what builds us, what breaks us, what makes us start again. That's what made us such great partners. We're very similar in that way.

I couldn't agree with her more.

At the time of the photo shoot, I was pregnant again, with my fourth child. This time, after having had three boys, I was having a girl.

I was thrilled to bring a girl child into the world. I felt, for the first time in my life – indeed, the bottom line had proven – that leaning into my girl-ness was a strength, not a detriment. In being myself - pregnant, tired, honest, out of shape and leaking milk – I had come into my own.

At the time I left Levi's, the Alicia ad was our highest performing ad ever. Women all around the world loved it. They flocked to buy our newly revamped women's collection. Every fit was meticulously designed at our newly implemented Innovation Lab, just down the street from our San Francisco headquarters. There was a fit and style for every woman, and they made butts around the world look great. We set a goal for ourselves to reach a billion dollars in sales of women's jeans by 2020. And we beat it by two years.

For the first time in my life, I could be my whole self in the workplace, and not only would it not be held against me, it would be an asset. I vowed to do it all the time.

CHAPTER 11:

LEVI'S WOKES – LET'S TALK ABOUT WOKE CAPITALISM.

In September of 2017 Saturday Night Live aired a digital short titled "Levi's Wokes." It was one of their mock ads, this time featuring brown, immensely oversized and shapeless gaucho-style burlap-looking pants, worn by Brooklyn/Silver Lake hipster-types, filmed in satirically contemplative black and white. I thought it was hilarious.

It began:

Introducing Levi's Wokes. Sizeless, style neutral, gender non-conforming denim for a generation that defies labels. Levi's heard that if you're not woke, it's bad!

Ryan Gosling, that week's guest host, wagged a scolding finger at the camera. The multi-racial cast continued:

"What's my size?!
Why don't you ask me about my accomplishments?!"
"My Wokes are size me. They fit everybody. Because they fit nobody!"
"What colors do they come in?" "Colors?" "I'm triggered!"
"This color? Can you label this color?"
"That is the color greb."
"They not brown. But they not not brown."
"It's a handful of colors none of which are dominant!"

I laughed. Then I watched it over and over again. Then I laughed some more. I was the CMO by this point and had been for four years. They were making fun of the advertising I was putting out into the ether. They were making fun of me and how I did my job. I didn't care.

But my phone was blowing up with texts of concern from friends and my marketing team at Levi's. Everyone thought we were being mocked and I should be worried, possibly about my job. But I was determined to be in on the joke and not the butt of it. I called the head of design at Levi's, my work friend and collaborator.

"Let's make some of those Woke jeans and send them to the cast of SNL."

We sewed up about twenty pairs and sent them out as quickly as we could, one for every cast member. We didn't need to worry about knowing their sizes because Wokes were size-less, shapeless, gender-less. We were in on the joke, culture creators ourselves. We'll invert the narrative and come out on top, hip enough to laugh at ourselves, we thought.

Besides, it wasn't us that they were making fun of, it was poser hypocrites who pride themselves on their re-usable totes and a "buy local" ethos while flying to remote locales twice a year on private jets, to go on exotic vacations on private beaches with private chefs cooking "authentic" local cuisine.

I didn't feel derided at the time because I hadn't thought much about wokeness in general or about woke capitalism at all. Mid-2010s wokeness felt like a tiny satellite circling around popular culture, mocking the annoyingly pretentious variety of hipster, not the everyday cool kids who authentically cared about stuff like environmentalism and equality.

Wokeness was a pretense, a posture appropriated by a few guilt-driven middle-aged white people with Priuses. (But only because they hadn't heard of Teslas yet.) "Woke" might describe a Hollywood celebrity touting "green" behaviors like recycling and veganism while wearing a new $10,000 outfit to every event and never wearing it again. They were ridiculous. They weren't us. We – Levi's – made commercially priced jeans sold at places like Kohl's and Sears, pants with a lifetime guarantee, designed for anyone and everyone for nearly 150 years. We were above trends and insults. We were of the people. We were Levi's.

The term "woke" was originally used in black communities in the 1940s, '50s, and '60s. It referred to being awake to bigotry and prejudice, and the coming revolution and racial reckoning. Early on in the 2010s it had a brief moment of earnestness, when it was broadened to apply to progressives of all races who had adopted genuine social consciousness, specifically around issues of inequality. But it quickly shifted to a sarcastic slight, meant for those poser hypocrites in expensive single-use outfits yelling at the rest of us to buy less and use less.

Okay, so what about woke capitalism? What's that?

Ross Douthat coined the phrase in a 2018 op-ed for *The New York Times*, "The Rise of Woke Capital." He wrote:

> Corporate activism on social issues isn't in tension with corporate self-interest on tax policy and corporate stinginess in paychecks. Rather, the activism increasingly exists to protect the self-interest and the stinginess — to justify the ways of C.E.O.s to cultural power brokers, so that those same power brokers will leave them alone (and forgive their support for Trump's economic agenda) in realms that matter more to the corporate bottom line.

"Woke capitalism" is corporate America's attempt to profit off of Millennial and Gen Z activism, often passive keyboard activism.

It exploits social justice politics and transforms it into social justice consumerism. And ultimately, investor profit. Companies positing to care about "progressive values" are really doing nothing more than striking a superficial pose meant to signal virtue while distracting from any company's true motive: financial gain for shareholders. Same as it ever was.

All of that is true. But there is more to it, in my opinion.

First, you've got a bunch of CEOs and executives who want to distance themselves from the greedy image of business leaders of the past. They want you to know that they are not like the ruthless banking moguls and oil tycoons from years gone by. They aren't destroying the planet, and they aren't taking advantage of consumers with sub-prime mortgages. They aren't stealing or grifting, they're helping! They aren't in it for themselves, they care about you!

Tech companies are well known for their "we're gonna change the world" cultiness. You don't just work at Google. You're connecting people to information that is life-changing, driving the digital revolution at the end of which we'll all be so much better off than we are now.

Corporate leaders want us to believe that they are do-gooders, not money grubbers. They'll get rich too, but they don't want you to think that is their mission. And, more importantly, they don't want to think that about themselves. They believe they embody the best qualities of Andrew Carnegie (So generous! So benevolent!), Henry Ford (a visionary who cared about his employees!) and Theodore Roosevelt (a progressive man of action!) all rolled into one.

Business executives would have us believe that they are our saviors. Bill Gates is eliminating malaria and saving the children in Africa! Howard Schultz is running for President to save our Democracy! Elon Musk is not only saving the planet with electric vehicles, he also is exploring new frontiers in space and defending free speech for the masses!

Big Pharma CEOs – well they're saving the world from covid. In fact, Chip actually told me in 2021, in the midst of the pandemic: "There are no more values-led CEOs in the world than those in Pharma." Never mind that not long before Pfizer was reaping unimaginably vast sums from covid vaccines and treatments, they'd paid out the largest healthcare fraud settlement in history, $2.3 billion, for fraudulent marketing, which included kickbacks to doctors to prescribe the pain medicine Bextra for uses unapproved by the Food and Drug Administration. Call it "marketing" if you must.

And never mind that *that* mind-boggling fine had lately been eclipsed by the combined $6 billion in fines paid by Purdue Pharma L.P., makers of OxyContin, for defrauding the U.S. government and giving kickbacks, as it profited from the epidemic opioid addiction producing mass death from overdoses. Additionally, the Sackler family, owners of Purdue, paid $225 million to settle civil litigation against them.

These pharmaceutical executives are the most values-led CEOs there are, or so many people somehow now seem to believe.

Somehow, some way, despite all the evidence of greed and corruption, business leaders have managed to re-brand themselves as altruists. Never mind that in 2020, CEOs made 351 times more than an average worker in the company they led – up from twenty-one times more in 1965. Indeed, in the last thirty years their average compensation has grown over *1,000 percent*, even as they have burnished an image as well-meaning humanitarians. How?

In partnership with a complicit press that buys into their companies' expensive "we're do-gooders" marketing campaigns, these CEOs have PR-ed themselves into philanthropic good-hearted hero status. This phony message has been amplified and embraced by consumers around the world, despite all the evidence that shows that these so-called do-gooders are really no good at all. It boggles the mind, but it's a testament to the power of marketing.

There was a time when doctors and lawyers were the pillars of the community, and that's what every mother, Jewish or otherwise, wanted her child to be. But now, business leaders seem to have taken that mantle. While Steve Jobs is widely known as kind of an asshole, he's also viewed as a visionary who changed the world. I can't tell you how many business leaders use his quote "Stay hungry stay foolish" as their email signature sign-off. It clothes naked capitalism with profundity and meaning. CEOs and C-suite executives were always rich. But now they're rich and beloved, and perceived as well-meaning and heroic. It's not lost on me that I was included in this misguided hero worship.

The 2008 economic meltdown was brought on by predatory lending practices targeting low-income home buyers, and it could have been a major setback for the newly shiny image of today's CEOs.

It led to Occupy Wall Street on the Left, and helped foster the Tea Party movement on the Right. Across the political spectrum, people took to the streets demanding change. And while these protests took over the headlines for at least a year, it didn't take long for the glamorous, young Elizabeth Holmes, the founder of a Silicon Valley startup called Theranos, to land on the cover of *Forbes*, billed as "The Next Steve Jobs." From there, she ascended quickly to the heights of pop culture stardom and accrued a reported net worth of $4.5 billion. On paper. Journalists by the score wrote fawning puff pieces which sought to convince the public that Holmes was an antidote to the corruption and chicanery exposed in the 2008 economic crisis. She was also a woman, an antidote to the male-dominated, misogynistic tech culture.

In 2015 she was named one of *Glamour* magazine's Women of the Year for her invention, a device meant to revolutionize healthcare with finger prick blood testing at your local Safeway. Afraid of needles used for blood draws? No longer a problem. Holmes, this business wunderkind, was about to make healthcare painless and stress-free. More, she had a compelling (although presumably fake, like everything else about her) story about the genesis of her triumph – an uncle who died of cancer who'd have been saved if he'd only been able to avail himself of this revolutionary technology that now she was giving to the world out of the goodness of her heart.

As the world knows, Theranos is now defunct, and Holmes has been convicted on four counts of fraud for lying about her company and product to secure more than a billion dollars in funding from venture capitalists – very rich, very greedy funders who were also eager to be viewed as saviors and healthcare heroes. Instead of being their ticket to sainthood, Holmes – exposed as a greedy corporatist and malignant narcissist, feigning humility to uphold her "I'm not a craven business lady, I'm a holy redeemer" image – will likely spend many years in prison. All along, she was just a money-hungry swindler. And all too many of us were swindled by her lies.

No matter. In this new Gilded Age, journalists – themselves often politically biased and ethically compromised – have continued to spread the fiction that corporate leaders and entrepreneurs as not just "good" people but near God-like figures. We the people eat it up, because it helps to fill the religion-sized gaping hole in our increasingly secular culture's atheist heart.

And today's ostentatiously woke CEOs are more than happy to play along, eager to prove to the public – and themselves – that they are not just guys out to make a buck. Woke capitalism signals that their guiding intention is to make this a better, more just world, even as it distracts us from their only true intention: enhancing their companies' bottom line, and their own.

Of course, the beauty of it all is that simultaneously it also endows consumers with a false sense of nobility, encouraging them to believe that buying the right stuff is actually activism. *You like t-shirts? Here – buy this organic cotton t-shirt that also shows you support the LGBTQ+ community because it has our logo but with a rainbow!*

Don't get me wrong, I'm not against capitalism. Far from it. I'm against the charade that is social justice capitalism. I want to buy stuff because it's the best stuff on the market. Win me over with your excellence. I'll even pay more for it. I'll express my political affiliation with my vote, not my sneakers or soft drink of choice.

But in the age of armchair, keyboard activism, woke capitalism lets consumers badge themselves as progressive activists without actually having to do anything. It's magic!

There's of course another piece of the puzzle, largely hidden from the public – the degree to which these CEOs are influenced by their Gen Z offspring. Many have kids who are attending highly woke private elementary schools and high schools – places like Children's Day in San Francisco, Trinity in New York and Oakwood in Los Angeles. These kids have been coddled and inculcated into gender ideology and critical race theory while denouncing white supremacy at their mostly white, and rich, fancy private schools.

They feel guilty about being white and privileged because they've been told they need to, and maybe they do need to feel a bit of gratitude for their "born on third base" status, but they are out to prove their worthiness by putting a woke sheen on their desire to stay rich and privileged. And so, they are all too eager to prove that they are virtuous and willing to "do the work" to have a raised and moral social conscience. That means needing to virtue signal even harder to prove one's seriousness. Usually "the work" entails not that much work at all, but necessitates ousting others for wrongthink. Witches must be burned at the stake, after all.

The kids go on to college, and graduate after four years of building safe spaces and protesting "micro-aggressions." Many believe that whenever they feel slightly unhappy, it is obviously the result of some grave injustice. And they feel justified in demanding punishment for anyone who offends them. They take this attitude with them as they enter the work force.

These young people have lived their lives under the impression that their every utterance matters, and that older people need to listen to them! Whether they have the life experience or wisdom that should merit such attention is irrelevant. They mock their parents and grandparents with the internet catch phrase "OK Boomer," signaling the outdated values of their hopelessly misinformed and misguided elders. They lay claim to inscrutable labels, like demisexual and recip-romantic (you guessed it, you only like someone after knowing they like you), which demand we all listen to them because they know things we don't. They have lived lives of oppression that we stodgy cisgender parents would never understand.

So, we better listen up or they won't visit us. Worse, they'll cancel us. Many of us are desperate to prove that we do not deserve this dismissive "OK boomer" meme. We are "with it," serious-minded "virtue"-osos too.

Today's executives reared these kids with an *I'm not your dad, I'm your friend* parenting philosophy, and they chase their children's approval. They want to impress their woke kids with their own pro-gressive bona fides. They want to be cool – peers not parents – in the eyes of their offspring; valued not for the materials goods that they provide, but for the values that they champion.

And now these young people are populating the companies led by *I'm not your dad, I'm your friend* CEOs. Surrounded by this cohort, CEOs are awash in approval and praise – but only if they can find a way to pander to the generation's every shifting demand.

Thus, the woke cancel culture that started on campuses has not just migrated into the culture at large, but has come to drive policy in almost every corporate boardroom.

Crucial to this is that these kids are social media pros, which makes them especially effective enforcers. They grew up with phones in their pockets, generating moment to moment likes on TikTok, Snapchat and YouTube. As students, these Millennials and Gen Z-ers knew that they could tweet from a classroom if a professor looked at them funny and garner not only peer attention but launch university investigations into tenured professors' classroom practices. Now they can post a picture of their boss on Instagram, calling her out for using the gendered term "guys." No one is safe. No one is immune.

These twenty- and thirty-somethings are ideological terrorists, policing their peers and elders relentlessly. They are "omnipotent moral busybodies" ridding the world of evil and they will not rest until they exorcise immorality for the good of those being exorcised. But as C.S. Lewis said, "I'd rather live under robber barons than under omnipotent moral busybodies." Amen to that.

Why do they do it? Because, as author and economist Thomas Sowell has said, those "who are contributing nothing to society, except their constant criticisms, can feel both intellectually and morally superior." By doing close to nothing – wearing the right t-shirt, affixing one's social media profile with the right badge (e.g. I am vaccinated; I stand with Ukraine) and by cancelling the "wrong" people by generating outrage with a finger tap, they are saved.

For their part, the CEO dads (yes, 95 percent of CEOs are men) are not social media experts. Their Corporate Communications leads manage their LinkedIn accounts, and they scan their wives' Facebook accounts on occasion to check out what the kids are up to. And that's the extent of their social media prowess. Which makes it all the easier for the woke mob to cow them online – and even in their own offices.

The outrage generated through call out culture and social media cancellation is real. And very satisfying for those who invoke it. But it also isn't real. It passes quickly for the most part, if its targets have the fortitude to hunker down and bear it. As Dave Chappelle says: "Twitter's not a real place."

But the CEOs don't know that. Their harried communications leaders present them with tweets and comments, and they have no sense of context. It's words on a "page." Could be in *The New York Times* or on CNN for all they know. It's bad stuff on the screen, with the potential to prompt reputational harm, causing the stock price to plummet. And they panic. Or most of them do.

Some do not. In October 2021, Netflix CEO Ted Sarandos said to employees in an internal memo:

If you'd find it hard to support our content breadth, Netflix may not be the best place for you.

This line in the sand was drawn in response to the employee dust-up over Dave Chappelle's 2021 comedy special *The Closer*, in which he declared himself a TERF – a trans-exclusionary radical feminist. He tackled the controversy surrounding gender ideology by stating that he's a feminist, he supports women's equality, he believes biological sex is real, *and* he also supports trans rights. The assertion: these two things – being pro-women's rights and pro-trans rights – are not in conflict.

In the 2020s, that's what passes not only for controversy but actual violence that kills trans people. According to the woke, "I'm a TERF" is a loaded gun pointed directly at the trans community.

In response to Chappelle's stand-up special, tens of employees protested at the Netflix headquarters, threatening to quit if the comedian's specials were not taken off the platform. Sarandos stood his ground, saying: "I think it's very important to the American culture generally to have free expression." And that was that.

No one has heard a peep on the matter since. In fact, *The Closer* garnered two Emmy nominations and holds steady at a 95 percent audience rating on Rotten Tomatoes, despite out of touch "elite" critics giving it a 40 percent. It was one of the most viewed shows on Netflix in 2021. So did it really take all that much courage for Sarandos to say: *Enough. Don't watch it. We're keeping this show on our platform because it has an audience, and we believe in free expression. Don't work here if you don't want to. The shows stays.*

In the end, it paid off for Netflix. They got street cred and eyeballs, money and prizes. It was the right decision, if you believe in a culture of free speech and artistic expression. And it was also the right business decision.

And yet . . .

Most CEOs lack the moral courage to do this. Because they know, deep down, that they aren't do-gooders, and they don't want that curtain lifted. So they kowtow to the very vocal minority – the scant few employees marching outside of headquarters or emailing the head of Human Resources. These CEOs are frauds and have no actual courage. The gutsy stance – tilting at windmills and fighting injustice – is a just a persona, a public façade, a wealth-generating marketing strategy. They love money and they fear the angry mob because that mob may interfere with their ability to produce inter-generational private-plane wealth. They want to make as much money as possible, but they want everyone, including their kids and their kids' cohort, to think that they really just want to make a difference in the world. *Oh gee, aw shucks, I happened to make gazillions of dollars. But that's just 'cause I'm really really good at heart.*

So, there you have it. Woke capitalism. I didn't know about Ross Douthat's column in 2018. I was busy as the CMO at Levi's making ads about voting. I *was* woke capitalism. And as is often the case, you can't see it when you're in it.

But I'd wise up pretty soon due to a head-on collision with the unrelenting, ever-righteous woke mob.

CHAPTER 12:

COLLIDING WITH THE MOB (THIS IS THE COVID-Y PART).

On February 25, 2020, San Francisco declared a state of emergency due to COVID-19 – despite having no local cases. On March 11, San Francisco banned gatherings of a thousand or more. On March 12, San Francisco Unified School District (SFUSD) announced that schools would be closed for three weeks. On March 13, San Francisco banned gatherings of one hundred or more. On March 16, the first "shelter in place" orders in America were announced for five Bay Area counties, which included the closing of outdoor playgrounds. Seven million people were legally mandated to restrict their activities to only what was "essential" – to just stay home. And outdoor play for kids was considered inessential.

On March 17, Governor Gavin Newsom said:

Don't anticipate schools are going to open up in a week. Please don't anticipate in a few weeks. I would plan and assume that it's unlikely that many of these schools – few, if any – will open before summer break.

On March 19, Newsom issued a statewide stay-at-home order for California's forty million residents. On March 24, it was announced that a teenager in L.A. County was the first minor to die of covid – though the cause of death would later be revised. The same day, the Olympics were postponed, and the first San Francisco death was reported – a man in his forties with significant underlying health conditions.

By March 25, just two weeks after the initial announcement of three-week school closures, the Bay Area and California closures were extended until May 1. Watching it all unfold, like many others, I was out of breath just trying to keep up with the accelerating restrictions.

During this time of rapidly escalating panic and the extreme narrowing of our lives, my oldest child came home from the University of California at Berkeley as the school went "virtual." My second oldest, a junior in high school, took to his bed for online schooling. My two youngest kids, ages five and three, were also at home, their pre-school shuttered for children of non-essential workers.

Along with countless others, I began the slog of working from home, clumsy on Microsoft Teams as a means of accessing meetings, and unnerved about the state of the Levi's business. How would this company, recently rebuilt, survive with all our stores closed? How many people would be left without jobs? Would I myself be unemployed? How would I pay for college? Health insurance? Life?

My oldest kids (the "bigs" as my husband and I called them) and I did our work at the dining room table, talking over each other, me listening to their school lectures, them listening to my daily executive team meetings trying to figure out what we were going to do. How would we protect people's jobs with no revenue coming in? How would we keep employees safe from the virus? How long would these closures last? How could we stop spending money, with none coming in, to ensure we didn't go under? Can we make masks? Should we donate bandanas to serve as makeshift masks for hospital workers?

Had anyone been outside? Why is there no toilet paper on the shelves at the grocery store? Or even any on Amazon?! Stock up on Tylenol, that's running out, too. Order groceries. But wipe them down with bleach when they get to your house. Leave the mail on the counter for three days before touching it. Don't go to the doctor. Don't let your kids outside. Don't even walk the dog. Don't don't don't!

It was a mad scramble. And everyone was terrified. Except me. Obviously, I knew covid was real. At the same time, I was used to studying data, and respected it, and based on the data that was readily available if you bothered to look beyond the headlines, I didn't understand what can best be described as mass hysteria.

"Shelter in place" rolled off everyone's tongue as if it was a thing we'd always known was a thing. Did this phrase even exist before this moment, right now?

Daniel attempted to entertain our young children (the "littles"), no easy task with playgrounds closed and no yard at our apartment. He also raged with mounting fervor about the harms being done to working class people, the civil liberties being infringed upon, the lack of clarity about any marker that would allow the restrictions to end, the possibility they'd go on indefinitely. And the age-stratified risk of covid making all this utterly inefficient, and unnecessarily harmful to kids. We'd followed the situation in Italy, one of the first countries hit hard in February, and knew the median age of death there was over eighty. We also understood what median meant.

I screamed at him: "You have to stop ranting!" I agreed with him on everything, but I was trying to keep it together, to work, to not go insane with four kids in our apartment all day and blaring, dueling meetings and classes scrambling my brain. When I went outside in search of food and toilet paper, the streets were empty. I bought jacks at our local convenience store thinking I'd teach the littles to play one of my favorite childhood games to help pass the time.

It felt apocalyptic. I came home, with no toilet paper, only jacks, and told my husband: "It's like people think if they set foot across the threshold of their homes, they're assured certain death. They think it's a war zone and they'll be struck down instantly. It's crazy out there." A woman had screeched at me to "Get away!" when I tried to hold her front door for her as she struggled to get her toddler laden stroller inside her apartment building.

I was dumbfounded. How could outside be dangerous? My husband ranted and paced some more in between taking the littles to play in a nearby deserted fountain at City Hall.

I took to reading anything that I could find about the virus. The headlines from *The New York Times* and the chyrons on CNN were all something to the effect of "We're all going to die!" *The New York Times Daily* podcast, which I had listened to on my way to work each morning and now on walks to Golden Gate Park, touted the World Health Organization's infection fatality rate of 3.4 percent as a reason to be afraid, very afraid. But, again, this did not fit with what I saw when I calmly looked at actual data. Why was everyone struck by such innumeracy?

Pre-March 2020, I was not in the habit of reading *StatNews*. In fact, I'd never heard of it. Presumably it was a trade publication for statisticians, decidedly not me. But on March 17 I came across an article by John Ioannidis, with this headline:

A fiasco in the making? As the coronavirus pandemic takes hold, we are making decisions without reliable data

By John P.A. Ioannidis March 17, 2020

I learned that the author was a Greek-American physician and scientist, and a professor at Stanford of medicine, epidemiology and population health, and of statistics and biomedical data science. He is also one of the most cited scientists in the world. His field of study is meta research, which basically means he researches research. His conclusion, and the defining assertion of his life's work, is that most published research does not meet basic standards for solid scientific evidence. In short, research is often deeply flawed. His seminal work, "Why Most Published Research Findings are False," is the most downloaded and read paper in the Public Library of Science. Of note, he was also an early critic of Theranos, the company founded by the now-disgraced Elizabeth Holmes. This guy was no lightweight. He wasn't stupid, and he certainly was not a quack. In fact, he seemed to be able to see things others could not.

His contention in the *StatNews* article was that we were implementing potentially devastating policies – lockdowns and school closures – without solid evidence that they were either necessary or effective. In our "better safe than sorry" approach, we weren't considering the unintended consequences – the enormous financial and social harms – that would inevitably come from extended restrictions. Given long timelines for vaccine development – usually many years – could we really afford to just wait? Maybe all these extreme measures weren't keeping the majority of us any safer from covid and were causing other disastrous impacts. It seemed to me that this line of thinking should at the very least receive consideration in state, national and international policy making.

Ioannidis further asserted that the infection fatality rate of covid could actually be as low as .2 percent, concentrated in the elderly, not 3.4 percent as was being claimed by the World Health Organization, driving a panicked response. And he argued that we needed to conduct better research to understand who was at risk and how much risk there really was, before shutting down the world and causing enormous destruction. He stated:

> . . . locking down the world with potentially tremendous social and financial consequences may be totally irrational. It's like an elephant being attacked by a house cat. Frustrated and trying to avoid the cat, the elephant accidentally jumps off a cliff and dies.

Ioannidis wasn't the only one making these claims. On March 20, 2020, Dr. David Katz, the founder of Yale University's Yale-Griffin Prevention Research Center (again, not a quack), wrote an opinion piece in *The New York Times* with the headline: "Is our fight against Coronavirus worse than the disease? There may be more targeted ways to beat the pandemic." In the op-ed he urged a more precision-based approach to fighting covid, rather than broadscale lockdowns and school closures, likening the blunt force of these tactics to all-out war versus the precision of a "surgical strike" to limit devastation. He reiterated the dramatic age stratification to emphasize the feasibility of a targeted approach to preventing severe outcomes and deaths. He ended with a plea for reason:

A pivot right now from trying to protect all people to focusing on the most vulnerable remains entirely plausible. With each passing day, however, it becomes more difficult. The path we are on may well lead to uncontained viral contagion and monumental collateral damage to our society and economy. A more surgical approach is what we need.

And on April 10, 2020, Martin Kulldorff, a Professor of Medicine at Harvard and one of the foremost epidemiologists and biostatisticians in the world, published an article on his LinkedIn page entitled "Covid 19 counter measures should be age specific." He was unable to find any scientific or medical journal willing to publish it and resorted to posting on his LinkedIn page. Despite his obvious credentials and well-researched analysis, he was rejected time and time again by medical journals and news outlets, a clear indication that the silencing of dissent about any variation in the possible path forward other than total lockdown was in full swing.

He wrote:

Among COVID-19 exposed individuals, people in their 70s have roughly twice the mortality of those in their 60s, 10 times the mortality of those in their 50s, 40 times that of those in their 40s, 100 times that of those in their 30s, 300 times that of those in their 20s, and a mortality that is more than 3000 times higher than for children. Since COVID-19 operates in a highly age specific manner, mandated counter measures must also be age specific. If not, lives will be unnecessarily lost.

All these highly credentialed, previously esteemed scientists and physicians were dismissed as either ill-informed, mistaken loons or corrupt frauds. Some, like Katz, muted themselves, presumably to avoid opprobrium. Others, like Kulldorff, continued to relentlessly use their voices throughout.

I fell into the rabbit hole of these pleas from respected doctors, statisticians and scientists. But the train had left the station on a panicked approach, which dismissed everything suggested by these well-intentioned and disciplined scientists as a cruel death march that would result in gruesome and unfathomable tragedy. It also shelved all that had been articulated in the CDC's pre-pandemic playbook. Written, as the name indicates, "pre-pandemic," in 2006, to ensure rational decision making not unduly influenced by panic, the playbook clearly stated that even with the very worst fatality rates, schools should never be closed for more than twelve weeks. For an infection fatality rate akin to covid's, not more than four weeks. The educational and developmental harm to kids was too great, impacting earning potential and, ultimately, life expectancy.

It was no easy task to stay informed. The headlines from CNN to *The New York Times* all screamed *Panic! We're all going to die!* But I committed myself to reading the actual data, which kept me calm about my own risk and my kids'. Still, it enraged me when it was decided schools would remain closed for the remainder of the spring semester. When everyone shrieked *It's just two weeks, two months, two however long it takes*! I thought not just of my kids but of those with far fewer resources. What would happen to children whose parents worked hourly wage jobs each day at the grocery store? Were these kids home alone trying to navigate online schooling with unreliable internet service? Would they log on at all? Where would they run and play with playgrounds closed? What of those who lived just one block away from me, in subsidized apartments, large families crammed into tiny spaces? Were they really safer this way? What about the kids who relied on school for meals? What would they eat?

New Traditions, the elementary school the bigs had attended, consisted of a student population with over sixty percent of kids that qualified for the "free lunch" program, as was true across the San Francisco public school system. The program also included breakfast and a snack to take home after school. What was going to happen to these kids? I cried daily pondering their circumstances, their fates, if schools didn't open soon.

My covid dissenting began on Facebook. I shared articles and videos from these heretical doctors and scientists claiming the fatality rate for SARS-CoV-2 was far lower than suggested by the alarmist reporting. They reasoned we should focus our efforts on those most at risk – the elderly and the vulnerable. And let everyone else go about their business. Don't worry about cases, they said. Worry about those susceptible to adverse outcomes, a far narrower population, making it more feasible to execute a plan to protect them. How could we protect the world from ever getting covid without causing disastrous unintended consequences? It seemed so utterly sensible and not at all controversial to me.

One of my earliest social media posts on covid was on March 25, 2020. I expressed what would turn out to be valid concerns about the adverse impacts of lockdowns:

Jennifer Sey
what I find upsetting right now among many things is that no one's fears or concerns are considered valid other than fears about getting, spreading, dying from Corona. anyone who brings up any other fears or concerns is pegged as totally selfish. is it selfish for a small business owner who supports her whole family - extended family - to be scared about her future, her child's future, her mother's future? is it selfish for a cancer patient who needs chemo but has it delayed due to corona to be angry? is it selfish for a woman who grew up in eastern bloc communism - Bulgaria - to be afraid that authoritarians are using this moment to grab power that they may never give back? is it selfish for someone in recovery who can't go to meetings to be more scared of falling back into addiction than of getting the virus? I think all of these fears are valid. Why do they all have to be erased or deemed selfish because they don't put Corona first in line?

Like   Reply   2y   👍 2

The examples I cited were all real examples of real people I actually knew. But it wouldn't have taken much empathy or imagination to conjure these situations. I didn't understand why, it seemed, almost no one was able to do so. The almost unanimous response was: "You're a murderer."

In response to my Facebook posts, some friends and family insisted that I'd been co-opted by the Republican Party. They suggested that I couldn't genuinely believe the things that I was saying, therefore I must be a pawn of the Koch brothers, either a paid mercenary or so inanely gullible that I was prone to their influence, and was doing it for free for likes and clicks to feed my ego.

On May 11, 2020, I posted about the fact that close to 70 percent of covid infections in New York City occurred post lockdown. I queried: "Are we sure this is working?"

From the husband of a friend from my gymnastics days I got: "You're going to get Trump re-elected with this garbage." Tellingly, he's since deleted his portion of our exchange.

Two weeks to flatten the curve became two months, and still, no one seemed to share my perspective. I argued with my brother Chris on Facebook, on the phone, via text. His wife, an emergency room physician in Los Angeles, was a "frontline hero" and at risk herself, as was their family. I was being reckless and insensitive to not take that into consideration, he said. And what about mom? Our mother had survived lung cancer (no she didn't smoke, she'd want me to tell you that) about fifteen years earlier. She'd had part of one lung removed during the illness and recovered despite being given a chance of survival of less than five percent.

"Mom's a goner if she gets it," he said.

"No, she's not. Even if she gets covid, her projected survival rate is about ninety percent. We would have been thrilled with that prognosis when she had cancer," I argued.

That did not go over well. I hated old people. I was selfish. I wanted to go about my unimportant business of getting haircuts and manicures while I put our kids' grandparents lives at risk.

I didn't care about getting my nails done. I just didn't want the world to spin off its axis. It seemed obvious to me that shutting the entire world down would cause unfathomable global harms including but not limited to food shortages, increased poverty, healthcare neglect and child abuse.

"I'm not saying *she* shouldn't protect herself. She can stay home. But what does that have to do with five-year-olds in kindergarten? I don't want mom to die, obviously, but I also don't want kids to be denied schooling. And what about poor people who aren't getting food in third world countries? Kids left home with their abusers? Don't they matter too?"

This was met with a virtual shrug.

"Same as it ever was. The poor and disadvantaged will suffer the most. It's a pandemic. We have to save who we can."

I hesitated to include any of this about my brother. I already have little hope of ever mending our relationship, but I like to think we might, one day. We had been close before covid, or at least I thought we were.

Chris and I had similar experiences growing up. He'd done gymnastics, too. We both went to Stanford together. He competed on the gymnastics team there, winning two NCAA team championship titles. We'd had our struggles over the years but nothing that couldn't be talked through. I understood it couldn't have been easy growing up in a family where my athletic ambition was the center of the family's emotional energy. When we moved to Allentown for my gymnastics in 1985, he didn't want to go. He liked his school and friends in New Jersey. He liked his gym. But he was left with no choice.

I'd be resentful, too. But I thought we'd wrestled all that to the ground in our twenties. I honestly don't know if underlying fissures and resentments were necessary for our rupture during covid. We certainly had a fundamental disagreement on covid policy. But why did it escalate as it did? I'm still not sure why my brother came to see me and my husband as not merely misguided, but as threats to society and, indeed, as the incarnation of evil.

And so, yes, we are one of those families that splintered during covid. As had happened back in the 1960s and 1970s with families divided over the Vietnam War. I still can't believe this is us. My family. Me and my brother. But here we are.

I've decided to include sentiments expressed by my brother that are public and readily available on social media. I can only assume he stands by it all, that he is proud of what he said, as he's left it in place. So, it seems fair to share and comment on. I also have decided to include it because I think it's relatable for far too many. And I, for one, feel a little less alone when I read about someone else's experience and find connection.

My brother reiterated his point about needing to save those we can, later in the year on Twitter. No shame in vociferously protecting the laptop "pajama class" while driving the poor further and further into inescapable poverty.

Christopher Sey
@csey16

···

Replying to @hannah_natanson and @JenniferSey

The rich have gotten richer. The poor poorer. Tragic, but same as it ever was.

8:48 PM · Dec 1, 2020 · Twitter for iPhone

2 Likes

He seemed to tweet the quiet part out loud with this one. Global pandemic policy and those that supported the harshest, most draconian restrictions seemed to say – screw the poor. Screw the children. Screw everyone but those who can actually work from home on a computer. And, it seemed to me, to be the most unfair, classist approach to pandemic management that I could imagine. My brother was scared for his wife who was caring for patients. I understand that must have been frightening. But front-line doctors can't make the rules for this very reason. They should influence the rules, provide insight from the trenches, but it's just one point of input. So many harms, that they weren't seeing, were being ignored.

I felt like I was losing my mind. Why didn't everyone see it?

I abandoned Facebook sometime in April, not wanting to get into such heated arguments with my family and friends. I sensed some of these relationships fracturing, possibly permanently.

My own father, in response to my husband's assertions that college spring-breakers who were at little risk from covid should, in fact, be permitted to engage in the decades-long tradition of partying outside on the beaches in Florida, wrote:

> The absolute stench of moral absence stinks in your selfish poorly reasoned bullshit reasoning. Science illiterates. Just keep operating on your Trumpian hunches!!

He not only said this to my husband, he said it publicly, on Facebook. I was stunned but I knew that my father's fear brought forth this furious nonsense. Still, it was cruel nonsense. And again, the Trump obsession. That seemed to be the ultimate insult. It was just all so stupid. But it seemed time for both of us – my husband and me – to escape to greener social media pastures populated with less familial toxicity and raw emotion.

I needed to find out if there were others out there who shared my views. Clearly few of my friends or family did, that much had been made clear. Was there anyone out there who was reading the data, suggesting a more balanced approach to protecting those most at risk while allowing low-risk young people to simply go about their business? I mean besides the scant few doctors and journalists I'd already discovered.

I switched to Twitter. The home of nuanced and balanced takes. This is a joke, if it needs to be explained, for anyone who has never been on Twitter. Two hundred and eighty characters does not allow for nuance. While the greatest benefit of this platform is allowing everyday folks to engage with experts, it may be the most toxic cesspool of all social media environments.

I only had about 1,500 followers at the time. Mostly gymnasts and gymnastics fans. After a decade of initially hating me for writing in my book about the sport's cruel and abusive training culture, with the revelation that Larry Nassar, the doctor for Team USA Gymnastics, had been sexually abusing young athletes for close to three decades, the gymnastics community had embraced me. Suddenly, in 2016, I was a hero, an early whistleblower who'd been right the whole time, with their full support. By and large, I accepted this pretense, or at least didn't publicly call it out as false.

But now I'd stopped tweeting about gymnastics. I switched to covid, an abrupt and confusing shift for those who knew me for my athlete advocacy. One of my very first covid tweets was this, on April 7, 2020:

8:46 PM · Apr 7, 2020 · Twitter Web App

2 Likes

I figured it was safe as it included a link to a newspaper article, which included a modeled study by University College London stating that school closures really didn't do very much to stop the spread of covid, but did a lot to harm kids. I did no editorializing. Just the facts as reported by a journalist. It got two likes and one comment, from a friend in the gymnastics world:

> After the dust has settled we can look back and see what worked and what we overreacted to. But the worst possible disaster would have been to make a mistake that hurt our children. There were too many unknowns. If nothing else we can look at this as a world-wide fire drill.

This was exactly my concern. That, in deploying the "precautionary principle," we were making a mistake that would hurt our children even more. That the fire drill would start an actual fire. That in abandoning the principle of "first do no harm" we were doing so much harm.

I couldn't stop thinking, or tweeting, about it. These kids, at home, many of them alone, isolated and on screens all day, were at the forefront of my every waking moment. I was desperate to find community, people who shared my concerns. I thought, if we band together, if we organize, maybe we can make a difference. It didn't work out how I'd hoped, but I was not wrong.

And while I recognized my peers at work might not approve, months passed without any mention. It was hanging out there, and I was aware of the possibility of a call from someone urging me to cut it out, but the call didn't come. To my mind, if I didn't hear anything, they either didn't notice or didn't care. I wasn't one to inflate my own reach and influence. I figured I'd continue until someone told me I had to stop. And even then, I might not. I imagined what the conversation might be. I'd explain, to whomever was given the unfortunate assignment of giving me a talking to, that this was merely an extension of my child athlete advocacy which they'd always supported. And they'd understand. Maybe. If not, I'd cross that bridge when I came to it.

But in the meantime, I just couldn't get the kids out of my mind.

CHAPTER 13:

LEVI'S ANTI-RACISM CONSCIOUSNESS IS RAISED.

O n May 25, 2020, George Floyd was killed when Minneapolis police officer Derek Chauvin kneeled on his neck for close to nine minutes. It was captured in videos that enflamed the nation. And suddenly nobody cared about covid anymore, at least for a time.

While Levi's has long supported LGBTQ causes, the company hadn't weighed in much regarding matters of race. But we were about to.

Our public advocacy, and action, for LGBTQ equality was long-standing. In 1992, Levi's became the first Fortune 500 company to offer same sex partner benefits. This was long before marriage equality was even on the radar of the political mainstream. And despite what we'd always said about Levi's not being politicized, the company had long been populated by leftie ideologues. But as I've said, I supported, and still support, actions that furthered equality for our own employees. However, this line blurred when we took external positions, as it had when we supported gun control initiatives.

In 2008, Levi's put its considerable weight against Prop 8, a California ballot proposition intended to amend the state constitution to ban same-sex marriage.

The *LA Daily News* wrote:

> The San Francisco-based jeans maker said Thursday that it has agreed to co-chair with Pacific Gas & Electric a group trying to drum up opposition to Proposition 8 in the business community.
>
> CEO John Anderson says the move is consistent with Levi's long history of supporting civil rights causes.

Despite Levi's opposition, the ballot initiative passed, keeping gay marriage illegal in California for the time being.

The movie *Milk*, starring Sean Penn, was released around the same time that Levi's gathered its forces to try to defeat Prop 8. The film chronicles the life of Harvey Milk, who was elected in January of 1978 to the San Francisco Board of Supervisors, making him the first openly gay elected official in the United States. He was assassinated less than a year later. The movie takes place mostly in San Francisco's Castro district, one of the most famous gay neighborhoods in the world. Levi's PR team dressed the cast in seventies-style undersized 501s (the buttons straining to remain fastened), bellbottom corduroys and hippie denim jackets. We hosted a premiere at the Castro Theater. We were all in.

And yes, I believed marshalling resources to try to defeat Prop 8 was the right thing to do on behalf of our employees, who were largely based in California. The company has a significant gay employee population, as is not entirely unusual in the fashion industry. Levi's had long tried to support their employees, and offering same-sex partner benefits was just one of their initiatives.

Did we make the most of this stance by sponsoring the *Milk* premiere and featuring Levi's jeans in all their rebellious glory? We sure did.

I still stand by supporting our own workers with policies intended to keep them safe, healthy and equal. Some might argue that dressing the entire cast in Levi's in such an explicitly progressive movie was taking a political stand. But it all made sense. We dressed the cast in what the people would have actually been wearing, and at the same time got a nice little progressive halo attached to the brand for being present.

Yet as I write this, I'm still puzzling over where I think the line should be drawn – when is it appropriate for corporations to move beyond protecting employees to taking overtly political stands beyond the walls of the company? Still, wherever that line is, it's pretty clear when we (along with just about every large corporation in America) crossed it.

It was in June 2020, following Floyd's murder.

To be sure, we at Levi's had been moving in that direction over the course of my tenure as CMO. As our business recovered, and we regained our leadership position within the fashion industry, we readily marketed things like equality and civic engagement along with new styles. We urged our younger fans to "use their voices" about issues they cared about, to use their vote – the unspoken subtext being "vote to get more progressive policies turned into law."

And, yes, I was in the middle of it all – I was the big wokester in charge of Levi's marketing wokes. Feel free to aim your vitriol at me. Maybe I deserve it. Anyway, I am used to it.

Levi's did not, and does not, have a large black employee population, and San Francisco itself is well below the national average in terms of the percentage of black residents, hovering at just under 6 percent, down from over 13 percent – close to the current national average – in 1970. Until recently, racism was not a stated issue of significant concern for the company. But we leapt on the anti-racism bandwagon with gusto that summer of 2020 as protests erupted around the country and the world.

We had actually started our racial reckoning in 2017 with the formation of a black employee resource group, along with other such groups supporting various categories of employees – among them Latinos, Asians, women, parents, immigrants and veterans.

I've been criticized by opponents of critical race theory, like Chris Rufo, for being part of such an initiative. Upon announcing my resignation from Levi's, Rufo asked me a question on Twitter:

"do you ... regret working to establish racially-segregated employee groups at Levi's?"

Let me answer here. No. I don't. Here's why.

I had been the executive sponsor of the black employee resource group since its inception, upon request from two black employees from my own team with whom I'd discussed the state of race relations in the hallways of Levi's.

My two oldest children are mixed race – my ex-husband is black – and when I mourned the murder of Philando Castille, who was fatally shot during a routine traffic stop on July 6, 2016, in a suburb near Minneapolis, with his girlfriend in the front seat and her four-year-old daughter in the back, I also worried about my own children being the victims of unwarranted police violence. Castille was pulled over at 9 p.m. and asked for his license and registration. He told the officer he had a firearm (he was licensed to carry one) and the officer told him not to reach for it.

Castille said: "I was reaching for . . ." (assumedly he meant his registration).

To which the officer responded: "Don't pull it out."

Then seven shots were fired. Castille was hit by five of them and he died at 9:37 p.m.

His girlfriend videoed the entire incident on her phone and streamed it live on Facebook. She screamed: "You just killed my boyfriend." Her child can be heard shouting: "Mom, please stop cussing and screaming 'cause I don't want you to get shooted."

It's horrifying. This is the one, of all the awful murders of black men caught on video and played on an endless loop on the nightly news, that affected me the most. It was the child's pleas to her mom that really haunted me.

I discussed all of this with my black colleagues and team members. We shared the same fears for our loved ones, and I couldn't help but worry about my sons when they headed to the corner store or came home a few minutes later than expected.

In 2013, on a vacation to Southern California, I witnessed my boys being racially profiled firsthand. I was in a convenience store with both kids, gathering snacks for our beach outing. I watched as the clerk followed them both around the store, hovering, tailing them, and closely observing their every move. I waited to be sure that what I thought was happening was actually happening. Could he have just been monitoring two pre-teens, whom he thought might shoplift some Doritos? Maybe. But I don't think so. I saw the way that he was looking at them. I approached when I felt confident that I understood what was motivating the clerk's suspicions.

"Do you guys have what you need?" I asked my children.

"Are they with you?" the clerk said to me, surprised.

"Yes," I confirmed.

That was enough. The white lady gave credence to the black boys' perusal of his shelves. They wouldn't snatch and grab, flee without paying.

Now, I wish I'd said something more, and taken the opportunity to explain to the clerk that what he was doing was wrong.

But instead, I'd made my point diplomatically, as is often my way.

Before the summer of 2020, Levi's had been silent on both matters of racially charged violence, and everyday discrimination against black people, though I'd discussed each with work friends and colleagues in the context of my fears for my own children. When we formed the employee resource groups, it was an effort to create support and a sense of community for various cohorts of employees, which was something that had been done informally for years.

As a thirty-year-old woman joining the company in 1999, I felt supported by female executives, who were few and far between. When I was passed over for a job, a vice president level marketing role in 2006, a long-tenured female executive whom I didn't even know reached out to me to offer support. She had noticed the unfairness. Though I'd successfully toiled as a marketing director for four years, when it came down to it, I was deemed unproven.

"Keep at it," she assured me. "You'll get there."

It wasn't worth filing any sort of discrimination complaint. It's just how it was. You had to be better. Men were promoted into their potential and women got promoted only after proving that they could do the job. I accepted it – what choice did I have? But I appreciated the show of support, and felt less alone as a woman climbing the corporate ranks after the senior executive talked to me.

And so, to me, formalizing this kind of networking made sense. Bring groups together. Create a sense of community within the community. That was our goal in forming Onyx, the black employee resource group (ERG) in 2017. So no, Chris Rufo, I don't regret working with black employees to try to foster a sense of community and provide some executive support and visibility to members of my own team. The goal was to make everyone feel included, not to make anyone feel excluded.

But that summer, in 2020, after George Floyd was murdered by Chauvin, was a turning point. We all watched in horror, from our locked down cities, as Chauvin put his knee on Floyd's neck, while the man lay handcuffed and face down in the street. Floyd pled for his mother before dying of asphyxiation. Other police officers stood by and watched. One officer, Thomas Lane, even pointed a gun at Floyd's head, while he was pinned and being suffocated, as if any more force was needed to restrain this dying man.

The nation went mad with rage. I went mad with it as well. I never watched the video. I didn't need to watch it to know how disgusting and gruesome it was.

It's important to note that by then we'd all been locked down in our homes since March. After three months separated from other humans, we were lonely, isolated, fearful, and barely keeping it together. And we were horrified by Chauvin's actions.

People took to the streets, not just in America, but around the world, en masse. And it wasn't always peaceful. Numerous people died during the protests, and vandalism and looting were rampant. The rage and helplessness in the face of such a horrific murder had bubbled over. The media presented the protests, which all too often became riots and arsons, as largely peaceful, softening the edges as a demonstration of support for the Black Lives Matter movement.

Furthermore, the protests were endorsed and encouraged by public health leaders, who were the ones responsible for keeping us locked down. In Democratic strongholds, where the protests largely occurred, we had not been to our offices, and our kids had not been in school, for more than ninety days. Restaurants were still shuttered, small businesses were going under. And we couldn't worship, mourn loved ones with funerals, or visit dying family members in the hospital. There were no graduations. Or weddings. Or high school football games. Or proms. Life had been put on indefinite hold because everything was too dangerous. And yet, more than one thousand doctors signed an open letter urging local government officials to NOT shut down the massive George Floyd protests. The letter stated:

We created the letter in response to emerging narratives that seemed to malign demonstrations as risky for the public health because of Covid-19. Instead, we wanted to present a narrative that prioritizes opposition to racism as vital to the public health, including the epidemic response. We believe that the way forward is not to suppress protests in the name of public health but to respond to protesters demands in the name of public health, thereby addressing multiple public health crises.

Former CDC Director Tom Frieden tweeted:

The threat to Covid control from protesting outside is tiny compared to the threat to Covid control created when governments act in ways that lose community trust. People can protest peacefully AND work together to stop Covid. Violence harms public health.

Of course, protests against lockdowns and school closures were deemed too dangerous and were shut down by police. Unlike the BLM protests, the threat from these sorts of protests was somehow *not* tiny compared to covid, even though they were much smaller. How did any of this make any sense? My husband summed it up well on Twitter, a few months after the fact, when the nation's attention had returned to covid matters and San Francisco's public schools remained closed indefinitely because of "science."

Daniel Kotzin
@danielkotzin   ...

This past summer, San Francisco refused permission for my son and 3 other children to have an outdoor, masked preschool graduation with their immediate families.

But thousands of BLM protesters were permitted to gather.

I will never forgive the unscientific, gratuitous cruelty.

8:29 AM · Feb 5, 2021 · Twitter for iPhone

ılı View Tweet analytics

22 Retweets   **236** Likes

Furthermore, why hadn't the nation responded this way when Castille was murdered in front of his own stepdaughter?

My take: many months into lockdowns, the nation was a powder keg, and Floyd's murder was the match that lit it all on fire. And fear of covid, while significant enough to prompt us to accept draconian emergency orders prohibiting any and all "non-essential" activity – we allowed our own loved ones to die alone! – was simply no match for the collective desire to prove how *not* racist we were by pledging allegiance to BLM (the organization and the general idea that black people's lives do indeed matter).

Every company in America renounced racism and their own supposed privilege in not fighting against it sooner. They said they'd do "the work" which apparently amounted to posting desperate apologies on Instagram promising fealty to BLM. These renunciations became very fashionable as corporate leaders across the country saw this as the perfect opportunity to burnish their newly woke image. I suspect some degree of guilt drove this mad dash to prove their newfound commitment to fighting racism. They knew they sent their kids to mostly white, mostly rich private schools, had no black friends and, generally had not thought much about racial dynamics up until this point, safely shielded from it all in their gated communities. This was the chance to sweep all that under the rug with a marketing campaign promising commitment to end racism and designed to appeal to young multi-racial folks who would hopefully become consumers of whatever brand in the future.

We at Levi's, along with so many other companies, made commitments. We would hire heads of Diversity and Inclusion and black executives; we would make every single one of our employees go through anti-racism training. We held virtual company town halls decrying our own white supremacy. We all committed to reading (or just buying?) Robin DiAngelo's *White Fragility*, which shot to number one on Amazon and stayed there. The book's publisher, Beacon Press, had trouble meeting demand for hard copies, as it continued flying off the virtual shelves. DiAngelo was flooded with requests to do keynote speeches at places like Nike and Goldman Sachs.

No one was more desperate to do the work that DiAngelo said that we needed to do than we were at Levi's.

CHAPTER 14:

"THE WORK."

We made a statement. We made several. Our CEO said:

Our company condemns all forms of racism – from the violent to the casual to the political. This isn't just about the shocking incidents captured on video. It's also about the implicit bias and quiet discrimination that happens every day.

I wrote a lot of the statements. I said:

We simply cannot sit idly by and think this is Black people's problem. It is America's problem, our greatest shame. We must do better.

I stand by this. We can and must do better. But that doesn't mean that we should orient *every* problem the country faces in a black vs. white binary. Math is not racist, as some educators have argued, some going so far as to put together a document entitled "Dismantling Racism in Mathematics Instruction" in May 2021. Part of anti-racist math is teaching kids about black mathematicians. Fine. But what about the actual math part?

If you work at Levi's in the finance department and you don't know how to calculate EBIT (earnings before interest and taxes) or ROIC (return on invested capital), but you do know about a whole bunch of black mathematicians, you won't keep your job for very long.

The document goes on to assert that focusing on getting the right answer is perfectionism (therefore damaging and racist), to teach math in a linear manner with necessary skills taught in sequence is racist, to value procedural fluency – e.g. how to do fractions or calculate percentages – over conceptual knowledge is racist.

But not knowing how to do basic math like long division is also called innumeracy, and it is very hard to hold a job, any sort of job at all, if you are totally innumerate. Not teaching black children real math will lead to real innumeracy and real unemployment. This is the real structural racism, if you ask me.

By 2020, anti-racism had become akin to religious fanaticism. As linguist, academic and iconoclastic cultural commentator John McWhorter puts it:

> . . . humans may sacrifice the black kid from the work of mastering the gift of math, in favor of showing that they are enlightened enough to understand that her life may be affected by racism and that therefore she should be shielded from anything that is a genuine challenge. This is not pedagogy; it is preaching. And in this country, religious propositions have no place in the public square.

But corporate America became churchlike in furthering the anti-racism doctrine.

At Levi's, we held town halls. I hosted one. I did an interview session with one of our black executives, a work friend. I mostly asked questions, but when I shared the story about intervening when my boys were being tailed in the convenience store, I was chastised by a few employees. I wasn't supposed to talk. In my attempt to demonstrate empathy and understanding I was told that I'd stolen the mic, talked over my friend, once again been part of the oppression. I felt confused and embarrassed. My friend, colleague and co-sponsor of the black ERG said "Nah. You did just fine. You're ok. Keep going."

I didn't know what to think. I'd spent the better part of my adult life as a member of a black family. My partner of sixteen years, now my ex-husband, is black. Our children, now men, are mixed race. I have engaged in discussions about racial discrimination and the actions that might move us forward for decades. I have done my best to live a life both conscious of bigotry and active in combatting it — in my own little world. Change starts at home, after all.

Floyd's murder did not prompt my awakening. I was awake long before. One Thanksgiving, as we discussed the perils of being black in America, my then-mother-in-law laughed at something I said.

"What?" I asked.

"You're right, but you know you're white, right?" she said. I did know, and I laughed too.

My ex-mother-in-law wasn't suggesting I was some sort of Rachel Dolezal, the white woman who presented herself as black, and may have really believed she was/is, despite having two white parents. My mother-in-law spoke with affection and acknowledgement that I had some modicum of empathy and understanding for the plight of black Americans, my children and then-husband included. As for Dolezal, it can be said that she did, as well. But she crossed a line when she tanned herself up with foundation, wore curly wigs and landed herself a gig as the local chapter president of the NAACP in Spokane, Washington.

It is hard not to cringe when watching an interview with Dolezal, this white woman in costume who convinced the world and seemingly herself of her genuine blackness. For a time. A generous interpretation is that her self-identification as a black woman came from sheer compassion which arose from her own life struggles and having had adopted black siblings. A less generous interpretation is that she was culturally appropriating a style of dress, language and overall self-presentation to swindle the public and leverage victimhood to gain prestige as a civil rights activist.

I find the whole thing utterly confounding and, frankly, I mostly think Dolezal is pretty unhinged. But it doesn't take a huge leap of faith to get that, when being a victim confers status, you're going to get white ladies assuming victimhood so as not to seem too privileged and therefore hated. Especially when people like Robin DiAngelo run around telling all of us white folks that we are damned if we do and damned if we don't. We are racists, no matter what. Who doesn't want to avoid that appellation?

But in this, as in so many ways, Levi's was ahead of the curve. Even before 2020's global anti-racism "awakening," back in 2019, we'd brought in Robin DiAngelo, the anti-racism guru herself, for a workshop. All of the ERGs were invited to participate in a consciousness-raising session despite the already prevalent criticisms of anti-racism training.

Simply put, critics argue it just doesn't work. Frank Dobbin, a Harvard sociology professor, has published research on attempts to combat bias for over thirty years in hundreds of companies. His conclusion: It doesn't do any good and may do some harm, because the training can actually activate stereotypes. Because "if people feel that they're being forced to go to diversity training to conform with social norms or laws" there may be backlash.

We were eager to send the message that we cared, that we were willing to do "the work," whether it worked or not. The basic program: the white lady tells us all how much white privilege we have, and we all feel really, *really* bad about it. We don't have to do anything with those bad feelings. We have to sit with them, "own" them. Wallow in them.

It seems to be the epitome of white privilege for a white person to walk around charging tens of thousands of dollars to tell people how racist they are. Blogger "Steve QJ" calls DiAngelo the "Vanilla Ice of Antiracism," which is about as funny – and accurate – a description as anyone could come up with. I won't even try to top it.

In reviewing her second book, *Nice Racism*, journalist Matt Taibbi describes DiAngelo's lifelong guilt over an embarrassing incident in college at a dinner party with a black couple as follows:

> Instead of trying to amp down her racial anxiety out of basic decency, this author fed hers steroids and protein shakes, growing it to brontosaurus size before dressing it in neon diapers and parading it across America for years in a juggernaut of cringe that's already secured a place as one of the great carnival grifts of all time.

This was written in 2021, but there was ample of evidence of this long before. It is hard to describe how much I was dreading this seminar. As the most senior member of the company in attendance, along with about fifty other, mostly white employees, I felt trapped from the get-go. Say nothing, admit you're a racist. Say you have black kids, your defensiveness reveals your racism. Say you're Jewish and have family that died in the Holocaust, further proof of your disrespect, trying to make it about you. This is what DiAngelo calls "credentialism," something white people do when they are hopelessly trying to prove that they aren't racist. This attempt to "individualize," she says, is a distinctly white trait. In her own words:

> The ideology of individualism is dependent on a denial of the past as relevant to the present. . . . Individualism denies the significance of race.

Good luck deciphering this gibberish presented as irrefutable truth. As far as I can glean, "individualism" upholds a righteous self-image and the racist hierarchy. As best I understand, the claim is: what goes unexamined goes unchanged. Shield yourself from examining your own racism and privilege by digging deep to find ways of relating – well, you're the worst kind of oblivious racist of all. You're the progressive well-meaning racist who doesn't even know she's a menace to society.

My oldest child told me beforehand: "Mom, never say that you have black children. That's the worst. Bring us with you as evidence if you like, but don't say it. Ever."

He was joking, or "facking and cracking" as my ex-grandmother-in-law used to say. Telling the truth and making a joke at the same time. I didn't say anything during the session. I left feeling mostly confused and directionless about what I was actually supposed to *do*. I couldn't understand how these workshops were supposed to actually help anyone, black or white.

By 2020, amidst all sorts of commitments to "fight racism" and improve the diversity in the company, we increased the frequency of these trainings. We had them for employees, we had them for executives, we had them for everyone. Of course, these all happened virtually, as we were still working from home. Massive protests with thousands of people were considered safe, but twelve executives in a room talking about how to not be a racist was apparently a grave danger.

During this time, and amidst all of our promises to be at the forefront of fighting racism, the Levi's executive team, of which I was a top-ranked member, went through another anti-racism training. It was a white guy leading it this time. We did it on Zoom and there were all sorts of exercises where you had to turn your camera off or on if you belonged to a particular group: "Someone in my family has gone to prison." Or: "Someone I know is a drug addict." And on and on.

We were supposed to be surprised when we saw who remained on camera after each question, an admission that we all had crosses to bear, secrets, challenges in our lives. But somehow the lesson was intended to convey that none of those crosses were so great as those carried by black Americans.

I hate this stuff. I hate ice breakers and trust falls and get-to-know-you gimmicks. But I went along. Until, in an offhand moment, the white guy leading the session said: "You know what group has the biggest problem admitting their white privilege?"

No. We didn't.

"White women," he told us.

That was about forty percent of us in the meeting.

"They've only newly come into power, and they don't want to give any of it up," he explained.

The implication being white men have plenty of power already and are more comfortable conceding some. I turned my camera off. I was livid.

He went on: "You know what group is the second biggest problem?"

No.

"Poor white people. They don't want to acknowledge that they have white privilege."

I turned my camera back on. I was even more livid. I thought, but didn't say: *Maybe they don't feel like they have any "privilege" because their communities have been decimated by unemployment and opioid addiction and corporate greed, and sometimes their electricity gets cut off or they can't pay for the medications that they actually need because they don't have enough money.*

I started to speak, thought better of it, and turned my camera back off. I felt like a coward.

What bothered me then, and now, is that it's all so black and white. Pun intended. You're either a "Grand Wizard" in the KKK or you see racism everywhere and battle it with every breath you take.

Anti-racism guru
Ibram X. Kendi

KKK Grand Wizard
David Duke

There is no in between. Which means that the continuum is not a continuum, but a door. You're on one side of it or the other. In or out. It might look something more akin to this:

David Duke
KKK Grand Wizard

Anti-racism guru
Ibram X. Kendi

Larry Elder
(black businessman and
former candidate for
California governor)
aka "White supremacist in
blackface"

Anti-racism guru
Robin DiAngelo

Chief Diversity and
Inclusion Officers

White suburban lady

Levi's executive

By today's "anti-racism" standards, Abraham Lincoln is already considered to be on the wrong side of this line. And, who knows, Martin Luther King Jr. might find himself there soon, too, for having said: "I have a dream that my four little children will one day live in a nation where they will not be judged by the color of their skin but by the content of their character."

There is plenty of racism in this country. I would never argue that there isn't. The thing is – we need real actionable strategies to overcome the impacts of racism, both structural and individual. Closing the education gap between white kids and black kids is a good place to start. If you can't read, you can't learn. And this has dramatic impacts on life outcomes. If a child can't read proficiently by the fourth grade, he or she is four times more likely not to graduate from high school on time. The median income for an adult without a high school diploma is about $30,000 a year, making it very difficult to break the cycle of poverty.

And here are the facts as of 2019: a sample of students was tested for reading proficiency in the eighth grade by the Education Department's National Assessment of Educational Progress (NAEP). This is done every two years and it's known as the nation's Education Report Card. Achievement levels are reported in four categories: advanced, proficient, basic and below basic.

Overall, 4 percent tested at the advanced level, 29 percent were proficient, 39 percent at basic and 28 percent at below basic. Pretty bad. This means that close to one third of the nation's children can barely read by eighth grade.

But wait, it gets worse. When you analyze the data for black students, 47 percent are below basic proficiency. Close to half of the nation's black children cannot read or can barely read. And the situation has deteriorated due to school closures. One Virginia study shows that reading skills were at a twenty-year low as of the fall of 2021.

National test results released in August 2022, by the National Assessment of Educational Progress, showed that reading scores for nine-year-olds fell by the largest margin in over thirty years as a result of school closures during the pandemic. And of course, high poverty and non-white students were the most severely impacted. On September 1, 2022, Sarah Mervosh wrote in *The New York Times*:

> In math, Black students lost 13 points, compared with five points among white students, widening the gap between the two groups. Research has documented the profound effect school closures had on low-income students and on Black and Hispanic students, in part because their schools were more likely to continue remote learning for longer periods of time.

These students are failing to learn because their schools failed to teach to them.

In *The New York Times* piece, Mervosh stressed the impact of this loss in learning with the following quote from Susanna Loeb, the director of the Annenberg Institute at Brown University, which focuses on education inequality:

> Student test scores, even starting in first, second and third grade, are really quite predictive of their success later in school, and their educational trajectories overall. The biggest reason to be concerned is the lower achievement of the lower-achieving kids.

Loeb added that being so far behind could lead to disengagement in school, making it much less likely that these kids graduate from high school.

Those of us who advocated for open schools said that this would happen from the very beginning. It was obvious. But we were dismissed and called racists by Democratic education leaders across the country. In 2021, when schools had been closed for about a year, then-San Francisco School Board President Gabriela López proclaimed:

> They [students] are learning more about their families and their culture, spending more time with each other. They're just having different learning experiences than the ones we currently measure.

By August 2021, Cecily Myart-Cruz, the head of United Teachers Los Angeles, asserted: "It's OK that our babies may not have learned all their times tables. They learned resilience."

But it wasn't okay then, and it isn't okay now. Real learning, as we all know, is the pathway to opportunity. According to the Bureau of Labor Statistics, as of 2020, the median weekly earnings for someone without a high school degree hovers around $600 per week, which is right around the national poverty line for a family of four.

If an innumerate adult can't get a job in the finance department at Levi's, an illiterate adult can't get a job anywhere doing anything. All of this is to say, opening schools would have had far more impact on actual structural racism than pointless Zoom training sessions about privilege.

Here's another example of the pointlessness of performative contrition. Today, land acknowledgments are very *au courant*. What's a land acknowledgment? Starting any speech with an acknowledgment that the place where the speaker is standing was once the home of an indigenous tribe. My son's high school graduation in San Francisco in 2021 started with one; it went something like this:

> Before we begin, we must acknowledge that we are on the unceded ancestral homeland of the Ramaytush Ohlone people who are the original inhabitants of the San Francisco Peninsula. As the indigenous stewards of this land and in accordance with their traditions, the Ramaytush Ohlone have never ceded, lost nor forgotten their responsibilities as the caretakers of this place.

What could this possibly do for the living Ramaytush Ohlone people? Acknowledging that their ancestors' land was taken from them hundreds of years ago helps no one.

Forcing poor Appalachians targeted by the Sackler family with opioid prescriptions, who then endured ongoing tragedies and mass death due to overdoses from opioid addiction, to admit that they have white privilege feels pretty pointless. How on earth is that going to help a single black nine-year-old-child living in poverty, like those who suffered record breaking literacy losses from school closures?

It's not. I'd prefer to fight to get public schools open, and then make them better.

But at Levi's, and in corporate America generally, and in the world at large, it all just started to snowball. We were all frantically announcing our racism, unburdening ourselves of this wrenching guilt, doing "the work" which apparently meant posting black squares on Instagram. Or demanding the firing of young black journalists from places like *Teen Vogue*.

In spring of 2021, a young black woman named Alexi McCammond was hired as the editor of *Teen Vogue*. At twenty-seven years old, she was an accomplished political journalist. She'd cut her teeth at the Washington, DC, news site *Axios*. In 2019, she was named the emerging journalist of the year by the National Association of Black Journalists.

During the interview process she revealed that she had tweeted some bad stuff as a teenager. Anti-Asian, stupid teenaged shit.

In 2011 when she was seventeen and in high school, she tweeted: "Outdone by [an] Asian #whatsnew," and "now googling how to not wake up with swollen, asian eyes..."

She'd apologized in 2019 when the tweets had surfaced. *Axios* said no problem.

And she apologized again in the interview process with *Teen Vogue*. No matter. Once she was appointed to this prestigious post, the mob went wild. Because there is no forgiveness in the world of wokeness. Journalist Diana Tsui posted on Instagram:

> Let's talk about Conde Nast [which owns Teen Vogue] HR and this questionable hire for Teen Vogue EIC [Editor in Chief]. She had a series of racist tweets in 2011. Maybe we can give her some benefit of the doubt as these were done when she was still a student. But her "apology," which was only after people caught them in 2019, referred to them as deeply insensitive. They are not insensitive, they are racist.

Corporate marketing folks, not to be out-woked, or in any way forgiving, cancelled advertising from *Teen Vogue*. My own team, without my knowledge (I didn't know a lot! I had more than one thousand people on my team in well over one hundred countries), joined the cabal to pull ad dollars from *Teen Vogue* if they didn't fire McCammond, who hadn't even started work yet. The publication succumbed to the pressure and pushed her out the door before she spent a day on the job. Technically, McCammond resigned. She said:

> [My] past tweets have overshadowed the work I've done to highlight the people and issues that I care about. I wish the talented team at Teen Vogue the absolute best moving forward.

But you know I know you know that she was given no other option. I found out my team had joined the "protest" the day before she resigned. I was furious.

Why did they join the pile on? I said something like:

"Guys [oops, I shouldn't have said that, it's bigoted and gendered, I was off to a poor start] . . . She's a smart, capable, accomplished person who also happens to be a black woman. We should cheer her appointment. She apologized for something she did as a teenager. That is setting an example. We should champion heartfelt apologies, learning from mistakes. We can't cancel everyone who ever said something indelicate. We'll all be cancelled."

Little did I know . . .

My team hemmed and hawed a bit. They claimed that they saw my point. But regardless, it was too late. McCammond had resigned. We'd contributed. I was mad.

Around the same time, I got an email from our CFO. He told me an employee on his team was concerned about an "influencer" we were using for Gay Pride month, considering him out of step with the values of the company. According to the employee, this social media star had expressed "violence" in his posts and the employee was very concerned that we would associate our brand with him. He didn't name names so I was left to sleuth a bit and troll all of the influencers we were currently working with.

I said I'd look into it, but it took some digging. In this age of social media, we employed hundreds of social media stars to endorse our products. I searched Instagram, our primary social media mode. Found nothing. Switched over to Twitter, a platform we rarely used because it's just not visual, which is the preferred purview for fashion brands. I found him. Or what I assumed had to be him by process of elimination.

All I could come up with was a gay fashion blogger from New York who was also Israeli. He had Jewish stars and Israeli flags in his profile. I was mystified. Could that be it? It had to be. The fact that he expressed support for the right of Israel, his native country, to exist was violence, according to some.

The antisemitism of the Left, which puts Jews in the "white" category in the racial binary, and not just white, but super white, had been nagging at me for years. Jews are placed at the top of the woke racial pecking order supposedly because they have money, power and influence. They do not deserve sympathy and they certainly do not deserve the status that comes from victimhood. According to some, like Whoopi Goldberg, the Holocaust was not an ethnic cleansing. It was just a bunch of white people arguing with each other. On *The*

View, in February 2022, Goldberg insisted that the Holocaust was "not about race" it's just "white people doing it to white people, so y'all going to fight amongst yourselves."

This dynamic had started to roil me in the summer of 2017 when a group of Jewish women were asked to leave the **Dyke March in Chicago**, a celebration within the city's Pride activities during the month of June. The Dyke March is seen as less corporate and more inclusive than the larger Pride Parade. But women carrying a rainbow flag adorned with a star of David were asked to leave by the parade's organizers. The organizers claimed that it wasn't antisemitism that made them do it; it was anti-Zionism.

The line between antisemitism and anti-Zionism can be blurry, but it wasn't blurry here. Although the Pride marchers' flag was adorned with a star of David, meant to represent their Jewish heritage, they carried a typical rainbow Pride flag. It was not an Israeli flag, which looks very different. The Israeli flag is blue and white; no rainbow.

This isn't an isolated incident. The contemporary Left is rife with antisemitism.

For example, take Ilhan Omar, a prominent left-wing Democrat and the member of Congress from the fifth district of Minnesota, who says things like: "It's all about the Benjamins" when responding to a journalist's question in 2019 about why U.S. political leaders support Israel. Her inference being, there is no good reason for the United States to support Israel. It is only done because the American Israel Public Affairs Committee (AIPAC) buys influence. Not because

Israel is the only democracy in the Middle East and shares many of our values.

As for financial influence, teachers' unions also give a lot of money to political candidates. In the 2021 gubernatorial recall special election in California, the teachers' unions gave over two million dollars to keep Gavin Newsom in office, rewarding him for keeping California public schools closed for the previous year, as they had wished. Do I like special interest groups influencing politics? Groups such as the American Federation of Teachers (AFT)? No. I don't like it. But treating AIPAC differently than other special interest groups is not only hypocritical, it reeks of antisemitism.

Further evidence of the anti-Israel/anti-Jewish push from the Left is the BDS (Boycott, Divestment and Sanctions) movement. In May 2021, the United Educators of San Francisco, the city's teachers' union, announced its support of BDS, when the majority of students were still doing Zoom school from their bedrooms. They were the first K-12 teachers' union in the country to make such a pronouncement. At the time they made this declaration in defense of BDS, the vast majority of San Francisco public school students had not set foot in an actual classroom for well over a year. But the union saw fit to expend time and energy on crafting this very important announcement which has nothing to do with its actual job.

Why not announce a boycott of Chinese-made goods? It is widely known and reported on that the Chinese government is engaged in human rights abuses of ethnic Muslims in China, the Uyghurs. The Chinese Communist Party (CCP) has pursued a policy of mass incarceration of more than one million Uyghurs with no sort of legal due process. Why doesn't the San Francisco teachers' union announce a boycott of anything coming out of China, like iPhones and Nikes, because of these human rights abuses? Could the fact that they *really* like their iPhones and Nikes have anything to do with it? What Israeli products are so integral to their lives that giving them up would be a real sacrifice? SodaStream? Feta cheese and couscous at Trader's Joe's? A boycott of Israeli goods doesn't require much from the protester at all.

Another reason is because criticism of China is considered unacceptable as it could be construed as racism because Chinese people are not white. But criticism of Jewish people, and boycotts of Israel, are laudable by many on the Left, because Jews are considered to be white, therefore privileged. And it is impossible to discriminate against privileged white people. And of course, there is clearly some antisemitism at play.

But more importantly, why is the teachers' union focusing on anything other than:

1) Getting schools open during covid.
2) Teaching our kids.

As I've shared, I am Jewish. Though, as my husband often says, I have less of a religious impulse than anyone he has ever met. And by "less" he means zero. Daniel was born in Israel and holds an Israeli passport. He served as a medic in the Israeli army in his twenties.

He is also secular but holds a deep pride in his heritage. And his father, now deceased, held leadership positions in the Anti-Defamation League and the Chicago Jewish Federation for many years. His dad also taught at the University of Tel Aviv in the late sixties and seventies, which is why my husband was born there. And speaks fluent Hebrew.

All of this is to say that we are both Jewish, and have personal connections to Israel. But that doesn't mean that we aren't critical of some Israeli policies, just as we are critical of some American policies. And, we are also proud of Israel, just as we are proud of America.

Back to our Levi's Pride influencer with Israeli flags in his Twitter profile. I reached out to the head of marketing and her social media lead regarding the complaint from the employee in Finance. I explained the concerns and gave my perspective that these concerns were not actually concerning. She told me that they'd already received complaints and had "de-emphasized" his role in our LGBTQ campaign in celebration of Pride month. In this case, "de-emphasized" meant we had stopped using him in the campaign entirely. Levi's Wokes had done it again.

I said: "Guys [again with the guys, oops], why? He's a fashion blogger. He writes about fashion. He's also gay. So what if he's proud of being from Israel?"

But again, I was too late. Again, we'd bowed to the mob.

I pulled my marketing leadership team together. I told them it was enough with the unforgiving intersectionalism. In a world of influencer marketing, we were never going to please everyone all the time. People have opinions. That's okay. We needed to stand by our people. They are using their voices as we encouraged people to do in our own campaigns. If we liked him for his gay fashion blogging, we could stand by his being Israeli. Can we please just get back to marketing jeans not pandering to the woke mob?

But the woke genie was out of the bottle.

In the world of woke-ism there is no forgiveness, as I was about to learn firsthand.

CHAPTER 15:

MY FIRST "TALKING TO."

Before George Floyd's murder, and before we embarked upon our anti-racist crusade, just a few weeks into the pandemic, with our sales having plummeted (down more than sixty percent) due to lockdowns, Levi's furloughed retail store employees to reduce costs. On April 8, Chip told *Yahoo Finance*:

> We just announced we are furloughing all of our salaried employees in our U.S. retail stores. But we are trying to do it with empathy. We are leading with our values.

A lot of good that empathy and those values did for the close to four thousand Levi's workers left without paychecks. But hey, it sounds nice.

On the exact same day these employees found out that they weren't going to be getting paid for an indeterminant length of time, the company announced that it was going to return $32 million to shareholders, revealing that Levi's was not, in fact, leading with its stated values. Instead, the company was forcing people of limited means to make sacrifices, while wealthy shareholders made no sacrifice at all. The laptop class crowed smugly: "We're all in this together," eager to assert their noble, selfless commitment to the public welfare.

But we weren't all in it together. And if I even suggested that the executive team should go to work in the office in solidarity with those who had to – people like Levi's distribution center workers shipping e-commerce packages – I was accused of being uncaring and selfish. In fact, I didn't think it was fair that I, and we, the "laptop class," could hide out at home pretending that we were the "caring" ones, while at the same time insisting that some go to work in-person, and others not be allowed to work at all (and not get a paycheck) even if they wanted to.

Shareholders collected enormous payouts for doing their part to "flatten the curve" (which really meant doing nothing at all), while those who could least afford it, like the furloughed salespeople at Levi's stores, had no option but to *not* get paid. As Stanford professor of health policy Dr. Jay Bhattacharya likes to say: "Lockdowns are trickle down epidemiology." So are dividend payouts, I suppose.

William Lazonick, an esteemed economist, was critical of companies like Levi's issuing dividends to already-wealthy shareholders rather than using the money to support employees. On May 5, he said to the *Washington Post*:

> "In a downturn like this, the first thing a company should do is give up any distributions to shareholders. [. . .] But in a crisis, companies will differ. Some will care . . . and some will rob the workers, who should expect that their continued employment will be the company's first concern."

Nevertheless, Levi's persisted. By the early summer of 2020, amidst the protests and pronouncements, the executive team, including me, was planning for widespread layoffs (or, to use the euphemism presented to disguise the truth: a "streamlining of our workforce") in a month's time.

In July 2020, after loudly proclaiming we were all about equality, we laid off fifteen percent of the company's employees, in order to reduce costs by $100 million. Levi's seized the opportunity to bolster its bottom line under the cover of covid, thus protecting the wealth of shareholders, while leaving workaday employees without jobs or income. Of note, a full 65 percent of the company is owned by the Haas family, the heirs of Levi Strauss, who are currently worth about $4 billion.

Later, in February 2021, Chip explained the layoffs to *Fortune* as follows:

We believe there's a real linkage between our values and business results. . . . [Because] of our values, it was very easy for us to declare that we're going to put our employees front and center through this.

How does terminating the employment of hundreds of people put them "front and center"? What "values" was Levi's "linking" to? The money "saved" by the layoffs went directly into the pockets of large shareholders. And it was lots of money. In fact, as reported by *Wallmine.com*, Chip himself cashed in about $43 million in stock in March 2021, a financial windfall generated, at least in part, by putting seven hundred people out of work only months earlier.

Date	Company	Insider	Transaction	Shares	Price per share	Total value
March 19, 2021	LEVI	Charles V. Bergh	Sale	356,926	$24.94	$8,901,734
March 16, 2021	LEVI	Charles V. Bergh	Sale	984,710	$24.98	$24,598,056
March 12, 2021	LEVI	Charles V. Bergh	Sale	359,649	$25.33	$9,109,909

Our head of Corporate Communications, Kelly McGinnis, was very busy during this time crafting messaging calling the layoff decision a "tough call" and planning employee all-hands meetings to explain to those who remained employed why this was all in line with Levi's stated "values."

Levi's CFO: 700-person layoff 'toughest call' of pandemic

Published July 10, 2020

My first "talking to" call finally came in in September 2020, about six months into school and playground closures. Private schools in San Francisco were all either opened or preparing to open, while public schools and public playgrounds remained stubbornly closed. This hypocrisy enraged me, and I'd upped the ante of late.

Jennifer Sey ✔
@JenniferSey

Most private schools in SF will open on Monday. Public schools won't. My kids will remain at home. I'm sad for them and their peers. I'd like to understand the plan to address how far behind many will fall. Is there one? Or do we pretend screen learning works just fine?

1:16 PM · Sep 18, 2020 · Twitter Web App

1 Retweet   **17** Likes

Nothing I said, or tweeted, got much traction. But employees had started to notice – I got a stray comment here and there like: *Why Jen? What's the difference? There's an election coming. Do you want Trump to win?* (It was always about Trump, never about the children.)

What's the difference?! I wanted to scream but didn't. Private school students were headed back for actual learning in actual school but the public schools remained shut indefinitely. The fact that they wouldn't acknowledge the obvious hypocrisy and inequality made me even more determined to keep fighting.

But I was screaming into the wind. The above tweet got 17 likes and exactly 1 retweet. No one really cared what I thought in the twitter-sphere. No matter. Kelly McGinnis, our head of Corporate

Communications, whose own kids were starting in-person school, found my views, and the fact that I expressed them publicly, too problematic to ignore. She called me, and when I saw her name pop up on my phone, I knew. None of us called each other randomly. And of course, we no longer "popped by just to chat." We'd been working virtually for several months. We set meetings, made appointments.

Kelly and I had worked closely together over the previous seven years. We distinguished between Levi Strauss and Company and Levi's in our spheres of responsibility. She was responsible for the company's corporate PR and overall reputation. She led things like quarterly earnings reports and communication around the company's sourcing and supply chain policies. The main focus of her efforts was getting stories placed within the trade press, in publications like *Sourcing Journal* or *WWD* (formerly known as *Women's Wear Daily*). Or to get stories placed that might influence the financial community, in publications like *Fortune* or in the Business section of *The New York Times* (the holy grail).

I was responsible for the brand communication, speaking directly to consumers around the world, reaching quite literally billions of people. I "owned" things like Levi's PR and advertising for the actual jeans on television, in magazines and online. The main focus of my efforts was to drive sales and brand image amongst everyday consumers around the world. Think *Glamour* magazine, Pop Sugar (a fashion and lifestyle website), Instagram, Superbowl. I led things like advertising campaigns in support of a Levi's product launch (new high-rise jeans), events at music festivals like Coachella and all the publicity that emanated from that.

Anything that would prompt people to want to buy Levi's was in my purview. Anything that would make the financial community want to invest in Levi's and keep the non-governmental organizations (NGOs – nonprofits invested in a social or political issue, like Greenpeace) out of our hair, was hers.

These two things were inextricably linked, so each of us rarely made a move without consulting, or at least informing, the other. Our partnership had been somewhat strained in the early days when I was a new CMO. I'm not sure why. Perhaps we were bumping into each other a bit without having clarified our individual non-overlapping responsibilities. I chalked it up to turf wars or the oft-whispered-about competition among female executives. With only a few slots reserved for women at the executive level, weren't we all in competition to ascend the ladder? If there's only one chair for a woman on the executive team, we women were elbowing each other out of the way for that slot. Or so it has been said. Personally, I've never felt that way.

In fact, I took special care to mentor women. When I first started at Levi's, a few (and there were only a few) female executives had taken special care to mentor me. Throughout my career I've often found the most collaborative working relationships I have had were with other women. My partnership with the head of Levi's Design, Karyn Hillman, is a major reason that the brand was brought back to life. We never felt competitive. We recognized each other's discrete talents and worked together to enact a shared vision – she brought it to life through product, I brought it to life through marketing. We knew neither of us could do the job alone. And we needed the other for the brand to be great, and for each of us to be great in our respective roles. When I got promoted in late 2020 to Brand President, I became Karyn's boss. It could have been awkward. It wasn't; it was completely seamless.

"I'm never going to tell you what to do," I told her. "We don't have to change how we work together, as it's worked so well thus far. I will not tell you how to make product. You are the expert, and my job is to stay out of your way."

When it came to Kelly, my colleague in Corporate Communications, I harbored no ill will or jealousy. I attributed our initial conflicts to a rocky start, a minor personality clash and a need to define our "lanes." I'd win her over. Or so I thought. Now I think maybe she'd been waiting for an opportunity to take me down all along. I certainly enjoyed more of the spotlight internally and externally than she did. My job involved speaking to the press, meeting with celebrities, motivating and exciting employees about the direction of the brand. Hers involved preparing others – the CEO, the CFO – to speak to the press and employees. She was behind the scenes making stuff happen, never in front of the camera. Was there some jealousy? I can't speak for her. I don't know. But even after we got through our brief bumpiness, she never fully supported me. She was not a fan.

Cut back to the call from Kelly in September 2020. I don't know whether she'd noticed my social media musings or if someone on her team brought them to her attention. At any rate, she called me, and I answered despite wanting to throw my phone across the room and hide in a defensive crouch, pretending this contentious ordeal was not about to begin. Somewhere, deep inside my brain, I knew the moment that I started this crusade that I might have to choose between having a job and having my voice.

This call was the beginning of a conflict within myself, with my colleagues, and eventually, with the woke mob.

I was not prepared to escalate it just yet. Inasmuch as I knew it was going to be a necessary conversation, I wanted a meeting to be scheduled, a meeting called: "Talking to Jen about her Twitter" or "Why you can't say schools should be open when you're the head of marketing at Levi's." I wanted to craft my talking points, think through how I'd respond to "you need to cut it out" before I just spoke off the cuff. An impromptu, pretend-friendly chat could lead to more anger and frustration than I wanted to reveal, possibly accelerating this undesirable dynamic – this battle of wills – that I really did not want. But I answered because that's what I do. I don't hide. I confront. With diplomacy.

Kelly: "Hey. So…"

Uh oh.

She paused. She was nervous. I was formidable and she knew it.

Me: "What's up?"

Kelly: "Yeah. So. About your Twitter. People are noticing."

Me: "Oh. Really? I guess I'm not surprised. I've sort of been waiting for this call."

What she said next was something to the effect of: *You're the Chief Marketing Officer. When you say things publicly, you're saying them on behalf of the brand and the company.*

I do remember exactly what I replied: "No. I'm a private citizen and public school mom. I'm speaking on behalf of children being harmed by public school closures. It is consistent with my advocacy for children in sports."

She was unconvinced.

"Are you telling me I need to stop?" I was taunting her to say yes.

"No, I can't do that. Just hold the line."

It was not clear to me what that meant exactly, and the conversation started to peter out. I didn't say okay, but I didn't say no either.

If Kelly had told me to stop, it would have unleashed something in me, quashing my well-practiced discretion. I had no contract with the company prohibiting me from using social media or from using it in a particular way. We had no employee policy regarding use of social media. I'd spoken out plenty about politics in the past, sometimes intemperately, but always from a left-of-center perspective.

I'd been public in my support for Elizabeth Warren in the recent Democratic primary, and no one cared. So they couldn't go the "we don't take sides in politics as a company and neither can you" route. [Note: Of course, I'm applying a logic which does not exist in the world of woke side-taking. My first and biggest mistake was not understanding this at the beginning. I thought if I applied logic and data all could be fine. I'd make it all make sense for people. I was very, *very* wrong.]

As a company we always made the point that we don't weigh in on matters of pure politics – like candidates or office holders. We don't donate to PACs or candidates, directly or indirectly. There were no restrictions on employees doing so, but LS&Co did not. I suppose this was to maintain the illusion of being apolitical in order to keep our loyal right-leaning consumers on board, since Republicans comprise slightly more than half of Levi's customer base in the United States.

However, in 2017 we did donate $1 million dollars to our own foundation, the Levi Strauss and Company Foundation, to support vulnerable populations – immigrants and the LGBTQ community. Nor was this out of the ordinary for the company. MarketWatch wrote:

Levi's is taking a $1 million stand against the Trump administration

Published: May 18, 2017 at 8:46 a.m. ET
—

I'm not sure who we thought we were fooling with the whole "we don't take sides in politics" line.

I'm not arguing about whether we should have donated the money or not. I am making the point that it is dishonest to say that you are not political, while "taking a stand against the Trump administration."

Just a few months earlier, in late 2016, we, as an executive team, were debating whether to weigh in on gun control. Our toe-dipping into the swirling rapids of the gun control waters was in response to an incident in one of our stores in Georgia. A shopper had carried a gun into a fitting room, it went off accidentally, and the man injured himself. It was very scary for sales associates and other shoppers and, of course, for the injured party. As a result, we debated, and ultimately made the decision, to post signs in our windows, as well as an open letter which was reprinted in *Fortune*, requesting our stores be a gun free zone. Chip wrote:

> ". . . while we understand the heartfelt and strongly-held opinions on both sides of the gun debate, it is with the safety and security of our employees and customers in mind that we respectfully ask people not to bring firearms into our stores, offices or facilities, even in states where it's permitted by law. Of course, authorized members of law enforcement are an exception."

Chip added that he knew some consumers would react to this request by calling for a boycott of Levi's. But, he concluded: "Most boycott threats around this topic ultimately blow over." (He was right about that. The threats do blow over. Oddly, he wouldn't apply that thinking to the handful of folks angry about my open schools advocacy.)

As I've said, I endorse rules that extend equality, and in this case safety, to our employees, so I supported this decision. I too knew any backlash would blow over soon enough. But I also knew that it was a landmine and that we needed to brace ourselves to be inundated with #boycottlevis hashtags everywhere. And sure enough, as soon as the first sign went up, we were widely characterized as anti-Second Amendment:

NRATV @
@NRATV

#NRA's @CamEdwards on anti-#2A @LEVIS "I'll spend my money somewhere else." Tell Levi's why you #DontDie4Denim #BoycottLevis

4:00 PM · Dec 2, 2016 · Twitter Web Client

63 Retweets   9 Quote Tweets   107 Likes

This was to be expected from the NRA. But the tweets and reddit threads flowed everywhere. We would post about a new jean style on Instagram and for days get nothing but "Levi's is anti-2A." There were lots of "Wrangler for me from now on!" type posts as well. Like this:

FollowDaMoney ➜ Guest · 6 years ago
My Wrangler store near me entertains open carry and I get my favorite pair for less that $20.

In February 2018, the tragic Parkland High School shooting in Florida, which left seventeen students dead, further ratcheted up the national conversation on gun control. Since we were already in for a dime on the issue, we now weighed going in for the whole dollar, by publicly and unequivocally announcing our support of gun safety laws.

As we debated whether or not to publicly take a stand on this issue, it seemed important to me that we not pretend such a decision was apolitical. Though I was a registered Democrat at the time and remain a gun safety laws supporter to this day, I warned that, make no mistake, we *were* weighing in on politics. It couldn't be more obvious that overwhelmingly it was people like us, liberal Democrats, who were gung-ho for tighter restrictions on guns and gun ownership. Whether we explicitly said so or not, we would be revealing our leftie cards. Even as I supported such a move, I argued that it would be better to just be honest about that and drop all the "we don't weigh in on politics" mumbo jumbo.

My peers disagreed, seemingly unable to even grasp the point. For them, *every* rational person was for tighter gun restrictions. It's a good bet many had never met anyone who disagreed – certainly not anyone in San Francisco.

"Political?" they responded. "We're just defending children from school shooters!"

To them it was just obvious common sense.

Of course, they were lying to themselves. But what else is new? When you convince yourself a lie is true, it is much easier to convincingly convey the lie – even as a company. So as a company we stood by the fiction that this was not political.

Chip's open letter appeared in *Fortune*, urging business leaders to take a stand, in September 2018:

. . . as business leaders with power in the public and political arenas, we simply cannot stand by silently when it comes to the issues that threaten the very fabric of the communities where we live and work. While taking a stand can be unpopular with some, doing nothing is no longer an option.

After this op-ed, Chip needed round-the-clock security because of death threats.

Still, it was more convenient to pretend that the company's policy of disavowing political involvement remained intact. As recently as April 2022, when asked if the company contributed donations to political campaigns, Chip replied:

No. This is pretty straightforward. We do not have a political action committee and to my knowledge, I don't think we have ever had one, and we do not make any political donations to any politician or political party.

Meanwhile, in October 2019, as reported by *The Tucson Standard*, Chip himself donated money to Arizona Democratic Senate candidate Mark Kelly. Indeed, Chip was ranked in his top one hundred donors.

This whole line of reasoning that we don't take sides in politics but stand up for [insert pro-Democrat talking point of the day here] is of course ludicrous. But if the position is that what we do as individuals is okay, why wasn't *I* as an individual allowed to weigh in on schools? Why, if Chip, as Levi's CEO, is free as an individual to donate money to Mark Kelly (as he has every right to), am *I* presumed to be speaking for the company? The rules weren't clear because there weren't rules. There were feelings.

The net net: we do weigh in on politics – all the time, without apology. We just don't say so because that might alienate our large Republican consumer base. Our CEO can overtly support Democratic candidates with money, but I couldn't speak out against the closed school policies of the California Governor, Gavin Newsom. Why? *Because we say so. It feels yucky, people get mad and we don't like it so you can't do it, Jen.*

None of that was said on my phone call with Kelly. But it didn't have to be. That was the message she delivered, likely with support and prodding from Chip. (He preferred having others have the hard conversations for him.) I was very disappointed and angry. But I held my tongue.

As the conversation was fizzling out with no clear resolution, Kelly was stuck issuing her concerns about my outspokenness on school closures, but unable to require any change from me. In my younger years, the issuance of concern would have been enough to stop me in my tracks. Now, not so much. Now, if you tell me I can't say something it just makes me want to say it more. Not merely because of the thing I'm saying, but simply to claim my right to use my voice.

Kelly hemmed and hawed a bit, acknowledging that she couldn't really tell me that I had to stop. I didn't know if she meant legally or because we were peers, and she wasn't my boss. She never said what was wrong with what I was saying, only that people didn't like it. I didn't care. People didn't like it when I wrote in my first book that Don Peters, the National Team gymnastics coach in the 1980s, was a pedophile. The then un-woke gymnastics social media mob argued he was a good man, and an even better coach, and I was just bitter because he hadn't liked me much. They screamed that I'd be sued for libel. This was in the days before #MeToo when, apparently, you didn't have to believe all women.

Peters did not sue me. But he was banned from the sport a few years later, in 2011, when my friend and fellow national team member, Doe Yamashiro, testified in an internal USA Gymnastics-led hearing that he had raped her.

I wrapped up the call with Kelly by reiterating that this really mattered to me. It was a value I would not abandon. The value I was referring to was advocating for vulnerable children. I'd done so very publicly for the past thirteen years in regard to athlete safety and no one at work had complained. To the contrary, they'd lauded my efforts, taking pride in being part of my advocacy by encouraging me to do it.

Kelly didn't argue this point and the conversation stalled. Neither of us really wanted it to continue, so we hung up. All in all, it lasted about five minutes. I conceded nothing but acknowledged receipt of the message.

Feeling I'd won this battle, I heaved a sigh of relief. I did not realize that I was already losing the war.

CHAPTER 16:

THE PUSHBACK ACCELERATES.

A month after my conversation with Kelly, and just a few months after laying off seven hundred employees, we were already preparing for another round of layoffs, this time to be presented as "re-structuring." Apparently reducing costs by $100 million was not enough. It's important to remember that we were already crawling out of the covid hole. Most of our stores were now open. Our sales were coming back, due to the strength of the brand (who might be responsible for that?). There was no business reason to shut me up. Or to lay off workers.

On October 19, just a few days before one hundred more people were set to be laid off, yet another executive took it upon himself to try to persuade me to keep my mouth shut: our Chief Legal Counsel. I liked him. He was quiet but used his influence when it mattered. He wasn't one of those people who felt obligated to have an opinion on everything. He typically weighed in only when he had unique insight or relevant knowledge about a subject.

However, it's never a good thing when the head of legal wants to talk to you. I had had very few one-on-one conversations with him. We interacted plenty in executive team meetings, but if he wanted to speak with me directly it was always about someone on my team who had been fired and was suing the company, or an issue with a celebrity's contract.

Even as we were all busy planning to terminate the employment of another one hundred people (purposely keeping the number low enough on this second round so as not to prompt the need for a public announcement, as required by the Securities and Exchange Commission when workforce reductions hit a certain percentage of the employee population), the Chief Legal Counsel set a time to speak with me. He used a vague title in the meeting request, but I knew what it would be about. I hadn't "held the line" as Kelly had urged me to do.

By then, public schools had been closed for close to seven months, and, although most private schools were now open, it was becoming clearer every day that San Francisco Unified School District (SFUSD) would not open at all that fall semester. So much for "two weeks to flatten the curve."

My high schooler had started his senior year from his bedroom. My five-year-old never got to meet his kindergarten teacher. He never saw his classroom, or interacted with his classmates in real life.

I remember a few things about the conversation with the head of legal very clearly.

He reinforced some of the same themes from my conversation with Kelly. "Jen," he said, "when you speak on anything, you speak on behalf of the company."

I repeated myself: "No, I'm a private citizen and public school mom. I have a right to defend children."

He did not dispute that.

"If you are telling me to stop, this is going to be a different kind of conversation. Less casual." My implication was that I'd need to include my own lawyer.

He said, "No, I can't do that."

He did offer some advice though.

"Make sure *she* doesn't get to Chip before you do."

This took my breath away for a moment. I was truly flummoxed. But then it all became clear. Kelly was running to our boss and showing him my social media posts, posts that up to now had garnered little to no traction.

Perhaps she was too busy to come to me again to discuss my open schools advocacy. I know she was occupied with carefully crafting our internal messaging about the imminent layoffs, making sure to elide any suggestion of cutting costs to save more money. It was going to be all about "streamlining" and "efficient ways of working." However, she apparently wasn't too busy to run to our boss. Repeatedly.

It's an indescribably awful feeling when you realize that a colleague is going behind your back to gossip and complain about you. To your boss no less. When our head of legal said to me that I needed to get to Chip before Kelly, I surmised a few things:

- There was a real bias to how it was all being positioned to Chip.

- Kelly really didn't like me much now, if ever.

- Kelly was my enemy. I couldn't fix that with logic or charm.

The warning from the head of legal made me realize that the conflict had indeed escalated, and it changed my approach. I decided to keep Chip informed myself. I wanted to help him understand my perspective, and that kids were being harmed. His own daughter was back in private school. Shouldn't the rest of the city's children have the same opportunity? I had confidence in my own ability to persuade.

But it wasn't just Kelly who was against me. It was all of San Francisco. It was every "blue" state and city across the country. She was part of a rabid, religiously fanatical woke mob intent on purging anyone who wasn't falling in line.

The calls continued. Next up was the head of Human Resources, Tracy Layney. The tenor of the conversations was always the same:

"You need to think about what you're saying. You represent the company when you speak."

"No, I don't. I represent me. I'm a person. I'm a mom."

Ok sure but, but, but, but . . .

"Are you telling me to stop?"

"No. We can't do that."

"Ok."

And on it went.

It was exhausting, but I was getting better at it and more practiced at my stump speech. Chip had still not talked to me directly on the matter. He sent minions to have the uncomfortable conversations, as was his way. Probably they reported back that I was intransigent, but maybe they sometimes put a sheen on it: she understands, she'll watch it, she'll toe the line. But then I didn't.

The only time Chip alluded to knowing about my advocacy was in an executive team meeting when he said: "You're acting like Trump." It was not in response to anything I'd done. It was a throwaway comment, but I knew at that point that he had been influenced.

In fall 2020, an article appeared in *Pro Publica* and *The New Yorker* titled "The Students Left Behind by Remote Learning." Its author, Alec MacGillis, wrote about a twelve-year-old boy from East Baltimore named Shemar. The child was good at math and his fourth-grade teacher tried to encourage him by telling him what a good student he was. She knew he had a difficult home life. He was often absent from school and his mother was a drug addict. They moved a lot, and he rarely got enough sleep because he and his mom would stay up late watching television. School was very difficult even before covid. And then covid restrictions and virtual learning made it impossible.

Shemar had no sober-minded, capable adult available to help him with the online complexities of logging into class and turning in homework assignments. He had no stable Wi-Fi. In short, he had no one looking out for him, like many children across the country in high-poverty areas, and often in non-high-poverty areas as well. In his case, his mom struggled with addiction, but in other instances parents were out working hourly wage jobs to keep food on the table, and there just wasn't anyone at home to provide the necessary support to navigate Google Chromebooks and Zoom school. MacGillis wrote:

> The biggest challenge was not technological. No one made sure that Shemar logged on to his daily class or completed the assignments that were piling up in his Google Classroom account. His grandmother, who is in her 70s, is a steady presence, but she attended little school while growing up in a sharecropping family in South Carolina. She was also losing her eyesight. One day, she explained to me the family's struggles to assist Shemar: Though three of his four older siblings lived in the house, too, they had jobs or attended vocational school, and one of them had a baby to care for; Shemar's mother was often absent; and his great-uncle, who also lived in the house, had dropped out of school in South Carolina around the age of 8 and was illiterate.

I cried when I read Shemar's story. And then I read it again. And again. I'd had children like Shemar in my thoughts incessantly for the past six months. It wasn't hard to imagine that in the public housing apartments one block away from my very nice apartment there were kids toiling away in similar circumstances. It wasn't hard to imagine that poor children were being harmed the most. They didn't have tutors or learning pods or strong Wi-Fi or white-collar parents with cushy tech jobs who could take breaks whenever necessary to help with a difficult assignment or in figuring out instructions for turning in homework. But somehow no one in San Francisco was imagining them and what their lives were like with no school, no supervision, no playgrounds, no one looking out for them. Or, if they did imagine them, they simply didn't care.

This is a moment, I thought. Real reporters in mainstream left-leaning publications are writing about this now. What lefty doesn't love *The New Yorker*? Now is the time for me to take this on inside the company. I can rally people around this position because it now has the imprimatur of *The New Yorker*. Furthermore, at this point, in the fall of 2020, my peers were sending their own kids back to school.

I was optimistic that they'd see it now and we'd put this conflict behind us. The conflict with my peers but also my conflict with the world. Alec MacGillis had painted such a vivid picture of the cruelty of these closed school policies I thought that now everyone would take notice, or so I hoped.

On October 23, I sat down to write a proposal, an "urgent yet inconvenient plea," emailed to Chip, and to our heads of Human Resources, Public Affairs, Corporate Communications and Legal:

I know we're so busy right now. We have so much happening. But we have committed as an organization to fighting structural racism. So I need to raise this. Please take a moment to read carefully if you can. Or when you can.

 Not sure if you are following what is happening regarding SF public schools. But in a meeting with the Board of Education a few days ago, it was made clear that not only will schools not open this year, but they will likely not be open broadly until possibly 2022. Next fall 2021 optimistically.

The ongoing commitment to keeping public schools closed in SF is the most structurally racist policy since mass incarceration. At this point 56 private schools have been granted waivers to open. It is predicted that all private schools and charters will open this year. That leaves the city's most in need, the city's Black and brown children and low-income families, without options. And they are the most harmed by virtual learning without the resources to make it viable.

 I cited an article in *The New York Times*, from just the day before, appealing to their need for legitimacy knowing just doing the right thing would not be enough. The headline read: "Schoolchildren Seem Unlikely to Fuel Coronavirus Surges." It went on:

Researchers once feared that school re-openings might spread the virus through communities. But so far there is little evidence that it's happening.

I ended with a request:

So, I'm asking, is there anything we can do? To urge reconsideration by the city. As part of our commitment to fight structural racism, here at home, in our own backyard?

1. Would we consider an op-ed in the *Chronicle* [the local San Francisco newspaper]? Our organization carries weight, as we've often said.
2. Would we consider making a donation to help schools prepare to open safely, which is oft cited as the reason they can't? Perhaps urge other large businesses here to do the same?
3. Would we urge the school district, SFUSD, to adhere to the policies and guidelines set by Newsom and the state of CA rather than those set forth by San Francisco public health, which are much more stringent and prevent schools from opening their doors?

I know I may be out of line in asking. And education has not been part of our platform of charitable giving or even speaking up. But it is so tightly linked to structurally racist policy [this was part of our giving platform] that I'd feel remiss if I didn't ask.

Thanks for reading. I know I included a lot here. But there is a lot happening and being written about this in recent days. As a mom of SFUSD students, with kids whose friends are deeply impacted, I'm just beside myself about it. It's impacting our hometown community, the parents who work at Levi's, and their kids – for years to come.

They were slow to respond. Then they said no. Not on the merits, but because our executives had kids in private schools. The suggestion being they'd look like elitists. Here's what Kelly responded with:

We're not seeing a lot of upside to LS&Co. jumping in on this one. . . . There's a lot of potential negatives if we speak up strongly, starting with the numerous execs who have kids in private schools in the city.

But doesn't everyone already assume executives are elitists? The fact that they believe that they can further an image as "of the people" altruistic populists by concealing facts about their lives like sending their kids to $60k/year private schools is evidence of their self-delusion.

It is also evidence of how frantic they were to cover up the massive lie that layoffs were necessary to "save the business," when in fact they were necessary to deliver payouts to already wealthy executives and shareholders. I guess they figured, we'll just pretend we aren't rich and spending close to a million dollars on our kids just to get them from elementary school through high school! No one will notice!

Privately I got an empathetic response from Tracy, our head of Human Resources:

This is beyond ridiculous!! I honestly don't even understand this…given the city is now in 'yellow' status. [Remember the incessant tiering?] What is driving this intractability with the Board of Ed?

I am deeply worried about these kids. My stepfather teaches 2nd grade at a Title 1 school in Fairfield, and even though he has done all that he can to master teaching 7-year-olds remotely, he says it is a fraction of what they should be learning. We also now know that transmission especially among elementary school students is very low. I honestly don't know what SF Unified is thinking. The city has worked so hard to drive down transmission and the kids cannot even go back to school.

Sounds like Kelly is on it. I honestly just don't understand this . . .

Tracy's empathy proved useless. She didn't publicly "take my side" with the group. I was left standing alone, again, looking like a stark-raving lunatic on a crusade to murder San Francisco teachers.

Kelly was *not* on it. We were knee deep in identity politics, at Levi's, in San Francisco and in the country at large. A presidential election was coming, and Democrats were suffering from "Trump derangement syndrome," as they had been since he took office. Every word President Trump uttered, or tweeted, was seen as authoritarian, tyrannical and racist.

So, when he tweeted in July "SCHOOLS MUST OPEN IN THE FALL!!!" I knew they wouldn't. If he said it, it was wrong. Not only was it wrong, it was evil and had to be stopped – by any means possible. Even child sacrifice.

If you don't believe me, here's a little case study.

On June 30, 2020, Dana Goldstein, *The New York Times* education journalist, reported that the American Academy of Pediatrics was pushing to open schools in the fall. Dr. Sean O'Leary, pediatric infectious disease specialist at the University of Colorado Anschutz Medical Campus, helped write the guidelines. He said:

> As pediatricians, many of us have recognized already the impact that having schools closed even for a couple months had on children. At the same time, a lot of us are parents. We experienced our own kids doing online learning. There really wasn't a lot of learning happening. Now we're seeing studies documenting this. Kids being

home led to increases in behavioral health problems. There were reports of increased rates of abuse.

This virus is different from most of the respiratory viruses we deal with every year. School-age kids clearly play a role in driving influenza rates within communities. That doesn't seem to be the case with Covid-19. And it seems like in countries where they have reopened schools, it plays a much smaller role in driving spread of disease than we would expect.

A week later, on July 7, 2020, President Trump hosted an event at the White House with Education Secretary Betsy DeVos. He said:

We're very much going to put pressure on governors and everybody else to open the schools. It's very important for our country. It's very important for the well-being of the student and the parents. So we're going to be putting a lot of pressure on: Open your schools in the fall.

Just three days later, on July 10, the American Academy of Pediatrics reversed its recommendation:

Returning to school is important for the healthy development and well-being of children, but we must pursue re-opening in a way that is safe for all students, teachers and staff. Science should drive decision-making on safely reopening schools. Public health agencies must make recommendations based on evidence, not politics. We should leave it to health experts to tell us when the time is best to open up school buildings.

But it was the American Academy of Pediatrics itself that was making recommendations based on politics, not evidence. When President Trump insisted on getting schools open, they rejected it. Why? Because he's Trump. Not because of any new data.

I refused to give into hopelessness as the months passed. I couldn't get images of children trapped at home with no school, no life and no hope out of my head. My peers at work may have wanted me to stop, but I only got louder. Who were they to tell me not to, especially with their own kids in school?

And besides, there was reason to believe that putting pressure on local government leaders and public health officials could have an impact. San Francisco playgrounds were closed for almost eight months. And ultimately it was parental pressure that got them open. On October 16, when San Francisco finally removed the yellow caution tape, unlocked the gates and let kids inside the city's 180 playgrounds, my husband's tweet was featured in the local newspaper:

Most horrifying of all is that the children are required to maintain a distance from each other and are not permitted to share toys. Children need social lives. Meaning they need to play with other children. That remains illegal in San Francisco as it has been for over 7 months.

Using our voices was working. But progress was slow and our work was not done. Even with playgrounds open, the rules, if parents chose to take their kids to play outside, were onerous and uninviting. Harvard epidemiologist Dr. Julia Marcus weighed in, tweeting:

Great to see SF playgrounds open today in the name of joy, fun, exercise. But: only 1 adult per kid, 30-min limit, no eating or drinking, and crying kids should be removed? Give people a break! This is a low-risk setting. Less absolutism, more pragmatism.

And so I continued. I was not about to accept mere crumbs, when our kids deserved so much more. I started a Facebook group called "Open Schools San Francisco"; I attended school board meetings "virtually" and asked questions in the chat that never got answered; and by December, I was appearing on local news programs agitating for public schools to open. The premise of these local news segments was that San Francisco was an outlier, schools across the country were opening, and here's a mom who says we need to open, too. I was not painted as some clueless lunatic who didn't care if kids and teachers died. And, importantly, I was never identified as a Levi's employee. I'd promised our head of legal in our October conversation that I would not identify myself that way in my advocacy, and I made sure that I didn't; I also ensured that I was always identified by local news channels simply as a mom of four.

I tweeted things like this, over and over:

 **Jennifer Sey** ✔
@JenniferSey

Over 50k public school students in SF have been out of school since Mar 13. Every day they fall further behind. Some won't graduate. Many will never catch up. This is a crisis - this city's future is being devastated. Kids deserve so much more. #openschools

>  **Jake Tapper** ✔ @jaketapper · Nov 24, 2020
> Health officials keep saying the schools should be the very last things to close, keep them open as much as possible.
> Show this thread

6:30 PM · Dec 13, 2020 · Twitter Web App

13 Retweets **2** Quote Tweets **93** Likes

I also led rallies. Although these rallies were sparsely attended, we were able to attract media coverage, which was always positive. But it was all to no avail. The San Francisco school board wasn't budging. They were in lockstep with the teachers' union, the constituency responsible for getting them elected to their posts. And the teachers' union was claiming there would inevitably be mass death if they were forced to return to the classroom, despite all evidence to the contrary from American states and even whole countries, like Denmark, that had already opened.

In fact, Denmark had opened schools just one month after the initial closures. The legal right to a quality education strongly factored into the government's decision. When announcing the decision to re-open, the government stated:

> . . . in current circumstances, schools and municipalities cannot guarantee that children receive the education in all subjects for which they are entitled.

By May 2020, not even three months into the pandemic, Reuters was reporting:

> Sending children back to schools and day care centres in Denmark, the first country in Europe to do so, did not lead to an increase in coronavirus infections, according to official data, confirming similar findings from Finland on Thursday.

However, in December of 2020, there was still no end in sight to the closures in San Francisco and other blue cities.

There had been endless warnings from the Left and the media about Trump's supposed authoritarianism. But in the end, it was the Left who shut public schools for what would end up being a year and a half. They were willing to betray the nation's public school students to spite Trump, and to prove that he was a dangerous tyrant willing to murder children and teachers. And to ensure that he wasn't re-elected.

I didn't care if people at work and in San Francisco called me a Trumper. I knew it was an attempt to muzzle me and other parents willing to fight for kids and open schools. It was stupid. And irrelevant.

It was also false. I hadn't voted for Trump.

But credit where credit is due. Donald Trump could not have been more right on the importance of opening schools. And everyone at Levi's could not have been more wrong.

CHAPTER 17:

MY APOLOGY TOUR.

In February of 2021, I moved to Denver with my husband and two youngest children.

My five-year-old had started kindergarten online in fall 2020. He hated it. He received about an hour of instruction a day, and his first encounter with "school" was not creating a positive educational experience. If a five-year-old can be depressed and screen-addicted, he was. So we moved to another state so our kindergartner could actually attend kindergarten.

My oldest child had moved back to Berkeley to finish his junior year online from his apartment. My second oldest, a senior in high school, stayed in San Francisco with his dad to finish up his last few months of high school. While public schools were still virtual in the city, other covid restrictions had relaxed somewhat, so he was at least able to spend time with friends. I didn't want him to be separated from his friends for his last bit of high school, and since I'd be visiting San Francisco regularly for work, I'd still see him.

While our Levi's offices were not yet open, and my team was still working remotely, we did have some in-person meetings – things like product line reviews that were close to impossible to do through a screen – so I'd be back to California every other week.

The fact is, regarding work, I was as busy as ever, and in the midst of all the controversy over my open-schools advocacy, my performance never flagged. To the contrary, having been promoted to Brand President in October of 2020, I now oversaw all of the brand's key functions – Marketing, Design and Merchandising. It was understood the job was a primary "feeder" for CEO. Meaning I was now a major candidate, if not the first in line, to replace Chip when he retired, which was not so far away.

Having come to the company in 2011, Chip was in his early sixties, and had accomplished what he set out to do: bring the brand and business back from the depths of near bankruptcy to take the company public.

From 1853-1971, Levi Strauss, and then his heirs, owned and ran Levi's. In 1971, Walter Haas, Levi Strauss's great great-nephew, took the company public for the first time. Then, in 1985, Walter's son, then-CEO Robert "Bob" Haas, took it private again. From 1985-2019, the Haas family owned Levi's outright. But, starting in the 2010s, the family didn't want to be involved in the day-to-day running of the company anymore. And they wanted cash, not shares.

Given the dismal state of the business when Chip took over, he had a lot of work to do to enable a successful public offering to get the family the cash that they wanted. And he did it. Between 2011 and 2019, Levi's added over a billion dollars in sales to the company's annual revenues, taking us to $5.7 billion per year. Chip then led a successful initial public offering (IPO) of the Levi's stock.

In the two days following the IPO, the Haas family sold close to twenty million shares of stock, bringing their net worth to $4.7 billion. These family members raked in $333 million in cash from the public offering. In fact, of the $623 million raised with the IPO (this is usually the stated reason to IPO – to raise money to invest back into the business for growth), over fifty percent of it went into the bank accounts of Haas family members. Mimi Haas, the largest family shareholder, owning over sixteen percent of the company, made the *Forbes* Billionaires list for the first time that year.

Chip did pretty well, too, going from very rich to very *very* rich. In December 2019, about nine months after the IPO, he said to the *San Francisco Business Times*:

> We choose the harder right over the easier wrong. This is a company that has driven profits through principles, and we manage the business for the long term. We're almost the antithesis of a publicly traded company, but it has served us well.

Since the IPO, Chip has liquidated over $42 million worth of stock. And there's plenty more where that came from. If this is taking the harder right over the easier wrong, then it doesn't really seem all that hard.

I, unlike some, have no real issue with rich people. That's capitalism. Some people, very few, will make *a lot* of money. What I *do* have an issue with is rich people masquerading as social justice warriors and fierce employee advocates, while they are laying off 15 percent of their work force at the same time as they are adding tens of millions of dollars to their bank accounts. You can't have it both ways. You're either a capitalist in it for the dough, or you're a do-gooder. People don't usually stumble upon $42 million without it being the goal. And most often, others are left in the wake of their avarice.

Dan Goldman is another Levi Strauss heir who profited immensely from Levi's IPO. His net worth is now valued at over $250 million. His assets include stocks and holdings in a variety of industry sectors, including oil and gas, large pharmaceutical companies, health insurance companies, military contractors and commercial banks.

Goldman, who was Democratic counsel during Trump's first impeachment hearing, used his windfall from the IPO to run for Congress in 2022 to represent New York's District 10, which covers northwest Brooklyn and most of Lower Manhattan. He would pour close to $5 million of his own personal funds into winning the Democratic party primary on August 23, 2022, greatly outspending all six of the other candidates combined.

Two weeks before Goldman's bought-and-paid-for win was announced, Jason Kaplan, a spokesman for former Representative Liz Holtzman – among his rivals in the primary – told the *New York Post*:

> Of course Dan Goldman is spending millions of dollars. It's easy when you were born with a silver spoon and a pair of blue jeans.

Goldman's claim is that he has:

> a deep appreciation for the opportunities my inheritance has provided me [. . . but] every American should have full confidence that our elected representatives are operating solely on behalf of the American people.

I guess "the American people" don't include laid-off Levi's employees.

As I've said, I have no issue with capitalism. But I do have an issue with using personal wealth to buy elections (especially when that wealth is unearned), which is exactly what Dan Goldman did.

He touted his "I do everything on behalf of the American people" ethos while growing his bank account by investing in commercial banks and Big Pharma, and disregarding the welfare of working people. All while feigning humanitarian concern for others. He is a true scion of woke capitalism.

Despite his own riches from the successful IPO that he had led, Chip had too much pride to retire without leading Levi's through a full recovery. During 2020, lockdowns drove our revenues down over 60 percent during the depths of closures. Which meant that we needed to get revenues back to $5.7 billion and, ideally, beyond it. I knew this was Chip's goal. He'd worked hard, for a long time, to revive this iconic brand, and it was all seemingly gone in an instant in the spring of 2020, as our sales bottomed out at $4.4 billion for the year. From a sales perspective, we were back where we'd been when he started at the company a decade prior.

Still, we were sure we could have a speedy rebound, and that expectation had to do with the strength of the brand loyalty and high favorability amongst consumers, both of which were largely due to my efforts over the previous eight years. And, in fact, once stores opened for good, we were well on our way.

It was a good bet that once the company came back, he'd hand over the reins – probably to me. I'd been told by Chip this was likely how it would go – if only I'd cut it out with the tweeting about covid school closure policies.

Only I didn't.

On February 27, 2021, I posted about our move on Twitter.

My thread was re-tweeted by CNN journalist Jake Tapper, generating some attention. A couple of weeks later, I was asked by Fox News's Laura Ingraham to appear on her show, *The Ingraham Angle*. I was red meat for Fox folks – a self-avowed leftie criticizing the Left's covid policies.

I didn't watch Fox or Ingraham, but I was well aware of their reputation in my circle. Pro-Trump, committed to airing right-wing propaganda, endangering America with fascist assertions about stolen elections and conspiracy theories. Ingraham was said to be one of the worst offenders – anti-trans, anti-LGBTQ, just plain old evil.

I consulted my fellow open-schools moms, a group of women across the country I had gotten to know through social media and activism over the previous year. We agreed: it was risky. There would be backlash. But I should do it.

The fact was, we had tried over and over to get ourselves, or any parent who was willing to be vocal about the harms of school closures, on more "mainstream," more "acceptable" platforms. We'd written the likes of CNN to no avail. No one agreed to cover the story. They all dutifully touted CDC talking points about the dangers of opening schools as proven facts. The only perspective beyond the CDC's that was represented was that of the pro-closure teachers' unions. But it was that perspective that molded the CDC's "opening" guidance, which was really guidance to stay closed until further notice, though that would only become fully apparent later.

On May 1, 2021, the *New York Post* ran this headline: "Powerful teachers union influenced CDC on school reopenings, emails show."

The article cited emails between the American Federation of Teachers (AFT) and the CDC. It said:

"Thank you again for Friday's rich discussion about forth-coming CDC guidance and for your openness to the suggestions made by our president, Randi Weingarten, and the AFT," wrote AFT senior director for health issues Kelly Trautner in a Feb 1 email — which described the union as the CDC's "thought partner."

So at the time I was asked to go on *The Ingraham Angle*, I and many other open schools moms were deeply frustrated and at wit's end. Not only could we not get our point of view represented in the "mainstream" media, but we were getting called racists every time we spoke up in defense of children, regardless of where we spoke.

To us, it didn't even seem as if our position should be controversial. Almost all private schools were open by then. As well as public schools in red states and schools all across Europe. Only public schools in blue states and cities remained closed.

We agreed that in this venue, I would at least be able to represent our view without being unduly attacked or sidetracked. I was a trained PR professional. I would prepare my talking points, tell my own family's story, and avoid falling into any traps Ingraham might try to set for me. If she tried to get me to say Democrats are evil, I wouldn't do it. If she tried to get me to say Ron DeSantis was our savior, I wouldn't. I would talk about my child's experience, and the general and increasingly severe harms being caused to other children, and call it a day. No weighing in on politics or politicians.

I did the show from our Airbnb rental in Denver on March 3, 2021, just a few days after we arrived in our new city. Ingraham led by saying it was increasingly obvious that it was more dangerous to keep kids out of school than to have them go back. She stated that kids were ten times more likely to die from suicide than from covid. And she said that this was more pressing in California than anywhere else in the country, where fewer than twelve percent of students were back in classrooms.

Everything Ingraham said was true. In fact, when all was said and done, California would lead the way with the most days closed for the highest percentage of students of any of the fifty states.

I told her moving was a difficult decision. I'd lived in San Francisco for over thirty years, but I'd lost hope that schools would open at all that spring, and I didn't want my son to miss the whole year of kindergarten. I said nothing I would take back. Nothing. In fact, I'm proud of everything I said, and I would say it again. And I would say it again on Ingraham's show.

The response was instantaneous. Employees at Levi's were furious. Livid. Apoplectic. I had consorted with the enemy, so now I *was* the enemy.

A few weeks later, on April 2, when Chip hosted one of his town hall meetings, it all came to a head. We had gotten in the habit of doing these virtual sessions every few weeks during the pandemic, as a way for him to answer questions directly from employees, and to create a sense of community and transparency during a time when we all felt separated. Generally, as one of Chip's direct reports, I was in the virtual "green room" during these sessions, and available to answer any questions employees had that pertained to the brand's activities. I missed this one as I'd taken a few days off to get settled in Denver, but I got a full report the next day.

An employee posted a comment:

> Can Chip please comment on Jen Sey's recent appearance on Laura Ingraham's show on Fox News? I was deeply disappointed and confused at the disconnect between morals & values the company projects and that of our leaders.

Chip was supportive of me. He said that I was a public school mom and a private citizen standing up for kids, and that I had a right to do so. That would be the first and last of Chip's public or private support for anything I said or did related to open schools.

Many employees voiced their disagreement with Chip. One posted a response during the session:

> She [Ingraham] is an especially divisive and bigoted personality who regularly attacks the very causes that Chip & the company champion. . . . I am embarrassed that my brand president gave her [Ingraham] credence by appearing on her show and to me it showed very poor judgement.

Another comment read:

> Jen's not just any employee – she's the Brand President,
> a public-facing leader of the company with a checkmark
> next to her name and a media-trained interviewee for us.
> Doesn't seem fair to pick and choose when we are and are
> not represented by such a publicly known leader.

Apparently, as the Brand President I didn't have the right to speak as a private citizen, according to some. No one seemed to think that it was problematic that private schools were up and running while public schools were closed. No one seemed to care that all the other top executives' kids, including Chip's, were in school. Those of us who just wanted the same for our kids, and dared to say so, were a problem. And I was even more of a problem because I'd said it to someone whom they considered to be *persona non grata*. That made me *persona non grata* as well.

The apotheosis of my anti-woke awakening came a month later when I was "asked" by my employee resource group co-sponsor, as well as our head of Diversity, Equity and Inclusion, to do what they kept referring to as an "apology tour." The internal complaints had continued to grow, and they wanted to give me a chance to answer questions directly. Or so they said. In fairness, they were both sympathetic to how uncomfortable this situation was for me. I would have to stand (virtually) in front of the black employee resource group, which I led, as well as other ERG members, who would all be invited, and perform what amounted to a walk of shame.

I suppose I could have said no. But I agreed for three reasons:

1. I still had faith in my own ability to explain myself.

2. I believe if we all talk and listen to others, we can build empathy and understanding, even if we don't agree at the end of the conversation. I try to live that every day.

3. I wasn't going to apologize. I would not bend a knee. I'd explain myself. I would not demonstrate submission with self-flagellation.

Public schools had been closed for over a year already. The entire spring semester of 2021 had passed, and in San Francisco public schools were still shut. It wasn't even clear at that point if they'd open in the coming fall. I was certainly not about to back down.

My one work friend left in corporate communications tried to help me prepare for my "apology tour." She emailed me:

There are people who just don't like what you're saying or where you said it. It's [about] the good/bad world we're living in, where Fox is Bad and MSNBC is Good. Was going on Fox (and that show in particular) an endorsement of what they stand for? Are you "one of us" or "one of them?"

Her view was that I needed to pledge a loyalty oath, essentially. In today's tribal world, I had to prove that I hadn't left the tribe, in order to prove myself worthy of working at Levi's. I honestly believe that she said it with kindness, with no real awareness of how utterly messed up it was to say that I needed to prove my woke credentials in order to be worthy of retaining my place in the company. She went on:

> My two cents would be, it's important to demonstrate that you're doing exactly what we say we stand for: using your voice on the topics that matter most. That's what you did with gymnastics, *Athlete A*, and now for your kids.

This colleague had been quietly supportive of the same open schools fight in Oakland, just east and across the bridge from San Francisco. And while she agreed with not only my views on schools, but my right to express them, even she was sucked into the "with us or against us" binary.

I rejected that binary then, and I reject that binary now. Had I actually been "one of them" because I was a registered Republican and watched Fox, did that mean I shouldn't be allowed to have a job at Levi's? For that matter, if I were a registered Democrat who disagreed with some of their policies, did *that* mean that I should not be allowed to hold a position at Levi's? In the world of Levi's Wokes, apparently so.

My peers who helped plan the session took great pains to disguise it as something other than what it was. We had new ERG leaders, and they positioned the meeting as a *get to know the new folks* kind of a thing. But everyone knew what it was.

I agreed that I would try to head off some questions at the pass by how I introduced myself. I would talk about my more than twenty years at Levi's, my advocacy for children in sports, my book and documentary exposing the culture of abuse in gymnastics, and the resulting movement demanding change. That would be my lead-in as to why I felt so strongly about advocating for kids and open schools during covid. Then I'd take questions.

I was nervous. Who wouldn't be? No executive in the company's history had ever before been coerced into standing up before employees to apologize for thought crimes.

Though I felt like I wanted to vomit the whole time, I suppose it went as well as could be expected. There were just two questions and one comment.

The first question was – you guessed it – about my decision to appear on *The Ingraham Angle*. The questioner wanted to know if I understood why this could be construed as offensive to black people and a demonstration that I was not sufficiently allied with black employees. Because, so went the implication, it was a given that Ingraham was a racist.

I said I took the invitation seriously, consulted my fellow open-schools moms, and though I knew it would be contentious and might be misconstrued, decided to do it anyway because it was a platform that could reach a large audience, as evidenced by the fact that they, who supposedly don't watch Fox News, had all seen it.

The asker granted that I hadn't said anything offensive during the interview. It was just offensive that I said it to Ingraham.

The second question was about my husband. He had an active social media presence and took a more dogmatic stance and aggressive tone than I did. He was outspoken about vaccine mandates being discriminatory. This was viewed as "anti-vaxx," the worst thing you can be in the age of covid, even worse than being a racist. The general view from the audience was that barring the unvaccinated from aspects of public life wasn't discrimination. Calling it such minimized actual discrimination like racism. It was a choice to go unvaccinated, and it wasn't a choice to be black.

My heart raced. I had expected some version of this question, and I answered honestly. The long and short of what I said was that married couples don't agree on everything (true), I am not responsible for what he says (true), I support his right to say what he believes as I support all of theirs (true), and he doesn't work for the company (true). What I didn't say overtly was that I agreed with him. I spoke the truth, I didn't lie. And, even more important to me, I didn't apologize.

The last remark was a comment, and it was basically a thank you. Thank you for being willing to do this. Thank you for speaking openly and honestly. Thank you.

My heart stilled for the first time in weeks. The lead-up had been nerve-wracking and the session itself about as stressful as competing in the World Championships as a sixteen-year-old back in 1985.

But, I thought, it had worked. I had been open and honest, and they had heard me. We can do this! We can build bridges and understanding, if we just talk to each other. I felt victorious. I received an email the next day that said:

> Jen, thank you for your raw honesty for answering what I thought were some tough and personal questions. As a gay man I am not a fan of Laura Ingraham as have been on the receiving end of her hurtful words and stances – however, your answer made sense to me. I have to admit I would have done the same as a parent in a similar situation. Your heartfelt answer and being so human and real about it is appreciated. I hope others at the meeting left with being able to see this now through your perspective. Thank you.

Whew. Okay, I thought, now let's get back to the business of selling jeans.

The apology tour had been a speed bump and provided some temporary cooling of tempers. But it wouldn't take long for it all to ramp right back up again. The old adage that if you give an inch, they'll take a mile was going to come at me full bore, at maximum speed and capacity, over the course of the next six months.

CHAPTER 18:

ON SPOUSES.

Everyone at work hated my husband. He was relentless about the cruelty of lockdown policies, and unforgiving towards those who insisted that they were necessary. He spared no one:

Daniel Kotzin
@danielkotzin
···

I am not a Covid denier. I am a lockdown denier.

I deny the right of the government to lock down healthy people.

I deny curfews, and travel bans, and business closures. I deny shuttered churches.

I deny dying alone. I deny cruelty to children. I deny forced family separation.

9:23 PM · Jan 17, 2021 · Twitter for iPhone

ılıl View Tweet analytics

6,639 Retweets   **450** Quote Tweets   **24.3K** Likes

247

He is a stay-at-home dad. He had no reason to be careful, no employer to mind. But why do so many people seem to accept as normal that if you do have a job, you can't say what you really think? Like you're not an actual person anymore, you're a mouthpiece for the company with no rights as an everyday citizen?

This whole idea that you can get in trouble for things your spouse says, or any another family member for that matter, had gained steam by 2020. "Woke-ism" demands that not only must you adhere to its principles, but your family members must, as well. It is cult-like. In fact, one of the seven signs you're in a cult is that the cult asks you to cut off contact with any non-believers. And if that means renouncing family members, then so be it.

This seems crazy: who would do this? Cult members, that's who.

Scientology has furthered a policy of "disconnection" for many years. And members do it. Disconnection is a core principle of this "faith," and mandates the severing of all ties with anyone, including and especially family, who are "antagonistic" towards Scientology. In this "religion" those antagonistic towards Scientology are called "suppressive persons," and stand in the way of an acolyte's spiritual growth. Suppressive persons must be shunned in order for the Scientology member to move to the next stage of their development.

How is this different from demanding a person denounce a family member or lose their job? Or denounce them, then lose it anyway?

In June of 2020, Aleksandar Katai was unceremoniously released from his contract with the Los Angeles Galaxy, a professional soccer team. He was not released due to poor performance or even something he'd done or said. He was fired because of things his wife, Tea, had said on social media.

On June 3, in the wake of the George Floyd protests, Tea took to Instagram. She captioned a photo of a looter hauling off boxes of Nikes: "Black Nikes Matter." Insensitive? Maybe, depending on your perspective. If *he'd* said it, should he have been fired for it? No. When his *wife* said it, should he have been fired? Not in any universe I'd choose to live in!

The couple is Serbian. They had both grown up in an economically unstable nation that was emerging from war and global sanctions, and had only recently moved to the U.S. The ways of Americans were presumably unfamiliar to them. So it's not that weird that they did not yet fully grasp the sensitivity of the racial conflicts in our country. They'd grown up hearing America was a land of freedom.

On June 4, the day after his wife's posts, a few fans took to the stadium to protest with a banner that said: "No racists in our club." That was enough. He was booted the next day. Katai tried to keep his job. He disavowed his wife, calling her comments "a mistake from my family." He said he took full responsibility for her actions, and apologized "for the pain these posts have caused the LA Galaxy family and all allies in the fight against racism."

Obviously, he did not understand that in this land to which they'd come, apologies prompt no forgiveness. They are simply rituals of self-flagellation, their role to prostrate the sinner.

Should this really have been a career-ending, life-altering offense? Of course not. But as I was soon to find out, in today's hyper-vigilant, upside-down morality play we call the workplace, there are no Get Out of Jail Free cards. Even when the offender is one's spouse.

In the spring and summer of 2021, as vaccine mandates were implemented, my husband was very vocal on social media. He said things like this:

Daniel Kotzin
@danielkotzin   ···

Requiring proof of vaccination is not about immunity, because it ignores the Covid-recovered. And it is not about safety, because the vaxxed transmit.

Vaccine passports are about power, control, and discrimination. They are moral abominations.

11:45 PM · Jul 20, 2021 · Twitter for iPhone

ılı View Tweet analytics

1,236 Retweets   **59** Quote Tweets   **3,548** Likes

He was not wrong. The mandates themselves were discriminatory, putting the unvaccinated into a class of people with fewer rights. But their impact was also racially discriminatory, as black Americans were least likely to be vaccinated in 2021. And, like me, my husband is keenly aware of the long history of racial discrimination in healthcare in the United States. The oft-cited Tuskegee Experiment, which took place between 1932 and 1972, was conducted by the United States Public Health Service and sought to study what happened when syphilis went untreated in the black male population. In 1943, four patients at the U.S. Marine Hospital on Staten Island were treated and cured of syphilis with penicillin. Within a year, 10,000 patients had been treated and cured. But the 400 "patients" in the Tuskegee Experiment went untreated, allowing the infection to progress beyond the initial site, beyond the subsequent skin rashes, to the late stages when a patient is no longer infectious, but the disease can advance to the point of dementia, blindness, deafness and death.

If among black Americans there is a deep-seated suspicion of public health authorities, there are very good reasons for it.

When vaccines for kids twelve and older became available in 2021, black families were least likely to vaccinate their children. As school districts threatened to bar the unvaccinated from attending school, black children were most at risk of being forced out of the public education system. In December 2021, the Los Angeles County school district (LAUSD) walked back its requirement for students twelve and older to be vaccinated by January 10, 2022, because it would have resulted in banning no fewer than 30,000, mostly non-white, students from campuses in the district.

LAUSD was forced to relent because only 60 percent of black students had been vaccinated. Along with just 68 percent of Latino students. Enforcing the mandate would have meant ejecting close to half of black children twelve and up from attending in-person school. These kids would have been pushed permanently off campus into separate and unequal, virtual schooling. If this isn't structural racism, I don't know what is. The district blinked and the mandate is now, thankfully, on indefinite hold.

When mandates like LAUSD's and others, including business mandates requiring vaccination in order to patronize restaurants, museums and any public venues, were announced and implemented, my husband was outraged. He compared such mandates to the banning of Jews from public life in Nazi Germany. Jews were demonized and deemed a "virus," forced to identify themselves by donning yellow stars of David on their arms, and prevented from participating in the everyday comings and goings of civilized society. The legitimization of this view of Jews as a viral contagion is what enabled the "final solution": that they needed to be eliminated.

Daniel Kotzin
@danielkotzin

Nazi propaganda:
Jews carry disease.
They hide who they really are.
They are selfish.
We cannot triumph while they still exist.

Covid vaccine propaganda:
The unvaxxed carry disease.
They hide who they really are.
They are selfish.
We cannot triumph while they still exist.

8:28 PM · Nov 17, 2021 · Twitter for iPhone

⦚⦙ View Tweet analytics

247 Retweets **21** Quote Tweets **620** Likes

I understand why some might see this as an insulting comparison. Yet, in Daniel's defense, there was no lack of commentary, not merely online but in reputable outlets, suggesting not just that those resisting the jab were selfish and anti-social vectors of disease, but that it might not be such a bad thing if they all died.

Michael Hiltzik, Pulitzer Prize-winning business columnist for the *Los Angeles Times*, penned an opinion piece in October 2021, now entitled: "Mocking anti-vaxxers' Covid deaths may be ghoulish, yes – but may be necessary." The original title, which has since been removed, was: "Why shouldn't we dance on the graves of anti-vaxxers?"

Hiltzik wasn't alone. When Dr. Jason Valentine of Mobile, Alabama, announced he would no longer treat the unvaccinated, social media cheered his decision. Even late-night host Jimmy Kimmel wished death on the unvaccinated:

> That choice doesn't seem so tough to me. Vaccinated person having a heart attack? Yes, come right in, we'll take care of you. Unvaccinated … Rest in peace, wheezy.

Indeed, there was a general vibe throughout 2021 that to bar people who chose to go unvaccinated from regular life was totally fine, even honorable. If you pointed out the unjustness, especially in a world where vaccination does not prevent infection or transmission of covid, you were the enemy. And my husband pointed it out a lot. He was the enemy, and I incurred guilt by association.

Daniel was not the only Jewish person to invoke the Holocaust. In the early days of the pandemic, Holocaust survivor Vera Sharav warned of the dangers of just following orders: "Adults now are not rebelling against things that are wrong," she said. She warned of the dangers of blind obedience and removal of personal choice.

But my husband and Vera were the minority. Most adhered to the belief that invoking the Holocaust appropriates the attempted Nazi genocide of European Jews to catastrophize minor grievances, thus denying, distorting and minimizing one of the world's worst atrocities in history. There's even a name for conversations online that eventually devolve into Holocaust analogies – Godwin's Law.

I think the point that Vera and my husband were making is that when you treat a group of people as "the other," bad things can happen. Really really bad things.

And if we apply the woke rule that you can say things about a group if you are part of that group, like black rappers using the N-word, then both Vera and my husband get to make the comparison. Except they don't. Because there is another unspoken rule which is: if you are white, and you say anything that goes against the woke ideology, you are not sufficiently committed to progress. Heck, if you are black and (gasp) a conservative, you are not really black. You're a white supremacist in blackface like businessman Larry Elder, Supreme Court justice Clarence Thomas and political commentator Thomas Sowell.

You can hate what my husband Daniel said. It's fine. I see his point, and I also see the point of the other side, that invoking the Holocaust is inappropriate. I don't have a strong view on that one way or the other. But, you know what? I didn't say it, he did. Yet I was scolded repeatedly for things he had said or tweeted.

Since he was vocal about being unvaccinated himself, I was also repeatedly asked: Are you vaccinated?

In fact, I am indeed "fully vaccinated." I submitted to a single shot of the Johnson and Johnson vaccine in May 2021 because, like many others, it was required for me to keep my job. And I had even shared this fact on Twitter, several times:

But my vaccination "status" wasn't really the problem (though perhaps my lack of enthusiasm at being forced to submit *was* part of the issue, because you have to *worship* it, not just *get* it, after all, to be considered properly devout, and a full-fledged "vaxxer"). The real problem, though: my husband was publicly and proudly unvaccinated, which made *me* an "anti-vaxxer."

First of all, why hurl epithets at someone for personal medical decisions? Second, really, a person is an "anti-vaxxer" because they've chosen not to take one vaccine? Third, if someone *is* an "anti-vaxxer," can they not hold a job at Levi's? Lastly, I am my own person. Am I not free to hold views discrete from my husband's? Am I implicated in his every utterance? Should a family member's words ever be a Human Resources issue?

This generation of "omnipotent moral busybodies" will police your words and your family members', and once they have decided that you need to go, that you are too toxic, they will banish you with religious fervor, eager to prove that they are indeed a certain kind of person, devout and superior in their seriousness.

Covid provided this opportunity for so many. While the young and healthy were never at any serious risk, the woke seized upon covid and reorganized our entire lives around it. It was the ultimate proof of their goodness. If caution was noble, extreme caution was saintly. They were willing to mask outside on a bicycle, never shake hands again, boost every sixty days forever and banish anyone who said that was an absurd way to live. They were willing to sacrifice children at the altar of covid fear.

My husband and I were not. So I had to go. My views were bad enough, but his were criminal. And I aided and abetted his crimes.

Still, in the fall of 2021, I somehow remained a candidate for CEO, at least theoretically. Chip himself made that clear. He told me over dinner that the top job was a real possibility. I had delivered stellar performance over my tenure, he said. I was an authentic leader that embodied the "profits through principles" culture of the company, and in doing so had legions of fans.

Chip told me that all I needed to do was: 1) get on the board of a public company; 2) get myself an executive coach and; 3) chill out on the social media rants. If I could do those three things, I'd be ready to take over in no time, he said.

While my continued advocacy for a return to normal for kids was supposedly "accepted" by Levi's at this point either as reasonable or something they just couldn't get me to stop doing, I was aware that my edging into other covid and lockdown-related territories caused much consternation. In fact, Tracy, our head of Human Resources, with whom I was now meeting regularly, urged me to delete anything related to the following subjects:

1. **The wrongheadedness of doctors threatening not to treat the unvaccinated.** There was a spate of articles and opinion pieces on the subject in the fall of 2021. But in a world where doctors treat active shooters who willfully harm others and drunk drivers who stupidly and inadvertently do, it seemed to me, hospitals and doctors declaring they would no longer treat the unvaccinated was an inappropriate triage methodology. It was a violation of

the Hippocratic oath, and it was wrong. Levi's said: *not allowed.*

2. **The profit motive of Big Pharma, citing Purdue Pharma as the driver of the opioid crisis.** In the age of covid, this was "wrongthink," as it was supposed to be obvious that these values-led CEOs just wanted to save us from death and destruction, not force the population to take medications that they didn't want or need. Levi's said: *not allowed.*

3. **Anything having to do with masks**. I avoided the matter of adults mandated to mask at work, but when it came to masking of toddlers, many still in diapers and just learning to talk, I repeatedly called it out as ineffective and damaging. Despite the lack of evidence that it did any good at all, this was "anti-science." Levi's said: *not allowed.*

4. **Anything suggesting that Public Health leaders might want to undertake a "get healthy" effort**. I dared to propose such a campaign for the clear and obvious reason that those categorized as "obese" were at significantly greater covid risk than those of average weight. This was deemed fat-phobic and bigoted – never mind that our own company offered incentives in the form of health insurance discounts to anyone who would offer testimony that they ate healthfully and exercised regularly. To be clear, there was no value judgement involved; I've been anorexic,

bulimic, overweight and underweight in my life. But it was yet another case of a true thing being unspeakable because "feelings." Levi's said: *not allowed.*

After our conversation, Tracy followed up with an email:

Hi Jen –

Per our discussion, here are the tweets that Kelly shared. Again, I would be most mindful of taking anything down that contradicts our policy like vaccine or mask mandates. I did think of one other thing – some of the employee feedback has been around the references to comorbidities like obesity, so that would be maybe something to look at too. Again, this is more about the 'go forward' but there may be some prior posts that are worth taking another look at.

1. Objection to employers/hospital mandating vaccinations
   e.g., https://twitter.com/JenniferSey/status/1436790582920232971?s=20
2. Objecting to medical professionals prioritizing vaccinated over unvaccinated https://twitter.com/JenniferSey/status/1434912326931685376? s=20, https://twitter.com/JenniferSey/status/1434344928297975808?s=20
3. Recurring objections to expectations re: masking, social distancing, vaccination, etc.
   e.g., https://twitter.com/JenniferSey/status/1432555112904499201? s=20 or https://twitter.com/JenniferSey/status/1432467201961840644?s=20
4. There are the call outs re: comorbidity that seem to blame victims and/or a call for public health campaign to address these issues vs focusing on vaccination https://twitter.com/JenniferSey/status/1432340708816420872? s=20
5. And a series of concerns about pharmaceutical companies' financial motives driving vaccination requirements
   e.g., https://twitter.com/JenniferSey/status/1430361129121845248?s=20

Thanks,

Tracy

To be clear, I never tweeted anything that contradicted company policy. I never tweeted anything about workplace vaccine mandates; my husband did. None of our employees were toddlers, so we had no toddler mask policy. However, working overtime to be a team player, I deleted the posts that Tracy said were unacceptable. Here's an example of one of the posts that I deleted, uncovered by me in the "Wayback Machine":

Why doesn't anyone in public health ever say "exercise, eat right, go for a walk every day?" We know that next to age, obesity is the next most significant indicator of negative

Covid outcomes. Why isn't the CDC sounding the alarm
bell and initiating a 'get healthy' campaign?

While I submitted to the deletions in a last-ditch effort to retain
my job and standing, I never did so by giving ground on any of the
issues in question. I wrote back:

I stand by rationing healthcare, denying it to those who
aren't vaccinated is wrong, but I will respectfully refrain.

Tracy agreed that I had a good point. But it didn't matter. Like
every single other Levi's employee, she refused to support me. It's
hard to put into words how angry and just downright mystified it
made me to be told, as I was over and over: *I agree with you, you're
right, but you can't say those things and I won't stand by you if you do.*

This is not a world I've consented to participate in. Why would
anyone?

Kelly McGinnis no longer asked me to consider my actions and posts. She probably knew that my days at Levi's were numbered. In the meantime, her own kids had been back to in-person school for over a year by then. At executive team meetings, she regaled us with the difficulties and miseries in her life: endless tutors and educational consultants to ensure her children would get into the right private middle school, the next step in their educational progression. There was no embarrassment or sense of irony in bemoaning these never-ending challenges, while earnestly insisting that I stop talking about the harms inflicted on public school kids who were getting no education at all.

Everyone at Levi's seemed to agree with Kelly. My husband and I were just too much trouble. *We* were the problem. Not the policies, not the harms being done, not the censorship. We, my husband and I, were non-compliant, something ultimately not just undesirable, but unacceptable, for a Levi's employee.

CHAPTER 19:

THE PREDICTABLE OUTCOME.

By the fall of 2021, many public school students had only just gotten back to full-time in-person learning, and it was a disaster. Among even the most conscientious students, older, hard-learned habits had been abandoned, and newer damaging ones were by now ingrained. Chronic absenteeism (absent more than 10 percent of the time) was as high as 40 percent in some major cities. Kids were hopelessly behind, and teachers had been encouraged to just pass them anyway. By spring 2022, fights were breaking out in the hallways of San Francisco schools.

Earlier, in February 2021, teachers at Newark Central High School, in New Jersey, were instructed by Principal Dr. Sharnee Brown not to hand out any F grades. The order was called the "No F and Missing Grade Mandate" and the instructions were clear: "During the pandemic, no student will have missing grades or

Fs." That month, 1200 out of 2000 recorded Fs disappeared from the grading system at this school. This practice, while done out of empathy, left students academically unprepared for their next grade.

By the spring of 2022, a fight at Everett Middle School in San Francisco's Mission District sent a student to the hospital with life-threatening injuries. Principal Esther Fensel said that the altercation was part of "an alarming and urgent rise in mental health concerns and behavioral incidents since the start of the pandemic not just at Everett, but across our district and our country." It isn't difficult to surmise that over a year of online learning left students not only academically unprepared, but emotionally, as well. Frustrations bubbled over. Fensel would announce her resignation not long after this incident.

I understand showing kids a measure of grace given all that they've lost, but simply passing students who can't read or do math will not serve them in the world. Quick fixes like grade adjustments will not drive necessary academic improvement. A failure to assist in re-integration, and to help kids manage reconnecting with peers after eighteen months of near total isolation will result in young adults ill-equipped to enter the workplace and the world.

What open-schools advocates had warned about was all coming to pass, and there seemed to be no plan to address it. A generation of permanently harmed kids would be left in the wake of disastrous closed school policies.

And while Kelly had given up on speaking with me directly about her ongoing concerns regarding my big mouth, she continued to monitor my online activity, and handed dossiers of my Twitter posts to Chip on a weekly basis. Schools were off limits in our very occasional and very limited one-on-one conversations, but she did ring me to tell me not to post anything about the vote to recall Governor Gavin Newsom, which was set for September 14, 2021.

The special election recall was at least in part a referendum on the governor's pandemic policies. It was an expression of frustration with his hypocrisy, most glaringly, the fact that he had kept public schools in California closed longer than any state in the country while sending his own four children to in-person private school. Furthermore, Newsom forced most businesses to shut down while allowing wineries to stay open, including his own. And, even though he had banned private gatherings of more than three households as well as indoor dining, he was caught eating at one of the most expensive restaurants in the world, French Laundry, with a group of lobbyists. Prior to covid, a meal at French Laundry cost $350; during covid the price was ratcheted up to $850. Governor Newsom claimed that the luxurious enclosed tent that they were in made it an outdoor meal, and that it was not a private gathering, because they were in a restaurant, making it in accordance with his rules. And he offered only the most perfunctory apology:

"I need to preach and practice, not just preach."

Nonetheless, he continued preaching and not practicing. The recall may have been started by the Right, but a multitude of other frustrated California citizens soon joined the cause. And I had posted about it:

Jennifer Sey ✓
@JenniferSey

"I feel that the recall effort has become less of a
partisan issue — say Republican, Democrat, etc. —
and it's been an educational issue." #openschools

nationalreview.com
Newsom Faces Recall Danger as Frustrated Parents Reach Breaking Point
Outraged parents, many of whom voted for Newsom, might push the recall effort
over the top.

8:27 PM · Feb 10, 2021 · Twitter for iPhone

In response, I received this text from Kelly, encouraging me to forgo any commentary on the subject.

Thanks!

One other note that's been
on my mind. You might
consider avoiding Newsom
recall mentions on your
Twitter feed. I'm thinking of
both government relations
and Haas Family
connections

Sure

Appreciate

Have you all watched
Operation Varsity Blues on

Not sure how you could call this anything other than suppression of political speech, as well as viewpoint discrimination, as no one would have cared in the slightest had I criticized President Trump. (Not *cared*? They'd have applauded!)

Of course, there were also other issues at play, like for instance that "the family" (what we called the Haas family) that still owns a majority stake in Levi's are fierce Democratic partisans and have longstanding personal relationships with Gavin Newsom. Recently minted billionaire Mimi Haas is Levi's largest single shareholder. Her son is married to Becca Prowda, the "Director of Protocol" (whatever that is) for Governor Newsom. Becca was appointed to the role in 2019, directly from her position as director of community affairs at Levi's. This is just one of many entanglements "the family" has with the Democratic Party and Gavin Newsom.

Newsom triumphed easily in the September 2021 recall, despite his evident hypocrisy. His main opponent, African-American businessman/radio commentator Larry Elder, was repeatedly characterized as "the blackface of white supremacy" because, apparently, if you're a Republican you are a white supremacist even if you are black.

I think I realized after Newsom's landslide victory that I had no chance of becoming Levi's CEO, but I still thought maybe I wanted it. And Chip kept holding out hope that it was possible. In October 2021, we met over dinner, and he tried to entice me, not with money, but with the promise of influence in the social and political sphere. He knew that was more alluring to me than riches. He said: "Think about the influence you could have! If you were CEO, you could have decided that the company should have weighed in on closed schools, like I did with guns."

I'll admit, it was tempting. Chip went on to say: "You're an activist at heart."

I said: "No I'm not. I just stand up for what I believe in. I don't compromise my values. That's not the same as being an activist."

He was unconvinced, the difference not readily apparent to him. But very clear to me.

Then Chip made a request. He needed my consent to do a background check on me and my husband. He said this was standard operating procedure for CEO consideration, and I do believe some sort of background check is standard.

The Levi's background check was to include an investigation into whether I had any questionable financial entanglements or a criminal record. But also, of course, they were going to investigate my social media activity, and that of my husband. Including my husband seemed odd. I have a hard time believing that if a man were the candidate that they would investigate his wife's social media presence in this way.

I had little doubt that Chip would come back in a few weeks and tell me that I couldn't be the CEO because of the findings in the report. And I told him as much. However, Chip insisted that I was still the lead candidate. But I knew the jig was up. It seems obvious to me now that holding out CEO was just another way to try to get me to stop. Ironically, the promise of more influence was an attempt to limit my influence.

However, at that point, even if I'd deleted all my accounts, I was a goner. By then I'd been at it for a year and a half, and screenshots live forever.

Plenty of trolls had made it their hobby to ensure that my heresies were recorded for posterity. The "Covidians," as they were called on Twitter, were true devotees, willing to go to unimaginable lengths to cement and signal their fealty to the cause. I'd been accused of everything from "grift," to "doing it for likes and clicks," to being too stupid to know any better (therefore incapable of leading an organization), to being selfish, to being a bigot. This "feedback" veered wildly, but I can assure you: I received no money; "likes and clicks" are of little significance to me, especially when compared to having a job that enables me to take care of my family; I'm not stupid. You can decide whether or not I'm selfish, and whether or not I'm a bigot.

The most passionate mob of trolls was a group of gymnastics fans who started a petition on Reddit to get me fired:

 IlaDC · 11 mo. ago

I blocked her months ago. I lost all my respect for her. Between her complete lack of understanding science to using other survivors' stories to defend her stance on Covid. She is sickening.

There needs to be a petition people sign that then gets sent to Levi's. Her behavior has far too many negative consequences for public health.

All of fifty-two obsessive gym fans were on board, and they'd committed to repeatedly calling the ethics hotline at Levi's until I was shoved out the door. This particular woke mob had made it their business to see me ousted.

Hardly incidentally, this cohort had hated me when my gymnastics book, *Chalked Up*, had come out, too, since having to think about the abuse endured by athletes interfered with their viewing pleasure. Though "cancellation" wasn't a term used widely in 2008, the push to cancel me had been relentless up until 2018, when long-time USA Gymnastics team doctor Larry Nassar was sent to prison for life and, overnight, I went from lying grifter to fearless heroine.

But as a critic of the sport, I'd never really been fully accepted, and my attacks on school mandates had brought these gym fans back in force. I could count on their being key members of my haters club.

My own brother had taken to piling on to the trolls who aimed to see me fired. Chris insulted both me and my husband repeatedly on our own Twitter pages. He said it was rude and ungrateful to challenge doctors and health officials. All he seemed to care about was the fact that he felt that we were dismissive of his wife's status as a frontline healthcare hero.

Both Daniel and I declined to respond to my brother's provocations on Twitter, but this was no longer some ordinary family squabble. Chris did not communicate with me privately to discuss my views, which he clearly found extremely problematic. By then, the fall of 2021, we hadn't spoken at all in over a year. We didn't email or text, either. The last time we'd emailed he'd told me that he wasn't interested in hearing me out on any covid-related matters. These were very difficult to avoid, as I had upended my entire life to move to Colorado so my younger kids could go to school, and I was on the brink of losing my job because of the stance that I had taken. Covid infiltrated everything. What else was there to talk about? Movies?

Chris and I were left with nothing to say to each other. The last time we'd spoken, he'd said, "social media is bad news," and I took it to mean he'd prefer not to communicate there because things tended to get ugly fast. I didn't take it to mean that I shouldn't post, only that *we* shouldn't engage. Which, to me, seemed fair and reasonable. I obliged.

Chris did not. He continued to respond to my and Daniel's musings, seemingly unable to help himself. And he took to consorting with my trolls, posting things like this, which I read when I was driving my second oldest child to college:

I'm very glad they [my husband and I] have been body checked and I seriously hope they stfu soon. Silence would benefit them. They might hear their conscience.

Christopher Sey
@csey16   · · ·

Replying to @90sWillysWonder

Way, dude
But FYI I'm very glad they've been body checked and i
seriously hope they stfu soon
Silence would benefit them. They might hear their
conscience.
Sorry for your crap

10:58 PM · Sep 20, 2021 · Twitter for iPhone

3 Likes

I could hear my conscience perfectly fine. It's what prompted me to continue to speak out in the face of family alienation, loss of friends, job insecurity and the general turning inside out of my life. But I was heartbroken by this betrayal by my brother as I wound my way through Nebraska and Iowa, en route to Chicago for the college drop off. I was a wreck, to put it mildly. In addition to sending my second off to college – always emotional for a mom – I was on the brink of losing my job and now my brother was actively trying to contribute to that end. I blocked him at this point, for a time, in an attempt to encourage what he'd told me over a year ago about wanting to avoid contentious interactions on Twitter. He saw my blocking him as an aggressive act. I saw it as self-preservation. For both of us. I knew if things continued as they were going, we'd have no chance at recovering. So I tried to force an end to it.

Noble actions on the part of the deeply unselfish covid-faithful included countenancing old and sick family members dying alone and afraid in the hospital, far from the soothing warmth of loved ones, and cutting off from the world children with near zero chance of getting the disease in order to "slow the spread." Joining the call to get your own sister fired from the job that enabled her to support her family was just another act of reverence. It seemed the cruelty of the faithful knew no bounds.

Unlike with my brother, my dad and I continued to speak throughout. He read the articles I sent to him, and we discussed our divergent views. Sometimes, he even granted I had a point. It got heated sometimes, but we always came back to each other. My mom and I found some peace in just not discussing these matters at all. In June 2021, my parents had come to San Francisco for my son's high school graduation. We muddled through our disagreements, as we always had. They loved me, and I loved them. And we all knew it, prioritizing our relationship over policy disagreements.

Certainly, the trolling by strangers and my brother would all show up in the background check. And had it been waved off by Chip and the board, and they'd decided to give me the CEO job anyway, my tweets, and those of my antagonists, would have been unearthed and amplified, with the intent of having me lose my job instantly, as happened to Alexi McCammond at *Teen Vogue.*

Of course, there was the chance that things would flip, and all of my foes would end up pretending they'd always supported my message and fought for what was right as had happened in the gymnastics community.

It could go that way again. Maybe, when the lies told by those pushing covid hysteria are fully exposed, along with the terrible damage they visited upon an entire generation, those of us who were right all along will receive our due. But I don't count on it. The woke are not big on self-knowledge or contrition, and the memory hole beckons. Indeed, it's funny – if that's the word – by late summer 2022, many of the Facebook responses from 2020 by my personal cadre of haters calling me a racist and a "Trumper" seem to have been deleted. And, in general, those who vilified people like me for speaking out against school closures have fallen silent. Or, they simply excuse the damaging policies with "well, public health officials were just doing their best." By 2022, it was no longer unacceptable to talk about the immensity of the damage done to children, among so many others. It had become the accepted truth.

But, along the way we'd skipped a step. For there has been no accountability for the damage done, no answerability on the part of those who made and enforced the policies, let alone those who encouraged them by shutting down dissenting voices on social media and within their own social circle. It is as if this horrible thing happened, but nobody did it. But in fact, these were policy decisions made by government leaders, largely in blue states and cities, and by the public health officials that they had empowered.

On September 1, 2022, *The New York Times* reported on the "Nation's Report Card" about the state of education with the headline: "The Pandemic Erased Two Decades of Progress in Math and Reading." Black and brown children, already at significant disadvantage in educational attainment, were impacted the most, increasing overall inequality. Because this is not just about declining test scores. Kids who don't learn to read and do math in grade school are at far greater risk of not graduating from high school, increasing the likelihood that they will live their whole lives in poverty.

Even when the damage from these policies is acknowledged, it is excused by Democratic voters and the media, who still claim that the Democrats are the party of education, kids and public schools. Despite the erasure of two decades of progress with the steepest drop in test scores in over thirty years, on September 6, 2022, in an opinion piece for CNN, Jill Filipovic proclaimed:

> Democrats need to respond [to Republicans] with their own clear message: That education is a right and is among one of the most formative and valuable tools we give our children.

It's true. Education *is* a right. It *is* one of the most valuable tools we give our children. But this isn't a messaging problem. This is an action problem. For over two years, Democrats have signaled in every way possible that education is *not* a right, and that it is *not* a valuable tool. And even now, in September of 2022, Democrats continue to onerously restrict kids and impede their educational development. Unvaccinated kids in New York City public schools still can't participate in sports or after-school activities. Toddlers in Headstart programs continue to be muzzled with masks, just when they are learning to talk.

As they attempt to burnish their message before the November 2022 elections, Democrats seem to believe that with the right talking points, they can convince voters that they didn't shut the schools for well over a year and that, yes, they are indeed the party that cares about kids. Despite all evidence to the contrary.

It may already be too late for many of the kids who have fallen desperately behind, and for the kids who have dropped out and are not going back. The extended school closures are going to affect their life options and their life expectancy. The kids most impacted are owed an apology, at the very least. But mere acknowledgment is insufficient; those who implemented these policies need to be held accountable. Not as a matter of retribution, but in the common interest, to guarantee such harms are never allowed to happen again.

I waited a few months for the follow-up from Chip on the background check, wondering each day precisely when the hammer would descend. I finally got a meeting request for January 24, 2022, from Chip's assistant. I suspect Chip had had the results for a few weeks, but was avoiding the unpleasant discussion.

At one point, I do believe that Chip had really hoped that I would be his successor. But he clearly hoped even more that I'd be obedient and stop challenging pandemic policies. He wanted someone outspoken and brave enough to use their voice and make hard calls when necessary. But not quite this much. A little less voice, a little more "yes sir," would have been the right combination to land me the job. Alas, that wasn't me.

On our video call, off the bat, Chip was sheepish. My hands shook beneath my desk, but I pasted a smile on my face. I was determined not to show any emotion, and I didn't. In the moment, when he told me it was over and there was no place for me going forward, I didn't have the wherewithal to ask to see the report. In any event, I strongly suspect that he would not have shown it to me.

I think he would have found some excuse, any excuse, not to share it, because there was likely some "gray" in the findings. It would probably have read as a judgement call. He may have feared that if he showed it to me, I might argue with him about the decision, and that I might actually be persuasive. But there was no point, because the decision had been made.

Chip asked that I stay while they found my replacement and maybe, in the interim, tone it down a bit on social media. In exchange, I'd earn more than a million dollars in severance, the "standard package" for an executive. This was unappealing to me for a whole host of reasons. Not least among them was that if I accepted their payoff, I'd inevitably be expected to sign a non-disclosure agreement (NDA) on the terms of the separation. Those "terms" would mean I could not disclose that I was pushed out the door for speaking up about school closures and challenging Public Health authorities. Those "terms" would mean I couldn't write this book that you are reading right now.

I nodded silently in the moment, when the deal was on offer. It was as much a nod of understanding as anything. I didn't know exactly what I was going to do. I was just trying to end the call. And as soon as I hung up, I started plotting my next move. I do wonder to this day what the report said.

I asked for the separation agreement three times between this call with Chip and my departure. It was never sent to me. But I realized almost right away that I wasn't going to sign it.

At this point, in addition to fighting for full transparency about the harms done from school closures in order to hold power to account, I was determined to speak out on the illiberalism and censorship that has seeped out of universities and into corporations across the country. And to advocate for others to speak their minds freely. Even – make that *especially* – if I didn't agree with them.

CHAPTER 20:

YOU CAN'T FIRE ME, I QUIT!

I was going to resign in spectacular, bridge-burning fashion. Publicly. Not behind closed doors with a *thank you hope to see you soon it's been amazing thank you for all the opportunities blah blah blah*. There would be no fawning but fake announcements about how I was leaving to spend more time with my family, which everyone in the business world and everywhere else knows means you got fired or let go or laid off or whatever the right lingo is for being left with no job.

I would not hide out at home licking my wounds, safely ensconced with a "soft landing," which in my case was a million-dollar bribe to keep me quiet. I had refused to be silenced for almost two years with the specter of losing my job always looming. I certainly wasn't going to silence myself now about *why* I'd been shoved out the door.

On February 13, 2022, I sent the following email to Chip, cc-ing the Chairman of the Board and Tracy, the head of Human Resources:

> Chip:
>
> After some deliberation, I've made the decision to leave Levi's. I am hereby submitting my formal resignation as President and EVP of Levi's, effective immediately. Please let me know what you would like me to do with my phone and computer, which I won't be using or reviewing after this email. Should you need to get ahold of me, please use my personal email also cc'd here.
>
> Jen

At the very moment I sent the email, celebrities including Justin Bieber and LeBron James were enjoying the Super Bowl at SoFi Stadium in Los Angeles, reveling barefaced after two years of isolation. (If you believe Bieber and James were actually isolating for the prior two years, well then I have a bridge to sell you.)

Despite the mask requirement and calls for caution at the game, over 60,000 people gathered to cheer and drink and party. The Super Bowl was a veritable "super spreader" event if ever there was one. Nonetheless, L.A. Mayor Eric Garcetti hobnobbed barefaced with a who's who of revelers. You'd think Garcetti would have been more careful about appearing in a photo without his mask, trying to set a good example or just not get dragged as a hypocrite. AGAIN. Just two weeks prior, at the playoff game that qualified the L.A. Rams for the Big Game, Garcetti was "caught" hamming it up for the camera mask-free with Magic Johnson. His response when criticized for his "rules for thee but not for me" behavior – he'd set the mask rule after all – *I held my breath for the photo.*

The next day there would be headlines about the ongoing charade of endless covid restrictions. It was all just noise at this point. Mayors and Governors and unelected public health officials would set the rules, ever more complicated and onerous and Byzantine, and break them. They'd make some dumb excuse no one believed, and then do it all over again the next day. Their "let them eat cake" attitude didn't seem to bother people very much. Everyone seemed to just accept the hypocrisy. It's as if they appreciated the act, the virtuous pose, even if wasn't backed up with action or belief. *At least they pretend to say the "right" thing*, a true sucker might utter. *That's better than not pretending.* But is it?

Also on the next day, preschoolers in Los Angeles would be required to wear masks for the entire day, and grade schoolers in Oakland would be required to wear masks and keep their distance from each other, even while outside at recess. But the folks who could afford Superbowl tickets, or simply knew the right people to be gifted tickets, didn't pay any mind to these children. They felt safe, ensconced among the clean, triple vaccinated and wealthy. Why heed the rules? They had beers to drink, a Mary J. Blige and Snoop Dogg half-time show to watch. They couldn't be bothered to think about why two-year-olds in diapers, who are just learning to talk, should endure forcible masking all day, something none of them could tolerate for a three-hour football game.

Did they really believe that covering the faces of toddlers in cheaper by the dozen Paw Patrol masks would prompt the end of the pandemic? If they didn't believe it, how could they just accept it without protest? Our kids' social, emotional and educational development was at stake.

For two years, I had never stopped railing against the cruelty and hypocrisy:

Jennifer Sey ✓
@JenniferSey

···

It feels a tad bit excessive to be in an official state of emergency while CA hosts the Super Bowl, the Rose Bowl, the Oscars and the governor goes on a book tour.

4:04 PM · Dec 12, 2021 · Twitter for iPhone

6,664 Retweets   **344** Quote Tweets   **32.6K** Likes

And so I was offered a separation package to leave quietly. But instead, I decided to quit, so that I could leave on my own terms. I would not be leaving Levi's quietly.

I had a plan. It had developed in the eleventh hour, but it was a plan, nonetheless. There would be another headline the next day, too. About me.

After sending my resignation email, I turned off my computer and phone and walked away from a job I loved, a million dollars in severance and a community I'd been a part of for over two decades. I wept as the whirring of my computer slowed then quieted – tears of both disappointment and relief that it was finally over. The conflict that had engulfed my final two years at Levi's was ending. Not how I'd hoped it would, but it was ending nonetheless.

It took a few hours to get a response. The email recipients were presumably enjoying the Superbowl, if not alongside the Biebers then in a likeminded spirit. Chip was possibly at the game. Before the pandemic, he often went. I had no idea if he was there or not. Knowing him, he probably opted to stay at home, much less carefree about the restrictions than those who'd enacted them.

I didn't want to know if anyone had responded. My work phone was shut down and put away in a drawer in my bedroom until I knew where to return it. I told my husband to hold my personal phone and not let me have it, even if I begged. I couldn't bear to read any response that might come through, but he had my permission to let me know if one did. I was afraid I'd change my mind if that was possibly on offer. I'd wiggle out of my plan. I'd let them placate me with money and platitudes and praise of my two decades of service. They'd offer a little more money, if I'd stay until they found my replacement (which as of this writing, more than seven months later, they still have not found) – *it's just two months, four months, a year, who cares! What's a few more months among friends. Oh and keep quiet. And don't be so dramatic. Why make trouble? We know you care about this issue of kids and school but it's gone too far. C'mon already. Just stop. C'MON, Jen, this is how it's done.*

A few hours later the email came. My husband read it to me from my phone:

Jen,

Wow, this is a shock, especially after our last few conversations. Can we discuss this? I'm copying [my assistant] – can you set up some time with her for us to talk sometime tomorrow (Monday?) Chip

Ignore. Ignore. Ignore. It took everything I had to ignore it, not to respond, not to smooth over the thing I had planned that hadn't happened yet but would in about twelve hours.

They had no idea what was coming.

CHAPTER 21:

MY PLAN AND WHY I MADE IT.

I was going to resign with an op-ed in Bari Weiss's *Substack* newsletter, "Common Sense," exposing Levi's silencing of speech and its rampant viewpoint discrimination, highlighting the company's lack of care for children, especially poor, black and brown ones. I would expose the hypocrisy of all of Levi's public declarations about inequality and the emptiness of its promises to be part of the solution.

It would be published the next morning, February 14, 2022, at 6 a.m. Eastern time, hours before anyone in San Francisco was ready for their workday.

Having executed hundreds of layoffs in my two decades at the company, I knew there could be no negotiating. The money always came with the demand for silence about the terms of the departure. There simply was no way I'd be able to accept their money without signing away my voice, the thing I'd been fighting to keep for the past two years.

This decision was not about money. It was about the fact that I'm a mom who has every right to speak up in defense of children. And it was about the fact that Levi's said my job meant I couldn't do it. I don't accept that. I don't accept that the more successful you are, the fewer rights you have as a citizen. Indeed, if rights can be denied to those with power and influence, who can't be denied? This would mean that the very fact of holding a job means giving up one's right to voice an opinion.

It had taken me a lifetime to escape the mindset that pleasing others is the paramount thing. All too often that means obliterating yourself. That's simply a trade I was no longer willing to make.

And so, on the evening of February 13, 2020, after I'd officially resigned via email, I braced myself for the storm to come – hoping it would draw at least as much attention to the message as to the one seeking to deliver it. My piece would appear in people's email inboxes in just twelve short hours.

In making my plan, I reminded myself that I'd made every effort to hold Levi's to their own stated principles. I'd also followed protocol. Like back in October 2020, when I'd written that proposal to Chip, Tracy and Kelly laying out the case that Levi Strauss & Co. should weigh in on the matter of persistent public school closures and was met with this from Kelly:

We're not seeing a lot of upside to LS&Co. jumping in on this one. . . . . There's a lot of potential negatives if we speak up strongly, starting with the numerous execs who have kids in private schools in the city.

And then Chip had agreed with her. And this became the company position.

And just like that, with that one email, everything changed for me. I saw the whole board. The grift was laid bare. And the charade was too much. I would not continue to unwittingly further it.

In pushing myself to follow through with my plan, I had to ground myself in what I'd put up with for the last couple of years since I'd spoken out – the attacks by my own community at Levi's.

A year earlier, in a virtual town hall, an anonymous employee had posted a question directed to me in the chat:

Jen, is our brand reputation with Gen Z/progressive consumers threatened by, for example, the conservative and trans-exclusionary viewpoints exhibited on your public Twitter account?

To this day, I have no idea what my covid schools tweets have to do with being trans-exclusionary. But if you're viewed as a "conservative," which I now was, you get billed as anti-everything. It all just gets lumped in. Open-schools moms = anti-trans and, of course, racist.

At Levi Strauss and Co, this supposedly inclusive company, one that touted all of its diversity and inclusion initiatives, my views, which veered from the San Francisco bubble's dominant narrative that schools and children were dangerous disease vectors, made me an alt right, Q-anon conspiracy theorist and an unemployable bigot.

And so there I was, standing in my living room. I'd officially resigned, and my plan was ready to be enacted in just a few short hours. But I wavered. I contemplated responding to Chip's "hey let's talk" email with an "Ok sure! Let's discuss!," thus opening up a less contentious and disruptive way forward.

But I stood firm and stuck to the plan. I reminded myself that I'd tried to hold on to my principles while working within the system. It didn't work. I needed to forge my own way. I prodded myself forward, remembering what Ruth Bader Ginsburg had said: *Fight for the things you care about, but do it in a way that will lead others to join you.* They hadn't joined me at Levi's, but maybe some would outside of Levi's? I had to try.

I nudged myself to proceed, to stand my ground, take one more step towards holding on to my voice, to not sign it away with an NDA even if that might still be on offer, which was unlikely anyway. I pushed myself not to reverse course. I rejected their labels meant to silence me for the past two years. I should not be afraid, now, to sever ties on my own terms to keep my voice. Even if I'd be expelled from corporate life forever. I'd figure it out.

I practiced deep breathing and cried some more. My husband hugged me tight and reminded me what I was fighting for. Which was, first and foremost, the millions of public school students across the country who were still onerously restricted, impeding their learning and development and emotional well-being. But also, beyond the children, I felt I could make an impact, however minuscule, in moving towards a culture of free speech in this country – where open debate and dissent would be not only tolerated but celebrated.

"Don't forget," Daniel whispered. "Don't forget about the kids. You can handle it. Don't forget, your voice matters. They can't silence you anymore. I'm right here with you. You can do it."

My computer stayed shut. My phone stayed with my husband. I put my five-year-old daughter Ruth to bed, took two melatonin, and went to bed myself. I did not set an alarm. I didn't need to. I didn't have to work the next day.

For the first time in my adult life, I was unemployed.

CHAPTER 22:

MY ANNOUNCEMENT
AND THE AFTERMATH.

I chose to publish the reasons for my resignation in Bari Weiss's newsletter, "Common Sense" because of *her* story. In July of 2020 Weiss had resigned from *The New York Times*. She left in a very public fashion, publishing a letter on her own website, after having been regularly bullied, harassed and deemed racist by her colleagues, in part for her views on Israel and on Jewishness more broadly. In her resignation letter she wrote:

> Showing up for work as a centrist at an American newspaper should not require bravery.

She went on to say:

Twitter is not on the masthead of *The New York Times*.
But Twitter has become its ultimate editor.

Her newsletter seemed like the perfect place for me to publish my own resignation story.

It ran as planned on February 14, 2022, and remains, as of this writing, the most popular article she has ever published. The story went viral. It was picked up by every major publication, including *The New York Times*, the *Washington Post*, the *Wall Street Journal* and NPR. I also appeared on cable news shows, including CNN's "Erin Burnett Outfront" and "Tucker Carlson Tonight" on Fox News. There were lots of others. The coverage was largely neutral to positive. On CNBC's "Squawk Box," Andrew Ross Sorkin agreed that the way that executives use – and get used by – social media is a tangled subject that needs to be sorted.

I believe my story resonated, in part, because the company is so iconic. Levi's, worn the world over, is a symbol of the American ideals of rugged individualism and freedom. There are bigger companies, but none so representative of how Americans see themselves. The conflict between what Levi's is revered for and what I had experienced in the prior two years laid bare, for many, the contempt for democratic values at the heart of woke capitalism. With a broad swath of actual Levi's lovers, it struck a chord.

For about two weeks after my resignation, Levi's was on their heels. Having gotten out first, I controlled the story. But hey, I was pretty good at marketing, so it's no surprise I was good at getting my story out there. Once they got their balance, Levi's tried everything: *we didn't fire her, she quit; she didn't quit, she chose to leave the company; we didn't say she couldn't talk about closed schools, we said she couldn't criticize Public Health.* Blah blah blah.

It was deeply disheartening that, although in no way directly involved, my brother again weighed in, making clear he was not at all happy with the generally positive tone of the coverage. He wanted to change that. So much so that he tweeted this at Kara Swisher, a business and tech journalist for *The New York Times*, with 1.4 million followers.

Christopher Sey
@csey16

Replying to @karaswisher

It's probably not that interesting to you but if interested in the Jen Sey affair i think the story deserves real scrutiny beyond twitter takes. Audience capture/pandemic/martyr-cult stuff. Not principled stances as proclaimed. Sad, deranged autobiographical marketing

10:40 PM · Mar 27, 2022 · Twitter for iPhone

The tweet is still up. You can find it. He was pitching a hit piece on me, his sister, to a reporter from *The New York Times*. There are no words. People tell me stories all the time about not talking to siblings for five years, ten years, more, then reuniting. So I guess there's hope. But it will be very hard for me to get past this.

I assumed corporate America would not be able to get past my actions and I'd never get another job offer again. But the calls to lead companies came in instantly. I would ask: "Do you know about my situation?" "Yes," the recruiters always said. "That's why we are calling." They were all in apparel or "image oriented" categories of business such as fragrance.

For now, I am choosing to forego corporate opportunities in order to retain my ability to speak freely. Frankly, I'm enjoying my freedom too much to give it up. Even if that freedom comes with less financial upside.

As Hunter S. Thompson said:

> There's a lot of things wrong with this country, but one of the few things still right with it is that a man can steer clear of the organized bullshit if he really wants to. It's a goddamned luxury, and if I were you, I'd take advantage of it while you can.

I will do just that for now, thank you very much.

Ironically, the day after my article appeared on Bari Weiss's *Substack*, three San Francisco school board members were recalled for their general incompetence and refusal to work on getting schools open during the pandemic. While kids toiled at home on Zoom, hourslong school board meetings (many of which I attended) focused on renaming schools like Lincoln and Washington High Schools (because they were named after "racists") and Dianne Feinstein Elementary (she may be California's senior Senator, but she did something indecipherable having to do with indigenous peoples in the eighties).

The school recall effort succeeded only a few months after the attempted recall of Governor Newsom had failed. Don't mess with our kids, voters seem to say. Board President Gabriela López, and board members Alison Collins and Faauuga Moliga, the only three eligible for recall based on time in office, were all removed with more than 70 percent of voters in this special election saying *we've had enough*. I don't know a single person who voted no. Private school parents, lockdown enthusiasts and even school closure zealots during 2020 realized that the board had failed in its most fundamental duty. Chip told me before my departure that he planned to vote to recall all three board members.

Even the Mayor of San Francisco, London Breed, who had sued the school district to try to get schools open in early 2021 and failed in her attempt, had come out in support of the recall prior to the vote. When it was over she said:

> The voters of this city have delivered a clear message that the school board must focus on the essentials of delivering a well-run school system above all else. San Francisco is a city that believes in the value of big ideas, but those ideas must be built on the foundation of a government that does the essentials well.

In my case, of course, none of that mattered; whether I was right or wrong was irrelevant. The problem was my lack of obedience and my willingness to make waves, rather than fall in line with the leftist narrative. If I refused to back off on fighting for open schools, what else might I do? The problem was that I could not be controlled.

Not only did I say things I wasn't supposed to, but in the fullness of time, I didn't say things that I *was* supposed to say. I have never put my pronouns in my email signature. No one at Levi's officially complained (that I know of), but I was repeatedly and strongly encouraged to do so. I assumed my she/her status was obvious as I presented as female, had had four children while working at Levi's and never demonstrated the slightest uncertainty on the matter. It felt redundant to me, and ridiculous. More, I didn't want to do it because I was told I had to. To participate in the nonsensical "just because" (it's "polite"?) is a dangerous precedent. If this is the standard, what can't we be compelled to do or say?

In 1943 the Supreme Court case of *West Virginia State Board of Education v. Barnette* ruled that the state cannot force children to recite the Pledge of Allegiance in school. This is a clear example of the compelled speech doctrine. The United States government cannot typically force people to say things that they do not want to say. Private companies can. However, I would argue that the principle of *not* requiring people to say things that they don't believe or want to say is one that should be supported by private entities as well as the government.

But today, coerced speech is as rampant as silencing of speech. I was told by one of my ERG peers that members were upset I hadn't commented sufficiently on the Derek Chauvin verdict in April 2021, when the police officer who killed George Floyd was convicted of murder. I didn't sufficiently express my anti-racism in employees' minds. My actions – sponsoring the black employee resource group, building a diverse team – were insufficient to prove my devotion to the cause of equality of opportunity. They viewed me as a "wolf in sheep's clothing," I was told.

I'm reminded of Lauren Victor, who, in August of 2021, was confronted by BLM protestors in Washington, DC, while out to dinner with friends. A mob of demonstrators surrounded her table, demanding that she raise a fist in solidarity with their cause. Victor had attended several rallies in the prior months. But, in this moment, when confronted with what looks like physical force, she refused to give in to the mob and raise her fist. As the marchers surrounded her table, she asked what they were marching for. They held no signs; it was unclear what their mission was. Angry as they were, no one answered her. On principle, Victor bravely refused to follow their demands.

On September 4, 2021, a week after the incident, she wrote in an opinion piece for the *Washington Post:*

> When they crowded around my table and started demanding that I raise my fist, it was their insistence that I participate in something that I did not understand

that led me to withhold my hand. In retrospect, I would have done the same thing even if it was crystal clear to me who they were and what they stood for. If you want my support, ask it of me freely. That's what we do in a democracy.

Not anymore, it appears.

Professor Stuart Reges at the University of Washington played fast and loose with these new unwritten rules around compelled speech. He is a professor of computer science at the university's Allen School of Computer Science and Engineering, and he is no stranger to courting controversy. In the eighties he wrote about being openly gay at a time when that could have put his burgeoning career at risk. In 2018 he wrote a piece for the online magazine *Quillette*, often billed as "libertarian-leaning," called "Why Women Don't Code." He's a provocateur by nature.

At the beginning of the 2020 school year, the university published a guide to best practices which strongly urged professors to include an Indigenous Land Acknowledgment in their syllabi to recognize the historic presence of Coast Salish people on the university property.

Reges didn't want to. He is critical of what he describes as "performative acts of conformity." Instead of using the language suggested by the university, or just not doing it, he poked the university in the eye by using his own statement, which did not deliver on their intent:

"I acknowledge that by the labor theory of property the Coast Salish people can claim historical ownership of almost none of the land currently occupied by the University of Washington."

Technically Reges delivered against their guidance. He included an Indigenous Land Acknowledgment. But the viewpoint he expressed intentionally – and mockingly – undermined the entire premise of the recommended statement. The university retaliated. They changed the land acknowledgment on his syllabus to their own, then introduced a competing class in the hopes of making his class redundant and leave his classroom empty. Then they launched an investigation into his alleged violation of their speech rules which prohibit speech that is "unacceptable or inappropriate," a purposefully vague description designed to empower university bureaucrats to decide what is and isn't allowed, depending on their whims and the "right-think" of the day.

The Foundation for Individual Rights and Expression (FIRE) is helping Reges sue the school. FIRE has been fighting for academic freedom for over twenty years. Having seen the ever-more illiberal drift on college campuses from both the Right and the Left, but primarily the Left – scholars and students targeted and terminated for their views – FIRE is standing in the gap to defend academic freedom. According to Greg Lukianoff and Joshua Bleisch, both leaders at the organization: "We are living through a crisis of academic freedom on campus unparalleled since the Red Scare of the 1950s."

It is arguably even more insidious to be held accountable for *not* saying something than to be savaged (on the internet and elsewhere) for saying things the woke disagree with. The insistence that one readily mouth whatever pablum one is ordered to recite is nothing short of tyranny. It presupposes absolute and complete obedience to authority. It is the antithesis of a free society, a violation of its core principles: that our words and views are our own and cannot be coerced or silenced or re-engineered. Otherwise our speech is merely an echo of the regime's – whether a university's, a corporation's or a nation's. It is propaganda posing as thought, a tool to spread the approved message.

Spare me that "Levi's is a private company, they can do whatever they want." I know that. I accept that the First Amendment gives private employers the Constitutional right to restrict the speech of their employees.

The question is, should they? And what are the costs and consequences when they do?

A culture of free speech, one where open debate and dissent is not just tolerated but celebrated, is not only the cornerstone of our democracy, in times of crisis (and the pandemic years certainly qualify) it is *the* essential tool in seeking truth. As George Washington said:

If freedom of speech is taken away, then dumb and silent
we may be led, like sheep to the slaughter.

Indeed, even in normal times, when free speech and free thought
are discouraged in companies, invariably the long-term health of the
business will be compromised. Without dissenters and naysayers
and devil's advocates, companies become authoritarian, guru-led
cultures. And no matter how smart, gurus at some point are as dumb
as anyone else.

Take Mike Jeffries. He was the CEO of Abercrombie & Fitch
(A&F) for more than twenty years, from 1992 to 2014. He took a
heritage brand established in 1892 as an outfitter for elite outdoorsy
gentleman – the likes of Theodore Roosevelt, Charles Lindbergh and
Ernest Hemingway – and singlehandedly reinvigorated and updated
it for contemporary consumers. The company had filed for bankruptcy in 1976, reporting a loss of $1 million. After changing hands
a few times, in 1988, it was purchased by Les Wexner's Limited
Brands, which hired Jeffries. By the mid-2000s, not only did he have
A&F back on its feet, but he had made it the undisputed leader in
youth lifestyle brands by creating a sexy collegiate image with homo-
erotic undertones — or, some might argue, overtones.

With Jeffries making every decision and controlling the brand's
image with an iron fist, A&F hit over $4.5 billion in revenue at its
height in popularity. Jeffries was hailed as a visionary genius.

But the brand's tightly managed "persona" came at a cost. Controversy surrounded the brand's sexy image as Jeffries's personal predilections seeped into its creation. In 2003, the brand was sued for discrimination against black, Asian and other minority job applicants who didn't fit a "certain look," which was inferred to be white, young and hot, based on who actually got hired. Other controversies ensued, including bizarre requests by Jeffries, who reportedly ordered flight crew on the company's private plane to look and dress a "certain way," presumably in line with how he wanted the retail sales associates to look. There was more, including racist anti-Asian t-shirt graphics, and a refusal to offer plus-sized clothing. In 2013, at the apex of the brand's controversies, a 2006 quote from Jeffries re-surfaced:

That's why we hired good looking people in our stores. Because good-looking people attract other good-looking people, and we want to market to cool, good looking people. We don't want to market to anyone other than that.

Jeffries retired in 2014, assumedly under pressure to do so. He'd run the business like a tyrant. No input solicited or allowed. And it worked for a time, when his vision was culturally relevant, a phenomenon. But then he lost his mojo. His personal tastes became out of synch with the culture, but he didn't change his management style to adapt, seeking input from those with a keener sense of the changing world. The guru was no more, his guru-dom discredited.

The fact is, in business we need rabble-rousers and dissenters, even whistleblowers. We can't get to the right answers if we aren't free to discuss the wrong ones. The wrong ones aren't dangerous unless they're allowed to fester. Inevitably they sink under the weight of truth.

Everyone has been to a brainstorming session where the facilitator starts by saying "Remember, there are no bad ideas." Well, today there are. *Lots* of them. And the punishment for uttering them is likely to be banishment.

It can't go on this way. We need free speech, both in daily life and in business, not just because it's right but because it serves us well.

Without free speech, we are left enslaved and in the dark. I chose to quit my job in a fiercely public manner because I felt it necessary to do my own small part in fighting against our headlong slide towards servitude and stupidity.

CHAPTER 23:

A BETTER PATH FORWARD FOR TODAY'S COMPANIES.

I used to always say people want to wear brands that share their values. This was my explanation for the fact that in 2017 and 2018 something we called the "Batwing tee" was selling like hotcakes. It was a plain white t-shirt with the Levi's brand logo on the chest.

Then we started making these same t-shirts with the names of cities on top of the logo. If you visited a store in Barcelona, you could get a Barcelona version; if you visited Miami, you could snag a Miami one there. They were souvenirs with the Levi's name splayed across the chest. I could think of no explanation at the time for why so many millions of people wanted to make themselves into a human billboard other than that they felt proud to align themselves with Levi's. Why? Because Levi's was doing good in the world.

I was wrong.

People buy certain brands and certain clothing items not for ideological reasons but because they fit well, are perceived to be "in style" (if a particular consumer cares about style), are comfortable and yes, if the brand is perceived as "cool." But today I believe in no uncertain terms that buyers do not care what your brand "stands" for unless it's coolness or status. No matter what they say.

In 2018, a bombshell *New York Times* article detailed harassment of women at Nike by male executives. The piece described a boys club led by Trevor Edwards, then Brand President. He had minions including Jayme Martin, one of Edwards's understudies who oversaw the global business and followed his lead in demeaning women at the company. The piece also implicates then-golden child CEO Mark Parker for letting a culture of harassment go unchecked. Outings to restaurants that ended up in strip clubs and a supervisor boasting about the condoms he always carried in his backpack created a culture wherein women felt marginalized and were often passed over for promotions, and the job would instead go to a "bro" down with the frat boy ethos.

Women in the company had had enough, and they put together a report that landed on Parker's desk. He apologized but also kind of denied it all. Still, the dossier resulted in an "exodus of male executives," as described by *The New York Times*. The exodus included Trevor Edwards, who'd been widely presumed to be the ascendant CEO once Parker retired.

About a year later, runner and six-time Olympic gold medal winner Allyson Felix shared her story of discrimination at the hands of Nike's leadership in a *Times* op-ed. Her contract with Nike as a paid endorser/athlete was set to run out in December 2017 and was in contract renegotiations, when she decided that she wanted to continue her career as a professional athlete while adding mother to her list of accomplishments. The contract negotiation was not going well. Despite all of her achievements, Nike wanted to pay her seventy percent less than what they had in the past. She accepted it. But what she couldn't abide was a clause that punished her for childbirth:

> I asked Nike to contractually guarantee that I wouldn't be punished if I didn't perform at my best in the months surrounding childbirth. I wanted to set a new standard. If I, one of Nike's most widely marketed athletes, couldn't secure these protections, who could? Nike declined.

She described pressure to return to training and peak performance in a rush after giving birth to her daughter by C-section at just thirty-two weeks due to severe complications from pre-eclampsia, if she wanted to get paid.

But wait, that's not all. Later that same year in 2019, a young running prodigy by the name of Mary Cain blew the whistle on Nike's Oregon Project, run by coach Alberto Salazar. The "project" aimed to train the very best young runners for Olympic glory. Cain was the youngest track and field athlete to qualify for a World Championship Team when she entered the program. In a New York Times video she describes a culture of abuse and humiliation that nearly broke her, due to Salazar's cruel approach to training athletes. The article states:

> After months of dieting and frustration, Cain found herself choosing between training with the best team in the world, or potentially developing osteoporosis or even infertility. She lost her period for three years and broke five bones. She went from being a once-in-a-generation Olympic hopeful to having suicidal thoughts.

Cain left the program. Salazar got fired. Then they shut the whole program down. In the span of eighteen months, three very public examples, splayed front and center in *The New York Times*, laid bare Nike's culture of misogyny, harassment and abuse. And this was in addition to Nike's well-publicized use of slave labor in China. The point being: If consumers cared even a little about the values of the brands that they wear, they would have rejected Nike straight away. Never bought a pair of their sneakers again, and tossed the ones they already owned in the trash. They didn't. In 2019, while all this was being exposed, Nike's revenue grew 7.5 percent.

True enough, Nike continued to strike the pose of a cutting-edge, ultra-woke company.

Amidst it all, Nike ran an ad campaign featuring Colin Kaepernick, the once-disgraced former quarterback now recast as a heroic defender of social justice, with the tagline "Dream Crazy." With the cultural tides now turned, Nike was eager to be associated with anti-racism. Maybe consumers bought it, or maybe they just liked the great graphics and slick messaging. But more likely they just didn't care about any of it and bought the sneakers because Michael Jordan is the best basketball player of all time, and Nike's shoes are perceived as cool.

A bit earlier, in 2016, upon Donald Trump's winning the election, people took to posting pictures of themselves on social media, burning their New Balance sneakers. Why? Because the company supported Donald Trum p, or seemed to. The Vice President of Public Affairs at New Balance had announced in *the Wall Street Journal* that President Obama had "turned a deaf ear" to them and that they were hopeful that President Trump would "move things in the right direction" in regard to their "Made in the U.S.A." supply chain endeavors. This was not okay.

Rabid anti-Trumpers set their New Balance shoes aflame in protest. And while I don't know it for a fact, I'd wager that many of them wear New Balance sneakers again. Because New Balance has since had a "normie dad shoe" resurgence. Indeed, dorky dad style became all the rage in places like Brooklyn in 2018. I'm fairly certain that these hipsters re-embraced the shoes because, well, they were cool again. In fact, the privately held company grew 12.5 percent in 2018, hitting $4.5 billion in sales.

At the end of the day, consumers don't really care that New Balance liked Trump or that Nike hired Colin Kaepernick or, for that matter, harassed women. They like the shoes. And that is why they buy them.

And probably that's how it should be. People buy luxury goods like Gucci and Prada because they confer status. Carrying a Gucci handbag is like saying "I make tons of money" or "I saved a month's salary to buy this purse!" That's the message being sent when a buyer coughs up $3500 for a tote. They definitely are not sending the signal that they support refugees just because Gucci does. There are much less expensive – and for the truly committed, actual – ways to support refugees.

Fast fashion companies like H&M sell piles and piles of unbranded clothing, straight off the fashion show runway but very cheap. No one cares that you can recycle your clothes in their store. What buyers like is that for a mere pittance they can get the latest styles from the Paris runways, replete with feathers and sequins. They don't even care that the clothes basically disintegrate after one wearing. They look good at the club, for just that one night.

Victoria's Secret, the lingerie brand, has lately fallen out of favor. Once revered and shopped the world over by young women buying into the anorexic-with-improbably-big-boobs brand image, this underwear brand is now struggling. But consumers rejected it not because their CMO was accused of sexual harassment and pushed out the door (he was), but simply because styles change. "Angels" prancing around on the fashion runway with wings and boobs exploding over the top of their push up bras are no longer cool. Plus, lace is scratchy, thongs and underwire bras are uncomfortable, and cotton, generously fitting "boy shorts" (the new favorite type of undies) feel much better on the skin. Fashion is fickle. Uber-sexy is out. Comfy is in. And who wants to shop in a store that looks and smells like a brothel, heavy with musky perfume and near porno-graphic imagery? By the same token, it's not an assertion of values to buy Third Love or Rhianna's Fenty underwear brands. It's just cool right now.

I'm glad that underwear brands like Aerie now embrace more realistic body types. I was anorexic in my teens and bulimic in my early twenties. Victoria's Secret didn't make me that way. My gymnas-tics coaches did. But it took me until twenty-five to reject the notion that my worth was related to the size of my butt, and it would have helped if I'd felt accepted earlier by the culture as reflected through advertising. At the same time, I don't for a second believe that some Kardashian in a thong won't take over our hearts and minds in an instant, once trends shift. And we'll all follow her lead. Because it will be the new cool to do so.

My point is, a company's role should be:

1. Deliver product excellence and pricing fairness.

2. Market those products.

3. Be inclusive, to draw on the largest possible consumer base.

4. Treat employees with respect and pay them a fair wage.

5. Don't lie about the primary mission, which is to make money.

Just own it! Don't be jerks about it, don't do anything illegal, but don't lie about your intentions either.

And do not think for one second that your social justice policies are driving people to buy your brand. They likely won't reject it when you fail to deliver on fair workplace policies (though you should absolutely try to do that) and they won't embrace your brand because you announce that you are pro-choice and willing to pay for employees to cross state lines to get an abortion. In fact, if you do announce that you are going to do that, you're apt to have half the folks that liked you burning your goods. But the truth is, no need to worry too much about that either. It won't last long.

Get back to being honest about your business goals. Get back to normie capitalism.

Normie capitalism appeals to consumers' sense of normalcy. Brands can and should include people in their advertising from all walks of life. Racial, gender, sexual and body diversity reflect the broad range of people who may be interested in buying a particular product, thus potentially appealing to the broadest possible swath of buyers. Normie capitalism says companies should take care of their employees, pay them a fair wage and ensure performance is evaluated based on contributions to the company's goals, not politics. Normie capitalism guarantees all employees feel welcome, can move up the ladder, or not (it's ok to do your current job well and stay right where you are), and provide for their families. All races, genders and even viewpoints allowed.

Normie capitalism strives to deliver the best product at a fair price and allows for some regulations to prevent the profit motive from getting in the way of consumer safety. Normie capitalism strives to make money for executives, shareholders AND employees, and is honest about that fact. (It might consider putting some limit on how much *more* a CEO can make than an average employee, just to spread the wealth around a bit, but that's just my little extra suggestion.) It certainly doesn't make a big show of taking *harder wrongs over easier rights* – while stuffing the bank accounts of shareholders and CEOs – and doing no such thing.

Lastly, normie capitalism recognizes that employees are more than employees. They are people. They have rights, including but not limited to, free speech, and they can have opinions and express them without fear of being fired.

Normie capitalism doesn't lie. Or it lies less. I guess Victoria's Secret might still promise that your boobs will look great. And Old Spice might still promise that you'll get the girl if you use the right deodorant. But no one believes any of that anyway. And somehow, there is something different and much more misleading about adopting social justice stances to sell merch. It's all a charade. It is deceitful and it pretends capitalism is altruism.

All of this is to say that the customer's function in a capitalist economy is simply to buy or not buy what companies are selling. Because anyone who thinks for a second that these companies care about the social justice platforms that they claim to be all about is deluding herself. Don't be fooled. They don't care about you or your causes. They care about money. Buy stuff you like. And if you really do want to make purchasing your form of activism, do a lot more research. And also, maybe stop buying Nikes.

Even better, go to rallies, write your Congressperson, write op-eds, go work at an NGO. "Just Do It!"

I'm not anti-capitalism. Far from it. I have chosen to work in a company for most of my adult life. (I may even work in a company again one day.) In all that time, I never stopped also working on the issues that I cared about, whether it was women's reproductive rights or child abuse in sports – outside of work.

It is not that we can't do good inside of work. In the workplace I tried to give women equal opportunity and pay them fairly, because those are explicitly work issues. But the "simple truth," as Caitlin Flanagan observes, "is that you cannot simultaneously dedicate yourself to making untold fortunes for a giant corporation and to championing a social good." So let's keep those things separate and distinct.

This is what I mean by normie capitalism:

Companies – Make great stuff people want to buy. Don't lie. Don't cheat. Don't be hypocritical. And for goodness' sake, don't fire employees for having opinions, even if those opinions are out of step with the mainstream in the moment.

People – Don't expect everyone to share your views in the workplace or in the world. Buy the stuff you like. Say what you think. Do it now. Defend speech by speaking up. Before it's too late.

CHAPTER 24:

WHY I STAYED SO LONG AT LEVI'S. AND WHY I ULTIMATELY LEFT.

I achieved a level of success at Levi's that I never anticipated when I was starting on my corporate path. I quit, on my own terms, knowing I'd done nothing wrong.

The fact is, I love Levi's. I believe that the company and its leadership are caught up in the middle of a cultural maelstrom. Call it wokeness or cancel culture or whatever you want to call it, but it's one where the public square is dominated by a mob, with no regard for due process. There is no justice or inclusion, only viciousness, and a world that completely ignores context and truth. And certainly does not allow for forgiveness.

Levi's is no better or worse than many other players contributing to this ugly dynamic. More like typical. They had the opportunity to exhibit moral courage and stand up to the angry employee and social media mob. They didn't.

But I think that they will find their way back. I really do. And I hope that the conversation that I am instigating will be part of finding that way back.

Levi's has a head start in that the company has such a long history of exhibiting some degree of moral courage. It's in their "genes," so to speak. It's part of why I stayed so long. And why I was so heartbroken to find out they'd been sucked into this new, cowardly mode of illiberalism that looks a lot less inclusive and democratic than we imagine America to be, and a lot more like rule by a tyrannical and aggressive minority. Still, I wear my 501s every day and retain high hopes for the company I inhabited, not just physically, but emotionally, for so long.

For twenty years it was the place I went every day, then for another two I went there "virtually." I got married, had two kids, got divorced, had two more kids, then got married again. All while working at Levi's. I wrote *Chalked Up*, about my time as an elite gymnast as a child, revealing the abuse and cruelty in the training culture, and was lauded for it by the company's leaders. I shared my life with everyone there, told them my stories.

And I told Levi's stories as if they were my own. I told the story of Levi Strauss, the Bavarian dry goods merchant who moved to California from Germany to seek his fortune. True enough, usually I didn't tell the part about how Levi Strauss screwed his partner Jacob

Davis out of his share of the patent and the profits. Maybe I should have.

But I told the part about how Levi Strauss donated a portion of the first profits that he he made from the company, a dry goods store, to an orphanage; and the part about how in 1897 Levi Strauss donated scholarship funds to U.C. Berkeley and stipulated that half of the money be reserved for women attending the college; and how the company introduced the first jean made specifically for women in 1934; and how, in 1991, Levi's introduced health and safety standards in their contracted production factories, where nearly all apparel workers were, and still are, women. Then, too, there was the story of how Levi's integrated their own factories in California during World War II, despite the fact that some employees protested, and some even quit. And I told the story of Levi's being the first Fortune 500 company to offer same sex partner benefits, in 1992. Time and time again, I asserted, Levi's was a beacon of equality.

Bob Haas, the great-great-grandnephew of Levi Strauss himself, a Harvard MBA and former peace corps member, was the CEO from 1984-1999. Early in his tenure, in 1985, he took the company semi-private after it had been public since 1971. He did it, he said, to escape Wall Street's never-ending demands for increased profits. He wanted to make investments for the long-term health of the company without worrying about quarterly ebbs and flows and the relentless pressures from shareholders. The stock climbed one hundred-fold and reached $265 a share. And Bob was a hero. For a time. And I still believe that he did it for noble reasons.

Bob was intent on showing the world that a company could make money while upholding progressive, humanitarian values. When shareholder-driven companies like Coke and McDonalds rushed into China in the 1990s, Bob did not. He not only decried China's human rights violations, but upheld his "profits through principles" vision by refusing to enter the market. In 1987, he led a major initiative to develop this "Aspirations Statement," intended to guide both Levi's leadership and the workforce overall:

Aspirations Statement

We all want a company that our people are proud of and committed to, where all employees have an opportunity to contribute, learn, grow, and advance based on merit, not politics or background. We want our people to feel respected, treated fairly, listened to, and involved. Above all, we want satisfaction from accomplishments and friendships, balanced personal and professional lives, and to have fun in our endeavors.

When we describe the kind of Levi Strauss & Co. we want in the future, what we are talking about is building on the foundation we have inherited: affirming the best of our company's traditions, closing gaps that may exist between principles and practices, and updating some of our values to reflect contemporary circumstances.

And then, in 1996, Bob led another leveraged buy-out (LBO) to take the company fully private. But he ended up saddling it with a crushing debt load, which ballooned to over $2 billion, leading to near bankruptcy in the early 2010s.

And for this, Bob was excoriated. In 1999, after Levi's steady decade-long decline had begun, *Fortune* magazine assessed his failure to go after financial opportunity in China with this headline: "How Levi's Trashed a Great American Brand." While Bob Haas pioneered benevolent management, his family's company came apart at the seams while he was at the helm. And he was the last member of the Haas family to lead Levi's.

Bob came to be viewed as not only soft, but as a failure as a leader, not business savvy enough to know when to set values aside. But I have always admired what he tried to do. And I reveled in telling the story about his refusal to enter the Chinese market even after we'd abandoned that-let's-not-do-business-in-China strategy and were battling it out for denim share on the Mainland. Levi's had values, we cared about human rights, but 1.4 billion future consumers simply promised too big of a potential windfall to leave on the table.

For the past two decades, Levi's has attempted to walk a line between Bob's profits-through-principles approach and just making money. But it proved to be an impossible line to walk. And in the end, Levi's fell into the abyss. We still feigned allegiance to the principles in Bob's Aspirations Statement. But, in reality, we'd left them far behind. It was all just posturing now. We still pretended to care about employees – and often cited his "profits through principles" mantra – even while laying them off during covid. Saying we cared was a ploy meant to conceal how little we actually did. This is the fundamental lie of woke capitalism.

By 2019, woke capitalism had subsumed Levi's. The Haas family just wanted money, though they tried to disguise that fact by leaning in even harder to present a humanitarian face, both to the world and to themselves. This is woke capitalism in a nutshell.

Now, there were only profits, no principles. They'd hired Chip to take the company public once again, thereby directly repudiating all that Bob had done, so that they could join the ranks of the country's billionaires. This wasn't Bob Haas's Levi's anymore.

What Bob Haas created encouraged love of the brand and its history. He fostered a real sense of community, and employees felt pride in being part of such a storied icon. It is what kept me there.

I told these Levi's stories because they were true and I loved them and they made me feel proud to work there. They meant something to me. They meant a business could operate with humanity and principle. A business could offer a high-quality product that didn't rot your teeth or poison your body, or tell you who to be, that was of lasting quality and style, and could be worn for a lifetime.

Levi's jeans bore the markings of your life, they told *your* story. Every paint spatter, hole, scratch, nick, the way that they conformed to your body and yours alone, over time, to get better with age. They were perfection. They still are. From the James Dean-style 1950s rebel to the Woodstock free-love contingent to *Dog Town and Z Boys* skater kids and the '70s punk rock revolutionaries, everyone with any sense of individuality, with something to say, wore Levi's.

I'd worn Levi's since I was a kid in New Jersey, enamored of Bruce Springsteen, as all New Jersey-ites were in the 1970s and

1980s. Bruce belted *Born In The U.S.A.* in his Levi's 501s, and we all felt proud of the freedom and individualism upon which the country was founded. I realize this promise was never reality for far too many Americans, that the story of America at its inception left out women, black people, gay people, poor people, everyone but property-owning white men. Nonetheless, the promise held, and we collectively worked towards making it true for all over hundreds of years, and we still strive to finish that job today.

But Levi's iconic imagery was not just about Bruce. The images that adorn the hallways at "the plaza," as we affectionately call the Levi's headquarters, are of The Beastie Boys, Madonna, Blondie, Kurt Cobain, the Ramones, Elvis, Snoop Dogg, Beyonce, JLo. Music royalty from across the decades all rocked Levi's because they were the denim embodiment of the American promise. They were for everyone. But you were always yourself in them.

And when the Berlin Wall came down in 1989, some of the young men celebrating their freedom wore Levi's atop the crumbling edifice. This wasn't product placement, though today some clever marketer would surely figure out how to insert their brand in that story. This just happened. Because Levi's really did mean everything good about America. And that meant freedom. Maybe the country didn't always live up to it, but that promise – just the idea of even making that pact with the citizenry – held power across the globe. The fact that we tried to live up to it, continued striving and pushing to embody the promise, was exceptional — or so we thought.

When less than pride-inducing stories emerged about Levi's, I urged us to be transparent. In 2020, amidst the protests in the aftermath of the murder of George Floyd and cries in the streets for true equality which had never been realized, this ad from the 1880s got limited traction on social media:

It was a real ad. It reflected the twisted racist mores of the times back in the nineteenth century. The company was guaranteeing to its consumers that Chinese laborers did not labor to make these pants. You could be sure that these pants, those you rely on to store your gold and build your future, were made exclusively by white labor.

I felt, and still do, that we should have used the opportunity to recognize past mistakes; and more, rather than simply condemn, to wrestle with the moral complexities of our collective past. To model true apology and seek authentic forgiveness. We should set an example, apologize for wrongs done. But couldn't we also note that it was over one hundred years ago, and in keeping with the values and beliefs at the time? Dumb question.

In the Jewish religion, we recognize Yom Kippur as the Day of Atonement. A sacred day reserved for forgiving the sins of others and repenting for one's own sins. In Catholicism, they use Confession to seek forgiveness. But in the world of left-leaning "woke-ism," there is no forgiveness.

And so, despite my recommending we "own" that piece of our past – then apologize and move on – we sat tight, hoping it would pass. And it did. One could argue that we made the right call. Why invite criticism when you can remain silent? Yet I can't help but feel it was a missed opportunity to correct and fight against the egregious and corrosive excesses of a culture that never allows for a shred of forgiveness. Punishment for veering from today's standards, even if it was over a century years ago, is permanent.

I told my own Levi's story with pride as well. The story of being seventeen and representing Team USA in Moscow at the Goodwill Games. The world was in turmoil, the Cold War was in full swing, but when I went to Moscow, it was with a suitcase packed with those tiny 501s I purchased with my mom at the Cherry Hill Mall. And, indeed, they amply provided evidence of the extraordinary value of Levi's in Eastern Bloc countries. Levi's were a symbol of the West, and of the freedoms afforded its citizens. A symbol of hope, they were worth as much as a car in some Communist countries. I still believe they can be that symbol of hope again.

After the Berlin Wall came down, Levi's made an ad in 1995 as part of its 501 Reasons campaign. A young man is seen driving a battered car through the streets of Prague. It was all the rage at the time for college students and new graduates to go live for a few months in Prague, a city once walled off to Westerners, but now a hipster paradise. Cheap beer at every meal, the chance to teach English to Czech students while living a bohemian existence pontificating, philosophizing and chain smoking with other barely employed twenty-somethings. It was pretty much the coolest thing you could do in the early nineties.

The guy is driving his beat-up car through cobblestone streets, and at the end of the thirty-second ad he gets out of the car to meet his friends. And he's pants-less, wearing nothing but boxer shorts. The voiceover read: "In Prague, you can trade them for a car. On screen: Reason number 7. Levi's 501 jeans."

It isn't revenge that drove me to reveal the story of my conflict with Levi's. It's that ad in Prague. It's me at seventeen in front of St Basil's Cathedral in Moscow. It's me believing in the values that Levi's purports to uphold, that always mattered to me more than titles and money.

Don't get me wrong. I made plenty of money during my time at Levi's, though a tiny fraction of what the Haas family and Chip made, as well as many of my peers. But in the end, I simply wasn't willing to sell my soul, or my principles, to try to match their fortunes.

And so I left. With no regret and only minor hesitation. I stayed true to what I'd always loved about Levi's.

My Levi's story is a different one now. It's about all this.

But in a way I think it's an even better one as far as representing what Levi's means, when it's at its very best. I held tight to what I'd always loved about the company and its history. I didn't abandon those values when it got hard. Levi's did.

I used my voice. And will continue doing so.

EPILOGUE

I was recently interviewing for a "real" job, in an attempt to stay sharp in case I end up needing to go that route. The interviewer asked me if I would have done anything differently at the end of my time at Levi's. I said "no," which I'm sure was not the answer she was hoping for. I think she wanted some repentance, an admission that I'd seen the error of my ways and could be trusted in a new leadership role going forward. I didn't offer that up.

I told her that if I were ever to lead a company or a division of a company again, I would make it my mission to create a truly inclusive environment, welcoming not only racial, gender and sexuality diversity, but viewpoint diversity as well. I stressed this would be in the service not just of my personal beliefs, but in the interest of product excellence and best-in-class business performance. I'd attempt to steward a return to normie capitalism.

I told her one of my hallmark phrases is "great ideas can come from anywhere." The point being, I want to hear from you because I know there is business benefit to this kind of culture wherein people feel comfortable speaking up.

She told me that she didn't think that was possible in the world right now. "Companies follow the culture, they don't lead it," she said.

I reject this. Certainly, as the leader of a company, I could say outright: *We welcome all. Be respectful, be kind, and freely say what you think on matters pertaining to our business. But also, outside of work, feel free to express yourselves on other matters as well. You're more than just employees. You're people. No one can take away your voice.*

Why on earth would that not be possible? Because of cancel culture? More and more it is becoming apparent that cancel culture has its limits. Take, once again, Ted Sarandos, the Netflix CEO, who laid down the gauntlet in October 2021, declaring to his employees *we're an entertainment platform and we're going to feature lots of content; some of it you won't like and that's okay. You don't have to work here if you don't believe in free expression.* And that was that. Everyone just got back to work, and Dave Chappelle remains on the platform.

The Spotify CEO, Daniel Ek, took a similarly bold stance when, in February 2022, Spotify star podcaster Joe Rogan came under fire for having used the N-word in past shows. Someone dug up content from years past to create a highlight reel of his racism. And yes, some of these old episodes make for very uncomfortable listening. But this all came on the heels of controversial covid interviews featuring doctors, like Robert Malone and Peter McCullough, outspoken dissenters from the mainstream narrative on vaccines and covid treatments, making Rogan a co-conspirator in distributing and making known their "dangerous" views.

Two hundred and seventy doctors signed an open letter to Spotify asking them to implement stricter rules around preventing the spread of "misinformation." They wanted Rogan punished.

But controversy just makes Rogan more popular, his listeners delighting in his willingness to engage those with perspectives outside the mainstream. He enjoys eleven million listeners per episode. (By contrast, *The Rachel Maddow Show* is the most viewed program on MSNBC, coming in at 1.8 million viewers per episode.)

Musicians like Neil Young and India Arie did not take kindly to any of Rogan's publicized "missteps," not the covid stuff nor the racial stuff. Despite Rogan's apology for the slurs, these artists took themselves off Spotify in protest and asked other musicians do the same. It didn't go very far. Ek told employees in an internal memo:

> "I want to make one point very clear — I do not believe that silencing Joe is the answer. We should have clear lines around content and take action when they are crossed, but canceling voices is a slippery slope. Looking at the issue more broadly, it's critical thinking and open debate that powers real and necessary progress."

In the end, Rogan claims he *gained* two million subscribers as a result of the controversy. Why couldn't other CEOs resist the mob in similar fashion?

I recently watched a documentary on the 1990s-2000s phenomenon "Girls Gone Wild." It was a company founded and led by Joe Francis who now lives in exile in Mexico for crimes involving sexual assault in the U.S.

"Girls Gone Wild" was a series of pre-internet videos advertised on mainstream cable channels like the E! network, featuring young women at spring break locales (think Daytona Beach) flashing their boobs. Francis or one of his camera operators would lure them into doing it, plying them with drinks and a chance to be famous. Behind the scenes, the real content of the videos was being recorded in the show's trailer, where the girls, often underaged, were coerced into sexual acts with each other and with the show's staff. Francis made money, lots of it, selling these low budget pornographic videos with zero cost expenditure on talent.

And here's the thing, Joe was considered a legitimate entrepreneur, despite the raunchy illegality of it all. He presented himself as empowering young women to express their sexual freedom. But there is no world in which coerced, drunken nudity for a crowd is part of any feminist awakening. Francis's grotesque distortion of sexual liberation was, in fact, the opposite.

When we look back at these videos, even the tame ones with girls lifting their shirts at nightclubs, we can see how wrong it is. Yet it was widely accepted at the time, with the ads for the videos running on shows favored by pre-teens — shows like "The Simple Life" featuring Paris Hilton and Nicole Richie, two spoiled Hollywood girls doing chores on farms.

It is nearly inconceivable now that this all was so recently considered to be acceptable. But things change, and in American culture they can change with startling speed, sometimes even for the better.

My hope is that in a few years, we'll look back at the horrific censorship of this time, the "wokeness gone wild," with the same horror. A little time and distance, I hope, will make it apparent to almost everyone just how wrong the censorship and cancel culture that we are experiencing now are. I'd like to think I can be part of instigating that transformation.

Which is why, given that I somehow tweeted my way right into the culture wars, I'm not going to stop now. To the contrary, I will take this misbegotten opportunity to offer a little advice on how we might inch our way back to some measure of sanity:

1. Say what you think. You may be surprised by how many people actually agree with you. Just say it. Say the thing. No one can join you until you step forward.

2. Advocate for others to do the same. If someone shows the courage to express a view that is considered verboten, provide encouragement. It's okay if you don't agree. You're protecting their right to free speech and guarding a culture of free expression.

3. Talk to people who have different opinions than yours. Heck, make friends with them. That is not only the best way to learn and grow, it also builds empathy. You will, at

least, come to understand the other "side" better, even if you don't change your opinion. Or theirs.

I have a friend, made in the last few years. She does all the things I've cited here. We disagree on a lot. She is a devout Catholic. I'm an atheist. She is vehemently pro-life. I'm pro-choice, but not without restrictions. She is also very smart. Harvard- and Oxford-educated. A lawyer and academic.

I didn't know this at the time, but before I left Levi's, she took it upon herself to write Chip an email. She shared it with me long after the fact. Here is some of what she wrote:

> I just want to do something small today to take a stand against what I view as a growing social media mob in an age when we need to be rewarding people for being sincere citizens [she's referring to me] willing peacefully to stand up for what they believe in, raising flourishing families, doing well and doing good in our workplaces, instead of rewarding social media mobs that try to sink people with increasingly meaningless labels.

She went on to say:

> I've always thought of Levi's as a conscious corporate citizen, and I hope that you will be one of the ones that

supports real social justice — which can only be achieved with a civil and diverse public square where people feel free peacefully to speak their true thoughts and persuade and be persuaded — instead of mob justice.

Chip never responded. But I like to imagine that he read it, and that next time, if there is one, he may think differently about matters. He may have her words scratching at his brain, and come to a different conclusion.

I haven't come around to my friend's views on most things, but I have developed a sincere understanding of why she holds them, and I learn something from her every time we talk. We all benefit from not viewing those who hold different views from us as monsters.

After the media maelstrom that was my departure from Levi's, it's all gone quiet, and I'm left with my own thoughts on the matter, trying to make sense of all that happened. I've had time to reflect, to learn, to assess what I could have done differently, and what I stand by (which is basically all of it).

It will always be hard and lonely to stand up to a media narrative and a community committed to tearing you down. "Use your voice" is a convenient platitude, but these days it too often means little more than joining the chorus of voices already in total agreement, and deaf to any others.

I understand full well that it can feel like you will be crushed by massive organizations and institutions if you question the prevailing narrative. Yet, chances are, there are others who are questioning it too, however quietly.

It all starts with the willingness of individuals to buck the crowd, to – if it comes to it – stand apart from friends, family, political party and an entrenched narrative embraced by the world. When I was in the midst of it, I didn't realize at first that one such person was me. I'm not special. I'm just some corporate marketing lady. But I found myself taking

Theodore Roosevelt's advice:

> In any moment of decision, the best thing you can do is
> the right thing, the next best thing is the wrong thing, and
> the worst thing you can do is nothing.

Don't do nothing. Don't acquiesce to the silencing, the cancelling, the intolerance, the blatant illogic of it all. Do not allow the vocal minority to assume the moral high ground. Don't stand by silently while "omnipotent moral busybodies" quash the reasonable majority with fear of ostracism.

Dissent, just a little bit, in your own way. It gets easier every time. I swear it.

Defend your friends and neighbors. Defend your principles.

Use *your* voice.

ACKNOWLEDGMENTS

This book poured out of me during the summer of 2022. It exists, and I am still standing, after a really rough few years because of the following people:

Gray Delany and everyone at **All Seasons Press** – You believed this book would be worth reading based on one chapter. Thank you for seeing something in it and trusting that I could do it.

"The Unicorn Sisters" – Laura, Vanessa, Kate, Jenny, A.J., Trish, Meredith, Emily, Lyric, Jessica, Michelle, Julie, Sarah Beth, Kory and Shveta. You showed up when I most needed it, drank High Noons with me, and made me laugh, which I *really* needed. I'll be forever grateful.

Jenin Younes – (aka @Leftylockdowns1) You're a total badass, our most frequent visitor in our new home and a darned good friend. Keep up the fight. We're all counting on you.

Maud Maron – Thanks for talking me off the ledge one dark night when I was in the throes of a meltdown. Your moral support, and sane and balanced advice, meant more than you know.

Dr. Jay Bhattacharya, **Martin Kulldorff** and **Dr. Tracy Beth Høeg** – Reading medical studies was never my thing, but your work became my source of sanity. You made me even more certain I wasn't crazy, and for that, I'm eternally grateful. Thank you for your persistence and courage.

Bari Weiss – Thanks for giving me a platform to tell my story. I'm here for parenting tips whenever you need them.

Judy Kotzin – Thank you for always calling to say, "I support you no matter what."

My parents – We've had bumps in the road, but we always get through it, and I've never doubted your love for me.

Levi's – Thanks for twenty great years. I'll work on forgiving the last two really crappy ones.

My four children – Everything, all I have to give, is for you. I love you all the much.

Daniel – You're the best husband, editor, agent, cheerleader, defender, apologizer and "partner in crime" a girl could dream of. Thank you for giving me a model of what a true partnership looks like. Plus, life is just more fun with you. I love you all the time.

REFERENCES

Portions of chapters 11 and 18 were previously published in modified form in my Substack *Sey Everything*. https://jennifersey.substack.com/

Prologue

Profits through principles: Chip Bergh, "Our Commitment to Profits Through Principles," LinkedIn, March 27, 2019. https://www.linkedin.com/pulse/our-commitment-profits-through-principles-chip-bergh/

Harder right over easier wrong: Chip Bergh, *Bloomberg Businessweek*. https://www.bloomberg.com/features/2017-how-did-i-get-here/chip-bergh.html

Use Your Voice: levi.com, May 2020. https://www.levi.com/US/en_US/blog/article/use-your-voice

Levi's Instagram: June 16, 2000. https://www.instagram.com/p/CBgYz3EjzQF/?utm_source=ig_web_copy_link

Tough call: Jane Thier, "Levi's CFO: 700-person layoff 'toughest call' of pandemic," *CFO Dive*, July 10, 2020. https://www.cfodive.com/news/levis-Harmit-Singh-layoffs-pandemic/581418/

It all started at Levi's inception: levistrauss.com, https://www.levistrauss.com/wp-content/uploads/2016/06/2016_CompanyTimeline_Long_F.pdf

Blackstone, Virginia: levistrauss.com, https://www.levistrauss.com/2015/01/19/a-proud-heritage-of-civil-rights/

Playgrounds closed: Aidain Vaziri, "San Francisco is reopening playgrounds. Here's the long list of rules visitors must follow," *San Francisco Chronicle*, October 14, 2020. https://www.sfchronicle.com/bayarea/article/San-Francisco-to-reopen-playgrounds-with-long-15645398.php

Closed Beaches: "Coronavirus California beach closure: Newsom orders Orange County beaches to close after seeing weekend crowds," ABC7, April 30, 2020. https://abc7news.com/california-beach-closures-newsom-closes-closure-gavin/6140174/

Disallowed surfing: "Santa Cruz bans surfing in Surf City during COVID-19 crisis," KRON4, April 10, 2020. https://www.kron4.com/health/coronavirus/santa-cruz-bans-surfing-in-surf-city-during-covid-19-crisis/

Filled skate ramps with sand: "California skate park filled with sand to deter gatherings amid 'Safer at Home order," ABC7, April 20, 2020. https://abc7news.com/venice-beach-skate-park-sand-safer-at-home-coronavirus/6117030/

Boarded up basketball rims: Baxter Holmes, "Coronavirus has stopped basketball across America," ESPN, April 7, 2020. https://www.espn.com/nba/story/_/id/29004540/coronavirus-stopped-basketball-america

Chapter 1: A day in the life of me living in, and at, Levi's.

Myt final promotion: "How I went from elite gymnast to global brand president of Levi's," MSNBC, June 25, 2021. https://www.msnbc.com/know-your-value/how-i-went-elite-gymnast-global-brand-president-levi-s-n1272382

The median tenure for a CMO: Nat Ives, "CMOs' Time in Their Posts Continues to Grow Shorter," the *Wall Street Journal*, April 29, 2021. https://www.wsj.com/articles/cmos-time-in-their-posts-continues-to-grow-shorter-11619692215

Initial public offering: Lauren Hirsch, "Levi Strauss shares surge, as jean giant makes return to the public market," CNBC, March 21, 2019. https://www.cnbc.com/2019/03/21/levi-strauss-shares-open-at-22point22-in-ipo.html

CMO Next List: *Forbes*, September 24, 2018. https://www.forbes.com/sites/jenniferrooney/2018/09/24/cmo-next-2018-the-full-list-of-50-chief-marketers/?sh=7b899bb656a3

2019 Top CMO List: *Forbes*, June 20, 2019. https://www.forbes.com/sites/jenniferrooney/2019/06/20/the-worlds-most-influential-cmos-2019/?sh=40c41563d3c8

2020 Top CMO List: *Forbes*, October 1, 2020. https://www.forbes.com/sites/forbesleadership-team/2020/10/01/the-worlds-most-influential-cmos-2020-resolute-leadership-in-transformative-times/?sh=feb28f8319a1

Chapter 2: The last call.

Athlete A: Rashika Jaipuriar, "Athlete A Wins Emmy for Outstanding Investigative Documentary," *Indy Star*, October 1, 2021. https://www.indystar.com/story/news/local/2021/10/01/athlete-a-wins-emmy-outstanding-investigative-documentary/5945215001/

Chapter 3: My asks.

The Turn: Liel Leibovitz, "The Turn," *Tablet*, December 7, 2021. https://www.tabletmag.com/sections/news/articles/the-turn-liel-leibovitz

The *Chicago Sun Times*: an open letter from 17 Chicago physicians, "As medical doctors, we believe reopening Chicago's schools is essential and safe," *Chicago Sun Times*, December 29, 2020. https://chicago.suntimes.com/2020/12/29/22204984/chicago-medical-experts-in-person-learning-optimal-safe-opinion

New York Governor Kathy Hochul: Maki Becker, "Hochul: Remote learning a 'mistake' that hurt women," *The Buffalo News*, August 27, 2022. https://buffalonews.com/hochul-remote-learning-a-mistake-that-hurt-women/article_590d859d-f4dd-5669-b1d0-2ffc0d09ec15.html

Chapter 4: Leaving gymnastics. The first thing I quit.

Chalked Up: Jennifer Sey, Harper Collins, 2008. https://www.amazon.com/s?k=chalked+up

U.S. National Gymnastics Champion: USA Gymnastics website. https://usagym.org/pages/pressbox/history/nationalchamps_women.html

Julissa Gomez: Maryann Hudson, "The Unthinkable Happens: Gymnast Gomez, 15, in Coma After Suffering Broken Neck During Warmups," *Los Angeles Times*, June 25, 1988. https://www.latimes.com/archives/la-xpm-1988-06-25-sp-5044-story.html

The Twisties: Emily Giambalvo, "Simone Biles said she got the 'twisties.' Gymnasts immediately understood," the *Washington Post*, July 28, 2021. https://www.washingtonpost.com/sports/olympics/2021/07/28/twisties-gymnastics-simone-biles-tokyo-olympics/

Chapter 6: My early work years. Humiliating but not terrible. And not woke.

Mickey Drexler: "Gap: Mickey Drexler," NPR, May 18, 2022. https://www.npr.org/2022/05/16/1099335113/gap-mickey-drexler

Levi's Board: levistrauss.com. https://www.levistrauss.com/who-we-are/leadership/

Swiffer: Chip Bergh, *Bloomberg Businessweek*. https://www.bloomberg.com/features/2017-how-did-i-get-here/chip-bergh.html

86% of fashion companies are led by men: Vanessa Friedman, "Fashion's Woman Problem," *The New York Times*, May 20, 2018. https://www.nytimes.com/2018/05/20/fashion/glass-runway-no-female-ceos.html

100% of the top CEOs of cosmetics companies are men: Allison Collins, "Are Women Moving Up Beauty's Corporate Ladder? In the top 20 beauty manufacturers, women hold only 15 percent of CEO titles," *WWD*, March 26, 2021.https://wwd.com/beauty-industry-news/beauty-features/are-women-moving-up-beautys-corporate-ladder-1234785408/

Chapter 10: Everyone has a Levi's Story. Even Alicia Keys. And Snoop Dogg. And Justin Timberlake.

Levi's had been in decline for over a decade: "Levi Strauss Revenue 2010-2022," *Macrotrends*. https://www.macrotrends.net/stocks/charts/LEVI/levi-strauss/revenue

Harvard Business Review **Case Study:** "Levi Strauss (A): A Pioneer Lost in the Wilderness," *Harvard Business Review*, March 2020 (Revised July 2022). https://www.hbs.edu/faculty/Pages/item.aspx?num=57955

"Go Forth" Campaign: "Levi's 'Go Forth' campaign by Wieden+Kennedy," *Campaigns of the World*, January 29, 2017. https://campaignsoftheworld.com/print/levis-go-forth-campaign/

"O Pioneers!": *Indoek*, September 1, 2009. https://indoek.com/article/levis-o-pioneers-go-forth-campaign/

Chip was brought aboard as a change agent: David J. Parnell, "Levi Strauss & Co. CEO, Chip Bergh, On Managing The Intersection Of Tradition And Innovation," *Forbes*, June 15, 2015. https://www.forbes.com/sites/davidparnell/2015/06/15/levi-strauss-co-ceo-chip-bergh-on-managing-the-intersection-of-tradition-and-innovation/?sh=1ce4d2f4743c

Live in Levi's: "The Levi's Brand Launches 'Live in Levi's' – A New, Global Campaign Inspired By Millions of Stories From Passionate Fans," Levi's press release, June 30, 2014. https://www.prnewswire.com/in/news-releases/the-levis-brand-launches-live-in-levis--a-new-global-campaign-inspired-by-millions-of-stories-from-passionate-fans-265190011.html

All women are naturally badass: "Alicia Keys Struts Her Stuff in Levi's to Promote Women's Collection," *AdAge*, July 10, 2015. https://adage.com/creativity/work/alicia-keys/42657

Levi's Music Project: Ray Rogers, "Alicia Keys & Levi's Team Up to Bring 21st Century Music Tools to Schools," *Billboard*, September 9, 2016. https://www.billboard.com/music/music-news/alicia-keys-levis-music-project-exclusive-video-7502883/

Billboard Magazine: "The 25 Most Powerful People in Music and Fashion," September 8, 2016. https://www.billboard.com/music/features/billboard-style-issue-most-powerful-music-fashion-7502864/

Chapter 11: Levi's Wokes - let's talk about woke capitalism.

Saturday Night Live skit – "Levi's Wokes": NBC website, September 30, 2017. https://www.nbc.com/saturday-night-live/video/levis-wokes/3594563

Woke Capital: Ross Douthat, "The Rise of Woke Capital," *The New York Times*, February 28, 2018. https://www.nytimes.com/2018/02/28/opinion/corporate-america-activism.html

Fraudulent marketing: Gardner Harris, "Pfizer Pays $2.3 Billion to Settle Marketing Case," *The New York Times*, September 2, 2009. https://www.nytimes.com/2009/09/03/business/03health.html

Sackler family. Beth Mole, "Sacklers — who made 11 billion off opioid crisis — to pay 225 million in damages," arstechnica.com, October 2020. https://arstechnica.com/science/2020/10/sacklers-who-made-11-billion-off-opioid-crisis-to-pay-225-million-in-damages/

CEOs make 351 times more than an average worker: Abigail Johnson Hess, "In 2020, top CEOs earned 351 times more than the typical worker," CNBC, September 15, 2021. https://www.cnbc.com/2021/09/15/in-2020-top-ceos-earned-351-times-more-than-the-typical-worker.html

The Next Steve Jobs: *Forbes*, February 29, 2016. https://www.forbes.com/profile/elizabeth-holmes/?sh=5e9a00a947a7

Glamour Magazine's Women of the Year Awards: Andrea Park, "2015 Glamour Women of the Year Awards," CBS News, November 10, 2015. https://www.cbsnews.com/pictures/2015-glamour-women-of-the-year-awards/

Holmes has been Convicted: Erin Griffith and Erin Woo, "Elizabeth Holmes Found Guilty of Four Charges of Fraud," *The New York Times*, July 8, 2022. https://www.nytimes.com/live/2022/01/03/technology/elizabeth-holmes-trial-verdict

95% of CEOs are men: Mandy Garner, "Men account for 95% of CEOs at global firms in US and Europe," *workingmums*, December 10, 2018. https://www.workingmums.co.uk/men-account-for-95-of-ceos-at-global-firms-in-us-and-europe/

Netflix CEO Ted Sarandos: Yolanda Baruch, "Netflix Offers The Door To Workers Offended By The Streaming Platforms Content: Netflix May Not Be The Best Place For You," *Yahoo!*, May 14, 2022. https://www.yahoo.com/video/netflix-offers-door-workers-offended-193427791.html

The Closer: Ellise Shafer, "Dave Chappelle Willing to Discuss 'The Closer' With Trans Community, but Says He's 'Not Bending to Anybody's Demands,'" *Variety*, October 25, 2021. https://variety.com/2021/film/news/dave-chappelle-netflix-the-closer-trans-employees-1235097068/

Two Emmy nominations: Robyn Bahr, "Dave Chappelle's Emmy Noms Show the TV Academy Isn't Swayed by Social Media," *The Hollywood Reporter*," August 21, 2022. https://www.hollywood-reporter.com/tv/tv-features/dave-chappelle-emmy-nominations-social-media-1235199415/

Rotten Tomatoes: ratings checked September 19, 2022. https://www.rottentomatoes.com/m/dave_chappelle_the_closer

Chapter 12: Colliding with the Mob (this is the covid-y part).

February 25, 2020: Kate Eby, "Coronavirus Timeline," ABC7, September 2, 2022. https://abc7news.com/timeline-of-coronavirus-us-covid-19-bay-area-sf/6047519/

Gavin Newsom: Casey Tolan and Paul Rogers, "Coronavirus: Newsom warns most schools could be closed until summer as lockdown expands," *The Mercury News*, March 19, 2020. https://www.mercurynews.com/2020/03/17/coronavirus-newsom-warns-most-schools-could-be-closed-until-summer-as-lockdown-expands/

Article by Ioannidis: John P.A. Ioannidis, "A fiasco in the making? As the coronavirus pandemic takes hold, we are making decisions without reliable data," *Stat News*, March 17, 2020. https://www.statnews.com/2020/03/17/a-fiasco-in-the-making-as-the-coronavirus-pandemic-takes-hold-we-are-making-decisions-without-reliable-data/

"Is our fight against Coronavirus worse than the disease": David Katz, *The New York Times*, March 20, 2020. https://www.nytimes.com/2020/03/20/opinion/coronavirus-pandemic-social-distancing.html

Martin Kulldorff: "COVID-19 Counter Measures Should be Age Specific," LinkedIn, April 10, 2020. https://www.linkedin.com/pulse/covid-19-counter-measures-should-age-specific-martin-kulldorff/

Pre-pandemic Playbook: cdc.gov. February 2007. https://www.cdc.gov/flu/pandemic-resources/pdf/community_mitigation-sm.pdf

One of my very first covid tweets: Jennifer Sey, Twitter, April 7, 2020. https://twitter.com/JenniferSey/status/1247717451384541184?s=20&t=Ub7FL2DxdNclOITTmZ1itA

Chapter 13: Levi's anti-racism consciousness is raised.

The first Fortune 500 company to offer same sex partner benefits: "Levi's partners with Self Evident Truths to celebrate LGBTQIA+ voices with its 2020 Pride collection," news24, May 4, 2020. https://www.news24.com/w24/style/fashion/trends/levis-partners-with-self-evident-truths-to-celebrate-lgbtqia-voices-with-its-2020-pride-collection-20200304

Weight against Prop 8: "Levi's joins group to defeat gay marriage ban," *Los Angeles Daily News*, September 25, 2008. https://www.dailynews.com/2008/09/25/levis-joins-group-to-defeat-gay-marriage-ban/

Murder of Philando Castille: *MPRNews*. June 16, 2017. https://www.mprnews.org/crime-law-and-justice/philandocastile

Open letter: Mallory Simon, "Over 1,000 health professionals sign a letter saying, Don't shut down protests using coronavirus concerns as an excuse," CNN, June 5, 2020. https://www.cnn.com/2020/06/05/health/health-care-open-letter-protests-coronavirus-trnd/index.html

Tom Frieden: Twitter, June 2, 2020. https://twitter.com/DrTomFrieden/status/1267796218496901121?s=20&t=UNbR7sRuCcyiU2kLWup13w

Chapter 14: "The Work."

"Our company condemns all forms of racism": Levi's Instagram, June 1, 2020. https://www.instagram.com/p/CA6ev9jgVsv/?igshid=YzA2ZDJiZGQ%3D

"We simply cannot sit idly by": Levi's Instagram, May 1, 2020. https://www.instagram.com/p/CA387zsgMGh/?utm_source=ig_web_copy_link

Dismantling racism in mathematics: "A Pathway to Equitable Math Instruction," equitablemath.org, May 2021. https://equitablemath.org/wp-content/uploads/sites/2/2020/11/1_STRIDE1.pdf

John McWhorter: "Is it racist to expect black kids to do math for real?", John McWhorter's Substack *It Bears Mentioning*, February 28, 2021. https://johnmcwhorter.substack.com/p/is-it-racist-to-expect-black-kids

Robin DiAngelo, the anti-racism guru: Daniel Bergner, "White Fragility Is Everywhere. But Does Antiracism Training Work?", *The New York Times*, July 15, 2020. https://www.nytimes.com/2020/07/15/magazine/white-fragility-robin-diangelo.html

Frank Dobbin: and Alexander Kalev, "Why Diversity Programs Fail," *Harvard Business Review*, July-August 2016. https://hbr.org/2016/07/why-diversity-programs-fail

"Vanilla Ice": Steve QJ, "Robin DiAngelo Is The 'Vanilla Ice' of Anti-Racism," medium.com, June 24, 2021. https://medium.com/illumination-curated/robin-diangelo-is-the-vanilla-ice-of-anti-racism-c163a76655f5

Nice Racism: Matt Taibbi, "Our Endless Dinner with Robin DiAngelo," *TK News by Matt Taibbi*, June 20, 2021. https://taibbi.substack.com/p/our-endless-dinner-with-robin-diangelo-806

What DiAngelo calls "credentialism": YouTube, February 21, 2017. https://www.youtube.com/watch?v=DwIx3KQer54

Education Report Card: U.S. Department of Education official assessment of educational progress, 2019. https://www.nationsreportcard.gov/highlights/reading/2019/

Virginia Study: "Examining the Impact of COVID-19 on the Identification of At-Risk Students: Fall 2020 Literacy Screening Findings," University of Virginia School of Education and Human Development, fall 2021. https://literacy.virginia.edu/sites/g/files/jsddwu1006/files/2022-04/PALS_StateReport_Fall_2021.pdf

National test results: Sarah Mervosh, "The Pandemic Erased Two Decades of Progress in math and Reading," *The New York Times*, September 1, 2022. https://www.nytimes.com/2022/09/01/us/national-test-scores-math-reading-pandemic.html

The profound effect school closures had on low-income students: Dan Goldberg, et al. "The Consequences of Remote and Hybrid Instruction During the Pandemic," Harvard University Center for Education Policy Research, May 2022. https://cepr.harvard.edu/files/cepr/files/5-4.pdf?m=1651690491

Gabriela López proclaimed: Isaac Chotiner, "How San Francisco Renamed Its Schools, *The New Yorker*, February 6, 2020. https://www.newyorker.com/news/q-and-a/how-san-francisco-renamed-its-schools

Cecily Myart-Cruz asserted: Jason McGahan, "Exclusive: Cecily Myart-Cruz's Hostile Takeover of L.A.'s Public Schools," *Los Angeles Magazine*, August 26, 2021. https://www.lamag.com/citythinkblog/cecily-myart-cruz-teachers-union/

Bureau of Labor and Statistics: Elka Torpey, bls.gov, June 2021. https://www.bls.gov/careeroutlook/2021/data-on-display/education-pays.htm

Alexi McCammond: Katie Robertson, "Teen Vogue Editor Resigns After Fury Over Racist Tweets," *The New York Times*, March 18, 2021. https://www.nytimes.com/2021/03/18/business/media/teen-vogue-editor-alexi-mccammond.html

Diana Tsui: Instagram, March 7, 2021. https://www.instagram.com/p/CMIKWZegh4n/?hl=en

Whoopi Goldberg: Jenny Gross and Neil Vigdor, "ABC Suspends Whoopi Goldberg Over Holocaust Comments," *The New York Times*, February 1, 2022. https://www.nytimes.com/2022/02/01/us/whoopi-goldberg-holocaust.html

Dyke march in Chicago: Peter Holley, "Jewish marchers say they were kicked out of a rally for inclusiveness because of their beliefs," the *Washington Post*, June 26, 2017. https://www.washingtonpost.com/news/acts-of-faith/wp/2017/06/26/jewish-marchers-say-they-were-kicked-out-of-a-rally-for-inclusiveness-because-of-their-beliefs/

Teachers' unions also give a lot of money to political candidates: Tiana Lowe, "Teacher's Unions reward Gavin Newsom with $2 million for its yearlong vacation," *The Washington Examiner*, July 28, 2021. https://www.washingtonexaminer.com/opinion/teachers-unions-rewards-gavin-newsom-with-2-million-for-its-year-long-paid-vacation

The United Educators of San Francisco: Aaron Bandler, "SF, LA Teachers' Unions Express Support For Israel Boycotts," *The Jewish Journal*, June 4, 2021. https://jewishjournal.com/news/337411/sf-la-teachers-unions-express-support-for-israel-boycotts/

Chapter 15: My first "talking to."

Levi's furloughed retail store employees: Brian Sozzi, "How Levi's CEO Chip Bergh is leading the jeans maker through the coronavirus pandemic," *Yahoo! Finance*, April 8, 2020. https://www.yahoo.com/lifestyle/how-levis-ceo-chip-bergh-is-leading-the-jeans-maker-through-the-coronavirus-pandemic-170515074.html

$32 million to shareholders: Peter Whoriskey, "U.S. companies cut thousands of workers while continuing to reward shareholders during pandemic" *The Washington Post*, May 5, 2020. https://www.washingtonpost.com/business/2020/05/05/dividends-layoffs-coronavirus/

William Lazonick: Peter Whoriskey, "U.S. Companies cut thousands of workers while continuing to reward shareholders during pandemic," the *Washington Post*, May 5, 2020. https://www.washingtonpost.com/business/2020/05/05/dividends-layoffs-coronavirus/

Chip explained the layoffs: Andrew Marquardt, "Leadership in crisis: Levi's leaders focused on company culture and empathy to make it through 2020," *Fortune*, February 24, 2021. https://fortune.com/2021/02/24/levi-strauss-covid-chip-bergh-ceo-chro-tracy-layney-business-leadership-pandemic

Chip cashed in: "Charles Victor Bergh Net Worth, *Wallmine.com*, May 6, 2022. https://wallmine.com/people/35668/charles-v-bergh

Layoff decision a "tough call": Jane Thier, "Levi's CFO: 700-person layoff 'toughest call' of pandemic," *CFO Dive*, July 10, 2020. https://www.cfodive.com/news/levis-Harmit-Singh-layoffs-pandemic/581418/

Upped the ante: Jennifer Sey, Twitter, September 18, 2020. https://twitter.com/JenniferSey/status/1307035677670989824?s=20&t=iDVjVCE44JRi8blkEQWj7Q

$1 million dollars to our own foundation: Katerina Ang, "Levi's is taking a $1 million stand against the Trump administration," *MarketWatch*, May 18, 2017. https://www.marketwatch.com/story/levis-is-taking-a-1-million-stand-against-the-trump-administration-2017-05-18-8884612

Chip's Open letter: Phil Wahba, "Levi Strauss CEO asks gun owners not to bring weapons into stores," *Fortune*, November 30, 2016. https://fortune.com/2016/11/30/levis-guns/

Donations to political campaigns: Liz Warren, "American Made Jeans Would Cost $150," *Sourcing Journal*, April 22, 2022. https://sourcingjournal.com/denim/denim-brands/levi-strauss-chip-bergh-shareholders-meeting-politics-offshoring-compensation-peta-340435/

Chip himself donated money: "Mark Kelly's Campaign Committee Receives $5000 from Chip Bergh," *The Tucson Standard*, October 2, 2019. https://tucsonstandard.com/stories/526285622-mark-kelly-s-campaign-committee-receives-5-000-from-chip-bergh

Chapter 16: The pushback accelerates.

Article appeared in *ProPublica*: Alec MacGillis, "The Students Left Behind By Remote Learning," *ProPublica*, September 28, 2020. https://www.propublica.org/article/the-students-left-behind-by-remote-learning

I cited an article: Apoorva Mandavilli, "Schoolchildren Seem Unlikely to Fuel Coronavirus Surges, Scientists Say," *The New York Times*, October 22, 2020. https://www.nytimes.com/2020/10/22/health/coronavirus-schools-children.html#click=https://t.co/8ghdOQQc5d

Here's a little case study: Dana Goldstein, "Why a Pediatric Group is Pushing to Open Schools This Fall," *The New York Times*, June 30, 2020. https://www.nytimes.com/2020/06/30/us/coronavirus-schools-reopening-guidelines-aap.html

President Trump hosted an event at the White House: Jordyn Phelps and Sophie Tatum, "Trump insists schools 'must open' in fall, says he'll 'put pressure' on governors to do so," ABC News, June 7, 2020. https://abcnews.go.com/Politics/trump-insists-schools-open-fall-local-authorities-hold/story?id=71648610

American Academy of Pediatrics: AAP.org, July 10, 2020. https://www.aap.org/en/news-room/news-releases/aap/2020/pediatricians-educators-and-superintendents-urge-a-safe-return-to-school-this-fall/

My husband's tweet: Mike Moffitt, "Medical experts bristle at SF's new playground restrictions," *SF Gate*, October 16, 2020. https://www.sfgate.com/science/article/Medical-experts-bristle-at-SF-s-new-playground-15654199.php

I led rallies: Michael Cabanatuan, "Latest San Francisco school reopening fight: How far apart should desks be spaced?" *San Francisco Chronicle*, March 5, 2021. https://www.sfchronicle.com/education/article/Latest-San-Francisco-school-reopening-fight-How-16004684.php

Media coverage: Luz Pena, "San Francisco public school students will not be returning to classrooms Jan. 5 as originally planned," ABC7, December 19, 2020. https://abc7news.com/san-francisco-unified-reopen-school-coronavirus-mayor-london-breed/8887079/

Denmark had opened schools: Emiliana Vegas, "Reopening the World: Reopening schools – Insights from Denmark and Finland," *Brookings*, July 6, 2020. https://www.brookings.edu/blog/education-plus-development/2020/07/06/reopening-the-world-reopening-schools-insights-from-denmark-and-finland/

Three months into the pandemic: "Reopening schools in Denmark did not worsen outbreak," *Reuters*, May 28, 2020. https://www.reuters.com/article/us-health-coronavirus-denmark-reopening/reopening-schools-in-denmark-did-not-worsen-outbreak-data-shows-idUSKBN2341N7

Chapter 17: My apology tour.

Moved to Denver: Jobina Fortson, "Bay Area Family Relocates to Denver So Child Can Attend School In Person," ABC7, March 1, 2021. https://abc7news.com/newsom-schools-reopening-ca-san-francisco-jen-sey/10381117/

Took the company public: Will Yankowicz, "As jeans giant Levi Strauss prepares to go public, new billionaire emerges," *Forbes*, February 14, 2019. https://www.forbes.com/sites/willyakowicz/2019/02/14/as-jean-giant-levi-strauss-prepares-to-go-public-new-billionaire-emerges/?sh=1545a18f2aa9

Haas family sold close to 20 million shares: Will Yankowicz, "Levi Strauss Heirs Sell $300 Million in Shares At IPO, Pushing Family Net Worth Past 4 Billion," *Forbes*, March 21, 2019. https://www.forbes.com/sites/willyakowicz/2019/03/21/levi-strauss-heirs-sell-300-million-in-shares-at-ipo-pushing-family-net-worth-past-4-billion/?sh=5ee455c94b35

Mimi Haas: Ed Lin, "Levi Strauss' Largest Shareholder, Mimi Haas, Sells Large Block of Shares," *Barron's*, October 16, 2020. https://www.forbes.com/sites/willyakowicz/2019/03/21/levi-strauss-heirs-sell-300-million-in-shares-at-ipo-pushing-family-net-worth-past-4-billion/?sh=5ee455c94b35

Forbes Billionaires List: Will Yankowicz, "Levi Strauss Heirs Sell $300 Million in Shares At IPO, Pushing Family Net Worth Past 4 Billion," *Forbes*, March 21, 2019. https://www.forbes.com/sites/willyakowicz/2019/03/21/levi-strauss-heirs-sell-300-million-in-shares-at-ipo-pushing-family-net-worth-past-4-billion/?sh=5ee455c94b35

Chip did pretty well too: Katie Burke, "A Denim Renaissance," *San Francisco Business Times*, December 20, 2019. https://www.bizjournals.com/sanfrancisco/news/2019/12/20/2019executive-of-the-year-chip-bergh-had-led-a.html

Chip has liquidated: "Charles Victor Bergh Net Worth, *Wallmine.com*, May 6. 2022, https://wallmine.com/people/35668/charles-v-bergh

Dan Goldman: Laura Nahmias, Levi Strauss Heir Would Join Congress' Richest with NYC Win," *Bloomberg*, July 30, 2022. https://www.bloomberg.com/news/articles/2022-07-30/dan-goldman-levi-strauss-heir-would-join-congress-s-richest-with-nyc-win?leadSource=uverify%20wall

Close to 5 million dollars: Gregory Krieg, "Dan Goldman, Democratic counsel during Trump's first impeachment, will win New York House primary, CNN projects," CNN, September 6, 2022. https://www.cnn.com/2022/09/06/politics/daniel-goldman-new-york-10th-district-primary/index.html

Liz Holtzman: Zach Williams, "Rivals blast 'shocking' Dan Goldman cash edge as early voting begins in NY10," *New York Post*, August 12, 2022. https://nypost.com/2022/08/12/rivals-say-dan-goldman-has-shocking-cash-edge-as-early-voting-begins-in-ny10/

Goldman's claim: Laura Nahmias, Levi Strauss Heir Would Join Congress' Richest with NYC Win," *Bloomberg*, July 30, 2022. https://www.bloomberg.com/news/articles/2022-07-30/dan-goldman-levi-strauss-heir-would-join-congress-s-richest-with-nyc-win?leadSource=uverify%20wall#xj4y7vzkg

I posted about our move: Jennifer Sey, Twitter, February 27, 2021. https://twitter.com/JenniferSey/status/1365813860905537536?s=20&t=3jC_nm95sf1O0DWgsiO7ZQ

The *New York Post* ran this headline: Jon Levine, "Powerful teachers union influenced CDC on school re-openings, emails show," *New York Post*, May 1, 2021. https://nypost.com/2021/05/01/teachers-union-collaborated-with-cdc-on-school-reopening-emails/

I did the show from our Airbnb: "Ingraham Angle," Fox News, March 3, 2021. https://video. foxnews.com/v/6236826699001#sp=show-clips

Chapter 18: On spouses.

Alexander Katai: "Alexander Katai cut by LA Galaxy over wife's 'racist and violent' Instagram posts," *The Guardian*, June 5, 2020. https://www.theguardian.com/football/2020/jun/05/ aleksandar-katai-wife-racist-social-media

Los Angeles County school district: Howard Blume, Melissa Gomez, "LAUSD posed to push back deadline for student COVID vaccinations to fall 2022," *Los Angeles Times*, December 10, 2021. https://www.latimes.com/california/story/2021-12-10/ lausd-plans-to-back-down-from-student-covid-vaccine-mandate

Michael Hiltzik: "Mocking anti-vaxxers Covid deaths is ghoulish, yes – but may be necessary," *Los Angeles Times*, January 10, 2022. https://www.latimes.com/business/story/2022-01-10/ why-shouldnt-we-dance-on-the-graves-of-anti-vaxxers

Original title: screenshot of original title, @Sheen6031, Twitter, January 10, 2022. https://twitter. com/Sheen6031/status/1480667398818738181?s=20&t=3ez9afRzwtrl5XKSyAPbew

Jason Valentine of Mobile, Alabama: Timothy Bella, "An Alabama Doctor Watched Patients Reject the Vaccine. Now He's Refusing to Treat Them," the *Washington Post*, August 18, 2021. https://www.washingtonpost.com/health/2021/08/18/ alabama-doctor-unvaccinated-patients-valentine/

Jimmy Kimmel: Timothy Bella, "Jimmy Kimmel Suggests Hospitals Shouldn't Treat Unvaccinated Patients Who Prefer Ivermectin," the *Washington Post*, September 8, 2020. https://www.washing-tonpost.com/arts-entertainment/2021/09/08/jimmy-kimmel-hospitals-unvaccinated-ivermectin/

Vera Sharav: John Miltimore, "A Holocaust Survivor Warned Americans about Blindly Supporting the War on COVID. We Didn't Listen," *Fee Stories*, March 10, 2022. https://fee.org/articles/a-holocaust-survivor-warned-americans-about-blindly-supporting-the-war-on-covid-we-didn-t-listen/

Chapter 19: The predictable outcome.

Just pass them anyway: Patrick Wall, "No Fs allowed: Some Newark high school teachers feel pressure to pass absent students during the pandemic," *Chalkbeat Newark*, February 4, 2021. https://newark.chalkbeat.org/2021/2/4/22267330/newark-failing-grades-pandemic

Everett Middle School: Andres Picon, "Fight at SF Middle School Sends Student to the Hospital, fuels debate over school culture," *San Francisco Chronicle*, May 5, 2022. https://www.sfchronicle. com/bayarea/article/Fight-at-S-F-middle-school-leaves-student-with-17153069.php

French Laundry: Eve Batey, "French Laundry Launches $850-Per-Person Indoor Dining 'Experience' Fit for a Bond Villain," *Eater San Francisco*, September 3, 2020. https://sf.eater. com/2020/9/3/21421335/french-laundry-yountville-thomas-keller-indoor-dining-rich-people

"I need to preach and practice": Taryn Luna, Phil Willon, "Newsom apologizes for French Laundry dinner, says he will practice what he preaches on COVID-19," *Los Angeles Times*, November 16, 2020. https://www.latimes.com/california/story/2020-11-16/gavin-newsom-apology-french-laundry-dinner-covid-19

Kelly McGinnis: Screen shot of text message received by Jennifer Sey from Kelly McGinnis, June 10, 2021.

Becca was appointed: Governor Newsom Announces Appointments, gov.ca.gov, June 12, 2019. https://www.gov.ca.gov/2019/06/12/governor-newsom-announces-appointments-6-12-19/

***The New York Times* reported The Nation's Report Card**: Sarah Mervosh, "The Pandemic Erased Two Decades of Progress in math and Reading," The *New York Times*, September 1, 2022. https://www.nytimes.com/2022/09/01/us/national-test-scores-math-reading-pandemic.html

Still can't participate in sports: Dana Goldstein, "At Headstart, Masks Remain On, Despite CDC Guidelines," *The New York Times*, September 7, 2022. https://www.nytimes.com/2022/09/07/us/head-start-masks-toddlers.html

Toddlers in Headstart programs: Karol Markowicz, "Continuing Covid craziness shows it was never about the science," *New York Post*, September 18, 2022. https://nypost.com/2022/09/18/continuing-covid-craziness-shows-it-was-never-about-the-science/

Chapter 20: You can't fire me, I quit!

L.A. Mayor Eric Garcetti: Tom Tapp, "LA Mayor Garcetti & Most Fans Are Maskless At Super Bowl Despite Pleas From County Officials," *Deadline*, February 14, 2022. https://deadline.com/2022/02/garcetti-maskless-again-super-bowl-los-angeles-1234933130/

I held my breath for the photo: David K. Li, Bianca Britton, L.A. Mayor Eric Garcetti defends maskless pictures: 'I hold my breath,' NBC, February 3, 2022. https://www.nbcnews.com/news/us-news/l-mayor-eric-garcetti-defends-maskless-pictures-hold-breath-rcna14729

Chapter 21: My plan and why I made it.

Bari Weiss's Substack newsletter: Jennifer Sey, "Yesterday I Was Levi's Brand President. I Quit So I Could Be Free," Bari Weiss's Substack *Common Sense*, February 14, 2022. https://www.com-monsense.news/p/yesterday-i-was-levis-brand-president

Chapter 22: My announcement and the aftermath.

She left in a very public fashion: Bari Weiss resignation letter, July 14, 2020. https://www.bariweiss.com/resignation-letter

The New York Times: Sapna Maheshwari, "She Was a Candidate to Lead Levi's. Then She Started Tweeting," *The New York Times*, March 25, 2022. https://www.nytimes.com/2022/03/25/business/levis-jen-sey.html

The *Washington Post*: Bryan Pietsch, "Levi's executive resigns, says firm pushed her out for vocally opposing coronavirus rules in schools," the *Washington Post*, February 15, 2022. https://www.washingtonpost.com/business/2022/02/15/levis-jennifer-sey-resigns-school-covid/

The *Wall Street Journal*: Jacob Gallagher, "Levi's Executive Jennifer Sey Resigns Citing Her Public Views on Covid-19 Restrictions," the *Wall Street Journal*, February 14, 2022. https://www.wsj.com/articles/levis-president-jennifer-sey-resigns-over-her-public-views-on-covid-19-restrictions-11644870629

NPR: Alina Selyukh, "Can a corporate exec speak as a mom about COVID rules? Consider the Levi's saga," NPR, February 21, 2022. https://www.npr.org/2022/02/21/1082107309/can-a-corporate-exec-speak-as-a-mom-about-covid-rules-consider-the-levis-saga

Erin Burnett Outfront: "Ex-Levi's executive says she had to quit her job to speak out," CNN, February 17, 2022. https://www.cnn.com/videos/politics/2022/02/17/jennifer-sey-levi-executive-covid-19-schools-vpx.cnn/video/playlists/erin-burnett-outfront/

Tucker Carlson Tonight: "Levi's brand president explains why she quit after turning down $1M," Fox News, February 16, 2022. https://video.foxnews.com/v/6297732386001#sp=show-clips

CNBC's "Squawk Box": "Former Levi Strauss executive Jennifer Sey on decision to leave company over Covid 'free speech' controversy," CNBC, February 17, 2022. https://www.cnbc.com/2022/02/17/former-levi-exec-jennifer-sey-on-resigning-over-covid-free-speech.html

The school recall effort succeeded: Thomas Fuller, "In Landslide, San Francisco Forces Out 3 Board of Education Members," *The New York Times*, February 16, 2022. https://www.nytimes.com/2022/02/16/us/san-francisco-school-board-recall.html

The Mayor of San Francisco: "Mayor London Breed on the San Francisco School Board Recall Election Results," Office of the Mayor, sf.gov, February 15, 2022. https://sfmayor.org/article/mayor-london-breed-san-francisco-school-board-recall-election-results

West Virginia State Board of Education v Barnette: 301 U.S. 624, https://www.lexisnexis.com/community/casebrief/p/casebrief-west-virginia-state-bd-of-education-v-barnette

Lauren Victor: "I was the woman surrounded by BLM protestors at a D.C. restaurant. Here's why I didn't raise my fist," the *Washington Post*, September 3, 2020. https://www.washingtonpost.com/opinions/lauren-victor-diner-dc-black-lives-matter-protesters/2020/09/03/fa0368de-ee21-11ea-ab4e-581edb849379_story.html

Professor Stuart Reges: "Lawsuit: Professor sues University of Washington after admins punish him for 'inappropriate' opinion," Fire.org, July 12, 2022. https://www.thefire.org/lawsuit-professor-sues-university-of-washington-after-admins-punish-him-for-inappropriate-opinion/

"Why Women Don't Code": *Quillette*, June 19, 2018. https://quillette.com/2018/06/19/why-women-dont-code/

We are living through a crisis: Greg Lukianoff, Joshua Bleisch, "He Made A Joke About Land Acknowledgments, Then The Trouble Began," Bari Weiss's Substack *Common Sense*, July 28, 2022. https://www.commonsense.news/p/he-made-a-joke-about-land-acknowledgements

Abercrombie & Fitch: "White Hot: The Rise and Fall of Abercrombie & Fitch"Netflix documentary, 2022. https://www.imdb.com/title/tt19034522/

2006 quote from Jeffries: Ashely Lutz, "Abercrombie & Fitch CEO Won't Apologize For Saying He Only Wants Cool Thin People To Wear His Clothes," *Business Insider*, May 16, 2013. https://www.businessinsider.com/abercrombie-statement-on-controversy-2013-5

Chapter 23: A better path forward for today's companies.

Harassment of women at Nike: Julie Creswell, Kevin Draper and Rachel Abrams, "At Nike, A Revolt Led By Women Leads to Exodus of Male Executives," *The New York Times*, April 28, 2018: https://www.nytimes.com/2018/04/28/business/nike-women.html

Allyson Felix: "Allyson Felix: My Own Nike Pregnancy Story," *The New York Times*, May 22, 2019. https://www.nytimes.com/2019/05/22/opinion/allyson-felix-pregnancy-nike.html

Nike's Oregon Project: Mary Cain, "I Was the Fastest Girl in America. Until I Joined Nike," *The New York Times*, November 7, 2019: https://www.nytimes.com/2019/11/07/opinion/nike-running-mary-cain.html

New Balance: Lisa Ryan, "People Are Burning Their New Balance Sneakers After the Company Said It Supports Donald Trump," *The Cut*, November 10, 2016. https://www.thecut.com/2016/11/why-some-people-are-burning-their-new-balance-sneakers.html

Turned a deaf ear: Sara Germano, "New Balance Faces Social Media Backlash After Welcoming Trump," the *Wall Street Journal*, November 10, 2016. https://www.wsj.com/articles/new-balance-faces-social-media-backlash-after-welcoming-trump-1478823102

Hitting $4.5 billion in sales: Erin Fitzpatrick, It's True: This Overlooked Sneaker Brand is Making $4 Billion," *Who What Wear*, August 16, 2018. https://www.whowhatwear.com/new-balance-sales-2018

Support refugees: "Gucci's Support For Refugees Globally on World Refugee Day," *Equilibrium*, June 24, 2021. https://equilibrium.gucci.com/gucci-support-for-refugees-globally-on-world-refugee-day

Victoria's Secret: "Angels Demons," Victoria's Secret documentary film, Hulu, 2022. https://www.imdb.com/title/tt19784922/

Chapter 24: Why I stayed so long at Levi's. And why I ultimately left.

Donated a portion of the first profits: levistrauss.com, https://www.levistrauss.com/wp-content/uploads/2016/06/2016_CompanyTimeline_Long_F.pdf

Company semi-private: Brenton R. Schlender, "How Levi Strauss Did An LBO Right," *Fortune* archive, May 7, 1990. https://archive.fortune.com/magazines/fortune/fortune_archive/1990/05/07/73489/index.htm

Aspirations Statement: Robert Howard, "Values Make the Company, An Interview with Robert Haas," *Harvard Business Review*, September-October 1990. https://hbr.org/1990/09/values-make-the-company-an-interview-with-robert-haas

Leveraged Buy-Out: Nina Munk, "How Levi's Trashed A Great American Brand, While Bob Haas Pioneered Benevolent Management His Company Came Apart at the Seams," *CNN Money*, April 12, 1999. https://money.cnn.com/magazines/fortune/fortune_archive/1999/04/12/258131/

Limited traction on social media: @Heddels, Twitter, November 9, 2020. https://twitter.com/heddels/status/1325902492392071168?s=20&t=UqbPwwwsBQqZVZae98Z5oA

Epilogue

The Rachel Maddow Show: A.J. Katz, "Here Are the Top-Rated Cable News Shows For Q2 2022," *AdWeek*, June 28, 2022. https://www.adweek.com/tvnewser/here-are-the-top-rated-cable-news-shows-for-q2-2022/510090/

Ek told employees: J. Clara Chan, "Spotify CEO Addresses Joe Rogan's N-Word Use, Doubles Down on Keeping Podcaster on Platform," *Hollywood Reporter*, February 6, 2022. https://www.hollywoodreporter.com/business/digital/spotify-joe-rogan-daniel-ek-1235087928/

Gained two million: James Hibberd, "Joe Rogan Claims Massive Subscriber Boost Due to Recent Controversies," *Hollywood Reporter*, April 22, 2022. https://www.hollywoodreporter.com/business/business-news/joe-rogan-spotify-subscribers-1235134232/

"Girls Gone Wild": "Rich and Shameless – Girls Gone Wild," TNT, 2022. https://www.imdb.com/title/tt19607980/

CPSIA information can be obtained
at www.ICGtesting.com
Printed in the USA
LVHW010115201122
733282LV00017B/361/J